UP THE TRAIL

How Things Worked
Robin Einhorn and Richard R. John, *Series Editors*

ALSO IN THE SERIES:

Sean Patrick Adams, *Home Fires: How Americans Kept Warm in the Nineteenth Century*

Ronald H. Bayor, *Encountering Ellis Island: How European Immigrants Entered America*

Bob Luke and John David Smith, *Soldiering for Freedom: How the Union Army Recruited, Trained, and Deployed the U.S. Colored Troops*

David R. Danbom, *Sod Busting: How Families Made Farms on the Nineteenth-Century Plains*

Phillip G. Payne, *Crash! How the Economic Boom and Bust of the 1920s Worked*

Sharon Ann Murphy, *Other People's Money: How Banking Worked in the Early American Republic*

Johann N. Neem, *Democracy's Schools: The Rise of Public Education in America*

Benjamin F. Alexander, *The New Deal's Forest Army: How the Civilian Conservation Corps Worked*

Jonathan Rees, *Before the Refrigerator: How We Used to Get Ice*

UP THE TRAIL

HOW TEXAS COWBOYS HERDED LONGHORNS AND BECAME AN AMERICAN ICON

TIM LEHMAN
ROCKY MOUNTAIN COLLEGE
BILLINGS, MONTANA

Johns Hopkins University Press | *Baltimore*

Printed in the United States of America on acid-free paper
9 8 7 6 5 4 3 2 1

Johns Hopkins University Press
2715 North Charles Street
Baltimore, Maryland 21218-4363
www.press.jhu.edu

Library of Congress Cataloging-in-Publication Data

Names: Lehman, Tim, author.
Title: Up the trail : how Texas cowboys herded longhorns and became an American icon / Tim Lehman.
Other titles: How Texas cowboys herded longhorns and became an American icon
Description: Baltimore : Johns Hopkins University Press, [2018] | Series: How things worked | Includes bibliographical references and index.
Identifiers: LCCN 2017046426 | ISBN 9781421425894 (hardcover : alk. paper) | ISBN 9781421425900 (pbk. : alk. paper) | ISBN 9781421425917 (electronic) | ISBN 1421425890 (hardcover : alk. paper) | ISBN 1421425904 (pbk. : alk. paper) | ISBN 1421425912 (electronic)
Subjects: LCSH: Cattle drives—West (U.S.) | Cattle drives—Texas. | Texas longhorn cattle. | Cowboys—West (U.S.)—History. | Cattle trade—West (U.S.)—History.
Classification: LCC F596 .L49 2018 | DDC 978—dc23
LC record available at https://lccn.loc.gov/2017046426

A catalog record for this book is available from the British Library.

Special discounts are available for bulk purchases of this book. For more information, please contact Special Sales at 410-516-6936 or specialsales@press.jhu.edu.

Johns Hopkins University Press uses environmentally friendly book materials, including recycled text paper that is composed of at least 30 percent post-consumer waste, whenever possible.

For Danell, who gives me grace and courage,
and for Sawyer, who gives me hope

CONTENTS

UP THE TRAIL

Prologue

THE CATTLE DRIVES OF OUR IMAGINATION are filled with colorful cowboys seeking adventure. Prodding and coaxing a line of bellowing cattle along a dusty path through the wilderness, these sturdy cowhands always triumph over stampedes, swollen rivers, and bloodthirsty Indians to deliver their mighty-horned companions to market. These gun-toting, lasso-throwing, ten-gallon-hat-wearing men on horseback ride free, unencumbered by city soot, noise, or crime. In this vision of America, Adam is a cowboy and the West is a verdant, if challenging, Garden of Eden.

All of this, except for perhaps the dust, would have been news to George C. Duffield, the Iowa rancher who organized one of the first long-distance cattle drives. In 1866 Duffield traveled to Galveston, Texas, where he purchased cattle to drive more than a thousand miles back to his Iowa farm. He had heard stories of cheap and abundant cattle roaming the Texas prairies and intended to drive a herd north, selling part of it to market and using the rest to stock his own herd. The wide spaces and lush grasses of the American prairie seemed to offer an opportunity for young men like Duffield to combine adventure with business and come out of the deal with a tidy profit.

Duffield was surprised to find parts of southeastern Texas "pasture poor and cattle thin," while other parts were the "most beautiful prairie that I ever laid eyes on" and "literally covered with tens of thousands of cattle, horses, and mules." Around evening campfires he listened to so many lurid stories of Indian attacks that he began to imagine hostile Natives swooping in at any minute.[1] On April 29, Duffield started northward with the one thousand steers he had bought at twelve dollars a head, a team of hired hands, and enough wagons, oxen, and supplies for a long journey. In the first eight days, the cattle stampeded three times. "Hunt cattle is the order of the day," he noted repeatedly in his diary. On May 13, he recorded in a typical entry, "Big Thunder Storm last night Stampede lost 100 beeves hunted all day found 50 all tired Every thing discouraging." The next day his men swam the cattle and rafted their provisions across the flooded Brazos River, losing most of their provisions in the swift current. Five days later as they continued north, four of his best hired hands quit, and Duffield noted, "Every thing gloomy."[2] At a nearby village Duffield purchased flour, meat, and supplies. This time the Trinity River took their supplies. Finally, on the last day of May, he coaxed the herd across the Red River, out of Texas at last.

Summer in Indian Territory offered no respite. A nighttime stampede scattered Duffield's herd, and several days of hunting lost cattle proved so discouraging that some of the hired hands deserted him. "Horses all give out & Men refused to do anything," he lamented. Somehow, five days later they made it to the aptly named "Boggy Depot," where some of his cattle got stuck in mud so thick that they had to use oxen to haul them out. The prairie nights were often "dark and gloomy," and on June 12 Duffield confided to his diary, "Dark days are these to me. Nothing but Bread and Coffee. Hands all Growling & Swearing—everything wet and cold." Amidst the bleak nights, perilous river crossings, scattered cattle, grumbling employees, and Indians, who claimed a few cattle as the price for crossing their land, he complained, "Have not got the Blues but am in Hel of a fix."[3]

Things picked up briefly when he was able to sell eleven cows for twenty dollars each at the Indian Agency. He used the money to buy more provisions and hire twenty Indians to help him get the herd across the Arkansas River and into Kansas, where blackberry patches and fish offered a welcome variation from beans and biscuits. In late July, however, Duffield and his men were ordered off the Shawnee Reservation and forced to backtrack into Indian Territory, where the "very saucy" Osage Indians demanded a "beefe for the right of way." Turning north again, they were pleased to buy chicken and vegetables from Kansas farmers, but this goodwill evaporated when Duffield's cattle stampeded and destroyed crops. All that Duffield could do was pay for damages and move on.

By late summer Duffield was "very sick," he recorded, with "severe shakes," a sore eye, and "cholic." Yet as the herd moved closer to Iowa he was cheered by seeing "some fine farms" and a meeting house, encouraging him enough to believe that he could "get Home some day yet." Finally, on the last day of October, he arrived in Ottumwa, Iowa, where he shipped one hundred head of cattle to his business partner and sent to rest of his dwindled herd by railroad to the Chicago stockyards. He does not record the exact number, but the few hundred cattle that that made up his surviving herd could hardly have covered his costs. Duffield's last diary entry, almost mercifully, concludes: "Got Home sick & tired & glad to get to rest. Spent Most of the day in Bed & feel badly."[4]

Nothing is more iconic to the idea of the American West than the cattle drive. Conjuring visions of cowboys, undaunted by the violence of nature or humanity, stories of the heroic man on horseback provide an image of a simpler time of individual autonomy, masculine freedom, and natural virtue. In a period of rapid industrialization, folk songs, dime novels, and eventually movies, the cowboy herds cattle alone on the open prairies, in tune with the rhythms of nature, master of his own destiny. Refusing to be a victim of the grinding industrial machine or the anonymous city, he uses pluck and grit to tame the semiwild longhorn cattle, defeat the wild Indians, and deliver beef to a hungry nation's dinner plate.

Duffield's experience defies this mythic story at every turn and illustrates what made driving cattle over long distances so difficult. Uncertain trails, an inexperienced labor force, lack of managerial expertise, distant and capricious markets—not to mention the inherent dangers of trailing hundreds of miles across farms and grassland owned by others—all point to the inherent improbability of the enterprise. Duffield did not encounter endless attacks of wild Indians as the legends of trail driving would lead us to expect. Although he considered native people a threat, even when he was using their grass to feed his herd, at a vital moment he used Indian labor and gained much-needed cash by selling beef to Indians. Cowboys, it seems, needed the Indians more than they realized.

Duffield persevered through obstacles and illness, but frequently exhibited a forlorn disposition. Occasionally he admired the beauties of nature, but more often he groused about storms, floods, stampedes, bad food, and parched lands. His not-always-trustworthy laborers grumbled, started stampedes for extra pay, searched half-heartedly for lost cows, refused to work, and left without notice. So much for cattle herders as faithful and true.

Was his just a long trail ride gone wrong? Duffield certainly had more than enough initiative, courage, and what the old-timers might have called "grit." What he lacked was an infrastructure that would allow his personal ambitions to find success. Successful cattle drives were ultimately a product of industrial capitalism, made profitable by a serendipitous collaboration of railroads, meatpacking plants, and consumer tastes. What Duffield needed was the system of laws, customs, markets, and cultures that would allow herders to move longhorns up the long trail. Only then could cowboys ride into the nation's pantheon of heroes.

1. How Cowboys and Longhorns Came to Texas

Texas cowboys did not invent cattle drives, but they did make them famous. In the two decades after the Civil War, North American cattle drives were the largest, longest, and ultimately the last of these great forced migrations of animals in human history. Spilling out of Texas, they spread Texas longhorns, cowboys, and the culture that roped the two together through the American West. Teddy Blue Abbott, who experienced it all firsthand, captured the immensity of the enterprise when he said it looked as if "all the cattle in the world seemed to be coming up from Texas."[1] Developed on the fringes of European society and transplanted to the edges of English and Spanish settlements in the Americas, cattle herding blossomed in Texas as nowhere else. In the Texas backcountry, the premodern herding traditions of the Iberian Peninsula and the Scottish Highlands collided in a creative, often violent, cultural fusion. Out of this cauldron emerged the cowboy. This young itinerant herder of cattle, who for centuries had been on the periphery of civilization, was transformed into one of America's most potent symbols.

Although folklore suggests that nothing could be simpler than collecting large herds of abandoned cattle in Texas and walking them north, these "rivers of Longhorns" did not surge northward in a natural process. Instead, they were an intricate part of two interrelated processes: the Gilded Age expansion of industrial capitalism and the consolidation of a war-torn nation. Before the cowboy could ride, markets had to be created, railroads built, financial systems adjusted, legal understandings altered, and political arrangements made. Nature also took a powerful role in shaping events: grass, cattle, horses, and a surprisingly powerful tick all played important parts. Popular culture remembers the cowboy as a hero who fashioned his own destiny, but those who actually herded cattle were buffeted by natural forces and economic circumstances. Teddy Blue and all of those cattle streaming out of Texas did not escape history; they were made by it.

Origins

Cattle came to America with Christopher Columbus on his second voyage and followed Hernan Cortez into central Mexico. As they expanded into vacant ecological niches, their numbers exploded. Less than one hundred years after Columbus, one Spanish traveler noted that cattle "wander by the thousands through the forests and fields, all masterless."[2] This invasive species, one of the agents of ecological imperialism, quickly dominated what had previously been Indian farmland and transformed the ecology and culture of the Mexican countryside.[3] One contemporary observer claimed, "You cannot exaggerate their numbers or imagine the spectacle before your eyes."[4] Learning to fend for themselves in the cane breaks, mesquite thickets, and bogs, from Mexico to Texas and Louisiana, these "Spanish," or "Criollo," cattle bred with astonishing fecundity, foraged among grasses, shrubs, and even tree branches for food, and defended themselves from predators with long, protruding horns. These durable beasts adapted to the subtropical heat and humidity as well as the heavy parasite load of the region. Natural selection made them fast, lean, and mean, the kind of animal that could find food in a drought, fight off wolves, and cover ground nearly as fast as a deer.

The other animal essential for the long drives also came to the New World with Cortez: the horse. As the Spanish conquered northward, some of their horses inevitably escaped and returned to the wild. Nearly nine thousand years after becoming extinct in America, horses returned to the very same landscape where equines had evolved millions of years earlier. On the prairies and mesas of their evolutionary origins, wild horses multiplied rapidly and spread into Texas and the Great Plains.[5] One early nineteenth-century map labeled the South Texas area "Vast Herds of Wild Horses." Horses and cattle, two species gone wild from Spanish conquest, ranged almost as far north as New Orleans, where, as one traveler testified, they "intermingled in wild confusion. . . . It is no extravagant declaration to call this one of the meadows of America."[6]

By Spanish custom, these free-ranging livestock were gathered annually and marked by burning brands into the skin or cuts on the ears in a distinctive pattern. Quasi-governmental association of livestock owners called the Mesta established rules for grazing, managed roundups, handled property disputes, and settled the ownership of unbranded calves. Essentially the forerunners of the nineteenth-century stockmen's associations, the Mesta registered and regulated brands, controlled the number of cattle and sheep that each person could keep on the range, and even regulated the kind and number of dogs that herders could possess.

Well-to-do Mexicans viewed the difficult work of minding, gathering, herding, branding, and driving cattle to market with disdain, leaving these tasks to a class of vaqueros, poor laborers who developed techniques of riding and roping later used by American cowboys. Combining skills brought from Spanish and West African herding traditions, these mixed-race Indian, Spanish, and African proto-cowboys revolutionized lower-class drudge work into a species of skilled labor by getting off their feet and onto the back of a horse. Trading the elongated lance, or *desjarretadera*, used to cripple cattle by cutting their hamstring muscles, for a *lazo* (lasso) thrown from horseback, *vaqueros* (sometimes Americanized to *buckaroo*) turned the saddle into a workplace, creating a unique set of skills that could not be easily replaced. The Spanish had initially prohibited anyone but gentlemen from riding horses, but now mestizo vaqueros made riding horseback an essential part of their job. By elevating cattle herding to an equestrian profession, vaqueros made it possible for later cowboys to enjoy the enhanced status of a mounted hero, even a chivalrous knight, while simultaneously reveling in the shady shenanigans of the ruffian outlaw.[7]

Vaqueros pioneered many of the clothes and habits later adopted by Anglo cowboys. They wore a *sombrero* to keep off the sun, covered their legs with a goatskin *chaparejos* (chaps), learned to throw a *lazo* (rope with a slip knot) while riding horseback, lengthened their stirrups to add more stability while riding, and used *la reata* (rope, or lariat) to hold livestock in place by tying it to a sturdy *poma* (pommel, or saddle horn). Once a year they conducted a *rodear*, or gathering, of the herd, branded the new calves and drove the surplus to market. Horses that ran freely on the range with no known owner were said to be *mestenos*, or "of the Mesta," a term later Americanized to *mustangs*.

Slaves who had herded cattle in their West African homelands contributed techniques in managing cattle and probably added the word *dogie*, a term for motherless calves, usually the smallest and poorest in the herd.[8] Long before cowboys made any of these words or practices famous, this rural underclass, quietly and quite apart from any participation from elite landowners, created the equipment and techniques that made later cattle drives possible.[9]

A second herding tradition came to Texas from the British Isles. This style of cattle herding originated in the Highlands and border country of Scotland and came to Texas by way of the American backcountry. Immigrants known as the Scots-Irish took refuge far from distant authority and practiced ancient traditions of open-range livestock production in coastal savannas, lowland pine barrens, and the Appalachian hill country, areas not suited to commercial agriculture.[10] These herders allowed livestock, both cows and pigs, to run free and become feral, and they sometimes migrated seasonally so that they could follow their herds. The legal tradition accompanying these herders required farmers to fence their crops to keep cattle out, rather than requiring cattle owners to restrain their livestock. These fence laws created a large commons, which allowed poor and rich livestock owners alike to benefit from nature's bounty.[11] These cattle were gathered twice annually in a "cow hunt," earmarked and branded, and perhaps herded to a local market. For these herders, the goal was self-sufficiency rather than the accumulation of wealth. As with the Mexican vaqueros, these "cowkeepers" had little status in society but valued their autonomy. Their distance from authority nurtured a strong sense of independence and a robust hostility toward governmental interference. Outsiders often viewed these backcountry frontiersmen as lazy, indolent, and unchurched. They derided this "very peculiar class" of "cowkeepers" with derogatory monikers such as "crackers," "rangers," and sometimes even "cowboys."[12] Nevertheless, when these southern cattle herders went up the trail, they carried with them two key ideas from their experience of an open range: semidomesticated cattle had great value, and cattle herders should be privileged with boundless autonomy.

Sustained contact between Anglo and Hispanic herders in nineteenth-century Texas allowed for the transfer of techniques and tools from Hispanic to Anglo herders. Celtic-Anglo herders tended to keep their stock closer, to gather it into moveable fenced enclosures called "cowpens," and they generally maintained a more docile herd than their counterparts farther south, in Mexico. Southerners commonly herded on foot, as their Celtic ancestors had done for centuries in the British Isles, used salt licks to attract livestock, and sometimes cracked long whips, up to sixteen feet long, to maintain control of the herd. Although they might ride on horseback, the horse was employed more for transportation than for managing the herd. Both traditions drove livestock—cattle, sheep, or pigs—long distances to markets. Herds numbering in the hundreds traveled along "drove roads," often the first highways, and stopped for the night at "drove stands" scattered some ten or twelve miles apart, about the distance a herd usually traveled in a day. The "stands" featured food, drink, and lodging for the herders, as well as pasturage or feed for the cattle. Local farmers learned to tolerate some trampling on their crops in exchange for a ready market for the corn or other feed they supplied and the possibility of obtaining a supply of fresh manure. Doing business with drovers sometimes made stand owners prosperous community leaders. In the Blue Ridge Mountains of North Carolina, for instance, the antebellum cowtown of Asheville saw approximately one hundred fifty thousand animals come through each year, creating a local livestock economy valued at $2 million to $3 million annually.[13]

One special difference between the Hispanic and Anglo traditions was the southerners' use of highly trained cattle dogs. These canine breeds, like the people who came with them, originated in the British Highlands and were common in the American South all the way to East Texas. Highly prized, they were intelligent, tough, and could move a herd on command. The best ones learned to "cut," or separate, a specific animal from the herd, a technique later made famous by horses. These dogs were also trained to "bulldog," or sink their teeth into a bull's lips, nose, or loose neck skin and hold on until human help arrived. With the herd's lead bull controlled, the rest would likely follow. In some instances, herding dogs were tough enough to catch and drag down a bison.[14] Eventually, mythologized cowboys would forge bonds of partnership with horses that had previously been reserved for canine companions.

The collision of these two herding cultures, the Anglo and the Hispanic, created both longhorn cattle and the modern cowboy. As Anglo-American livestock herders moved westward through the southern backcountry and into the Texas borderlands in the 1820s, they challenged both Mexican authorities and native peoples for control of this land. Their spirit of self-sovereignty, personal honor, and clan loyalty gave Anglo-Texans a sense of superiority over those they encountered.[15] Perhaps self-deluding and certainly romanticized, these Texas cattle herders pictured themselves as independent and self-governing, exempt from social etiquette, opposed to political oppression in any form, protectors of women and the innocent from Indians and desperadoes, and possessed of an innate sense of morality that never erred.[16] This sensibility was honed during the Texas Revolution against Mexico of 1835–36, when cattle-raising came to be known as a "*cow boy* system" (first as two words, later hyphenated, and finally one word), as soldiers from both sides of the Rio Grande raided each other in order to provide beef to feed their troops.

After the war, as cattle raids continued on both sides of the border, the Texas Republic declared that Mexican livestock was public property and encouraged soldiers, and specially constituted "rangers," to take any cattle south of the Nueces that were "without real owners."[17] Neglecting the reality that some of these "wild" cattle were claimed by Mexican ranchers, "hardy and adventurous" Texans "formed themselves into small companies, and started on the arduous and fatiguing enterprise of collecting these wild but really fine cattle." These bands collected wild cattle and stole domestic cattle on expeditions "to the very doors of the Mexicans" and soon "became the terror of the Mexican border."[18] The practice was so widespread that one US Army officer observed that these early "cow boys" were "all in the cow stealing business." They might claim to "steal only from the enemy," he concluded, but "to the contrary, they steal from Texans as well as Mexicans."[19] Whether crossing the Rio Grande to steal tame cattle from Mexican ranches or driving wild cattle from the brush, these first "cow-hunts," as they were called, did not distinguish between wild, stray, or domesticated cattle. All were on the open range, free for the taking, just as if they were game animals.

Both Anglo and Mexican ranchers stole cattle, sometimes driving herds fifteen miles or more into either Mexico or Texas, only to have these same well-exercised cattle stolen back and herded to their original homes. Occasionally the tensions of this back-and-forth livestock larceny erupted into serious violence. Juan Cortina became famous along the border for his seizure of any and all nearby cattle, as well as for championing the rights of Mexicans in Anglo Texas. Just before the Civil War and again in the early 1870s, Cortina's struggles for land, dignity, and cattle sparked open warfare, which resulted in dozens of casualties and was put down only by armed Texas rangers. One group of Anglo ranchers in South Texas defined this tug-of-war over cattle as a struggle between good and evil. For them, "Mexican bandits" robbed "American settlers" in a contest between "savagery and civilization."[20] For ranchers south of the Rio Grande, the situation was reversed. One American army officer recognized the Mexican perspective: "They believe the country was wrongfully taken from them, the stock of wild cattle and horses, which have produced immense herds now grazing there, belonging to their forefathers, they have a right to take them back."[21]

This ongoing transborder cattle theft, exaggerated by events such as the Cortina wars, crystallized for Texans a prideful certainty of their own rights and a callous disregard for the lives of those they considered to be inferior. The Texas Rangers who fought Cortina and returned cattle to ranches north of the Rio Grande came to think anyone with a Mexican appearance and accent "must be guilty of something illegal, presumably murder, robbery, cattle-rustling, or invasion."[22] This sense of racial righteousness led another early chronicler to conclude, "Many of these first cowboys thought no more of killing a Mexican than . . . killing a rattlesnake."[23] When Texas cowboys started up the trail, this sense of cultural superiority and racial animosity was tucked in their saddlebags.

At first the term *cow boy* suggested life at the fringes of the law, a rough but romantic reputation. As with the vaqueros of Mexico and the gauchos of Argentina, a hint of violence came with the territory. While some applauded these "hardy and adventurous cow boys" for having the ambition and foresight to gather the seed stock for what would become a profitable business, other Texans feared the immoral taint. The *Dallas Herald*, reflecting the views of respectable society, lamented that "from her first settlement" Texas had been "cursed with the presence of a roving class of worthless characters. . . . A pony, a pair of spurs and a six shooter constitute the necessary outfit of this class of persons." In the same vein, the *Denton Monitor* offered this advice for parents: "Do not allow your boys to load themselves down with Mexican spurs, six-shooters, and pipes. Keep them off the prairies as professional cow hunters. There, in that occupation, who knows that they may forget that there is a distinction between 'mine' and 'thine.' "[24] Given this hostility to the title of *cowboy*, many antebellum Anglo cattle herders preferred to be called *vaquero*, signifying skill and craftsmanship in managing cattle, rather than *cowboy*, with its connotations of theft, violence, and youthful excess.

Another product of this violent cauldron was a breed of cattle that made cowboys famous: the Texas longhorn. Descended from the Spanish cattle brought to America by Cortez, these cattle had grown wilder and meaner than their ancestors. In the decades after Texan independence from Mexico, they mixed with "American" cattle brought to Texas by herders from throughout the South. Allowed to roam freely in the mesquite thickets, brush country, and wooded hills of the Texas range, they adapted to their disorderly circumstances and evolved a sturdy self-reliance.[25] Hard hooves and long legs allowed them to travel great distances in search of food and water, which their keen sense of smell allowed them to find at great distances. During times of drought, they were resourceful enough to use their horns to pull down branches from a cottonwood tree in order to eat the leaves. They were known to consume the blossoms of cacti if necessary. Longhorns traveled alone or in small bunches and did not hesitate to use their outward-facing horns to fend off predators, including wolves, mountain lions, or humans on foot.[26]

Although longhorns might be found in different degrees of domestication, it was the truly wild animals that gave the breed its reputation. Feral cattle who had never known the human touch and who remained unbranded and uncontrolled were known to Spanish ranchers as *cimarrons* (wild, unruly, or runaway, later applied to escaped slaves) because they had completely returned to nature.[27] These animals were not only without owner but were often considered too wild to capture and turn to human purposes. As truly wild animals, they were in a class with deer, bison, or other creatures whose "instinct for the wild was too strong." Although they were dangerous to a man on foot, a few sport hunters who found a challenge in tracking the elusive creature reported that longhorns were more evasive than deer and harder to kill than buffalo. Colonel R. I. Dodge claimed that "the wild cattle of Texas" were "fifty times more dangerous to footmen than the fiercest buffalo." Another soldier noted that shooting a "wild Texas cow" was harder than killing "the most cautious and wary old buck. To kill a buffalo is but child's play compared with it."[28] Big-game hunters visiting Texas sometimes aimed for wild longhorns, considering them to be one of the most prized trophies.

The raw freedom that the wildest longhorn cattle enjoyed eventually spread a reputation of rugged independence to the entire breed, as well as to the cowboys who followed them, reversing traditional ideas about nature. In the early nineteenth-century, Americans held a widespread belief that humans could—and should—improve upon raw nature by turning land and animal to a higher moral purpose.[29] By the middle of the century, Americans were beginning to rethink such ideas. Popular culture had made heroes out of frontiersmen Daniel Boone and Davey Crockett, and Henry David Thoreau explored the possibilities of finding moral clarity by living apart from civilization. In this new celebration of untamed nature, previously despised wild cattle were now lending a sense of "barbaric virtue" and "primitive strength" to the once lowly occupation of cattle herder.[30] The longhorns—wild, independent, and free—gave this same reputation to the men who herded them.[31] Longhorns and cowboys, these co-creations of the Texas frontier, were forged together. It remained to be seen whether cattle drives would be a harbinger of civilization or a departure from it.

Cash on the Hoof

The English language speaks to the deep connection between livestock and money. The Latin word *pecunia*, from which comes the word *pecuniary*, is derived from *pecus*, or "cattle herd."[32] In the vernacular, cattle were often referred to as "cash on the hoof." In antebellum Texas, where money was scarce and cattle abundant, this became literally true. A "cow and a calf," or a paper promise to pay the equivalent, became a kind of substitute currency, widely accepted and transferred in much the same way as printed money. Called "cow paper," this informal, semilegal tender may have inspired the two-dollar bill printed by the Republic of Texas, which pictured a mounted rider chasing a horned steer.[33] In early Texas, as in other cattle frontiers, accruing wealth in cattle was often preferred to amassing wealth in land; not only did cattle represent portable wealth, but their natural fecundity meant that they multiplied faster than other forms of capital. This meaning is continued in the contemporary stock market, where a "bull market" is the metaphor for seemingly natural increase of the value of stocks. Today's paper stocks, like the livestock of nineteenth-century Texas, can create the illusion of a rapid multiplication of value. Yet however valuable this "cow paper" might have been as a means of barter in a subsistence economy, the natural increase of longhorn cattle could only translate into wealth if the "cash on the hoof" could be transformed into money in the bank. Because of Texas's position at the western edge of American society, markets remained distant, expensive, and uncertain.

For that reason, cattle's greatest commercial value was in the hide and tallow markets. Cows were slaughtered, skinned, and boiled. Their hides were dried for leather, their fat rendered into tallow for candles, and their meat dumped into the river as worthless. When one hide and tallow plant near Beaumont filled the Neches River with cow carcasses, the scanty population of the region did not complain of the stench, perhaps because the practice created large, beef-fattened catfish in abundance. The port at Galveston regularly recorded four or five times as many cattle hides exported as beef cattle.[34] In a creative but ultimately failed attempt to create value out of the abundant supply of cattle, Gail Borden Jr. developed a "Meat Biscuit" made of dehydrated beef mixed with flour. Despite winning an award in London, the "Meat Biscuit" was reported to taste "insipid and without flavor." With no orders coming in from the anticipated customers, armies and overland travelers, Borden's experiment languished. Despite a decade of effort and a plant in Galveston, he found no market for his Texas beef in any form. Borden recovered successfully, however, making a fortune by adapting a condensation process, originally developed to dehydrate meat, to put condensed milk in a can.[35] That business, however, thrived with dairy cattle in Connecticut rather than longhorns in Texas.

Other ways to transform longhorns into a commercial commodity proved spotty at best. Steamships carried live cattle from ports in Galveston and Indianola to markets in New Orleans and the Caribbean, but the high freight rates and tendency of these cattle to lose weight in transit made this option less than lucrative. During the 1850s trail drivers took perhaps as many as fifty thousand Texas cattle to feed the multitudes of California immigrants. Many of these trail drives combined herds of cattle with prospective miners eager for a way to get to the goldfields. A cow costing as little as $5 in Texas might sell for anywhere from $25 to $150 in California. But this market carried a high risk, as Apache cattle raiders and desert heat exacted a heavy toll in herds that passed through the Southwest. In 1852 James D. Mitchell, described as "a trader, dealing in horses, mules, cattle, and negroes," purchased five hundred cattle and set out for the West Coast. During the six-month journey, more than two-thirds of his men died of cholera. The survivors feared Indian attacks and were beset with hardships that were "beyond belief." Because they were passing through plains still rich with buffalo, they were compelled several times to corral their cattle and wait three or four days for the larger, wilder bovines to pass. In California, Mitchell received from $75 to $150 per head, but these profits were quickly diminished by high prices for other goods. In any case, the proceeds could never compensate for the loss of life or hardships of the journey.[36]

Even before the Civil War ambitious men had tried to make money from the abundant cattle by driving them north. Tom Candy Ponting led the best-known cattle drive, which anticipated the long drives to come. Born in England, Ponting started his cattle driving career at the age of fifteen with a trip of more than one hundred miles from his home in Somerset to a market in London. After immigrating to Illinois, he became involved in the midwestern cattle trade. Hearing about the cheap, plentiful cattle in Texas, he put his assets in gold pieces, traveled to Texas, and bought longhorns. In 1853 he started a four-month journey with 700 long-horned steers. First he drove them north through Indian Territory, where he purchased 80 more cows, then continued northeast through Missouri to Illinois, where the herd gained weight on stored corn. He sold most of them to the meat market in Chicago, but the 150 fattest steers he drove to Indiana, where they were loaded onto railroad cars and shipped to New York City. "These were," Ponting believed, "the first Texas cattle that were ever in New York."

This pattern of taking lean cattle over long distances to feeder farms and then to urban markets was no doubt familiar to Ponting from practices in his native Britain. Similar, too, were the herding techniques used by Ponting's drive. He drove a supply wagon, pulled by a belled ox that doubled as a lead steer, with the herd following along. Although he was nervous about traveling through Indian Territory, the native people proved useful when he hired several of them to build a raft to ferry the herd across the Arkansas River. When possible, his men stopped at farmhouses to purchase butter, eggs, and bacon. Near Saint Louis, he hired a ferry to carry his livestock across the Mississippi River. Surprisingly, he made the entire two-thousand-mile journey with no serious incidents. The New York newspapers delighted readers with reports of the possibilities of more beef drawn from the distant reaches of the continent, and the local butchers toasted Ponting for the success of his drive. These first Texas cattle brought good prices and made profits for Ponting, despite costing nearly twenty dollars per head to transport. But the New York butchers' initial enthusiasm waned after more experience with longhorns. As Ponting admitted, he got a good price because "Texas cattle were very deceiving, most men would guess them heavier than they were."[37]

The arrival of Texas cattle in New York came at a fortuitous moment, when Americans were learning to like beef more than pork. Before the Civil War, pigs had been the primary source of meat on American tables, but now beef became the meal of choice for the middle and working classes of New England, the Mid-Atlantic, and the Midwest. Cookbooks recommended beef while maligning pork as difficult to digest and unwholesome. One claimed that "beefsteak deserves the highest rank among breakfast fares. . . . This

Bible and chemically sanctioned food, purposely designed for man, is very satisfying to the stomach and possesses great strengthening powers." The popular magazine *Good Housekeeping* informed its readers that pork "does not generally meet the approval of intelligent people and is almost entirely discarded by hygienists."[38] Beef was the health food of the day, providing manly and all-American strength for middle- and working-class families alike. Immigrants preferred a meal of beef and potatoes, evidence of their newfound prosperity in this land of plenty.

Yet the cow that reproduced so abundantly in Texas was not successfully adapted to fit the nation's demand for beef. Meatpackers generally paid low prices for longhorns because they found them lean and stringy. The most generous evaluation for Ponting's longhorns came in New York, where the *Daily Tribune* reported that they had "something of a wild look" and were descended from "a most excellent breed of cattle from the South," even though the meat was "somewhat like venison, and apt to be a little tough cooked in the ordinary way."[39] It should have been no surprise that the longhorn, celebrated by some as being as wild as a deer, had meat as tough as venison. Other reports were less charitable. In Saint Louis, where longhorns fetched only fifteen or twenty dollars per head in 1854, the newspaper explained the low price because they were "about the nearest to wild animals of any now driven to market. We have seen some buffaloes that were more civilized." A few years later, the *New York Times* noted that a recent shipment of longhorns into the city "were barely able to cast a shadow . . . they would not weigh anything were it not for their horns."[40] Their reputation had gone from wild to ghostly. Horns and hooves on a lean body thrived in the Texas brush, but they made unsavory fare for the nation's beefeaters.

Texas Fever

As the longhorns trailed north, they carried with them another barrier to joining the nation's stream of commercial livestock. As early as 1853, farmers in western Missouri noted that Texas longhorns infected their own cattle with a mysterious but deadly disease. Although the longhorns had no visible signs of illness, in the wake of their passing, local cattle would become lethargic, their eyes would glaze over, and their head and ears would drop. Finally, their legs would weaken, until they staggered helplessly. As the disease progressed, they stopped eating, their temperatures rose, and their urine turned blood-red. Within eight to ten days, as many as 90 percent of afflicted cows were dead. The disease had a variety of names—Spanish fever, southern fever, acclimation fever, splenetic fever, and red-water fever, because of the urine—but most of all Texas fever, because of the association with Texas cattle. The etiology of this malaria-like disease would not be understood until decades later, when scientists described the cause of this mysterious illness to be a protozoan (*Babesia*). The disease was carried not by the cattle themselves but by cattle ticks (*Boophilus*), which attached themselves to the bovines. Both protozoan and tick had evolved in Africa and attached themselves to the Spanish cattle that came to the Americas. As these cattle moved north out of Mexico, they unwittingly carried the tick with them throughout the Southeast, wherever the climate was warm and wet enough to sustain it. The northern boundary of the cattle tick, as later defined by the US Department of Agriculture, very nearly corresponded with the usual definition of the South. If cattle ticks could vote, they would have almost all joined the Confederacy.[41]

As long as cattle remained in the South, the ticks and the fever they carried went largely unnoticed. Calves from birth were routinely exposed to the disease and became immune to the deadly symptoms. Humans suffered no ill consequences from eating the meat of tick-ridden cattle. Yet because southern calves suffered from repeated attacks of babesiosis during their formative years, they lived with repeated, long-term, low-grade infections, which stunted their growth. Outsiders to the South frequently commented on the poor quality of southern cattle: they were small, "scrubby," and "lean." Carrying only four hundred to six hundred pounds of beef, they were mere "pony cattle," one northern livestock judge pronounced. If southern cattle were inferior, this judge continued, then Texas cattle were "poor even by Southern standards . . . largely semi-wild and probably worth only one-half as much as animals in other Southern states."[42] In line with their own biases, visitors attributed these deficiencies to southern sloth, mistreatment by slaves, the free-range grazing system, or the lack of proper attention to animal breeding. A better explanation may simply have been a medical one: having suffered from a persistent, low-grade infection, the cattle simply did not put on weight as rapidly as their northern counterparts. An early twentieth-century scientific study found that babesiosis caused cattle to weigh up to 20 percent less than cattle not raised with the disease.[43] Those New York and Saint Louis butchers who complained about the lack of meat on the longhorns' lean bodies were seeing the effects not only of a wild breed but also of one that grew up bearing ticks that carried growth-sapping protozoa.

The cattle tick caused more immediate and obvious problems when Texans first attempted to trail longhorns north to distant markets. Because a herd of Texas cattle passing through cultivated farming regions often left a trail of hideous disease and death to local cattle in its wake, farmers in Missouri and Kansas formed "vigilance committees," which forced the Texas herds to turn back. Rifle-bearing farmers and grassroots opposition to Texas herds, sometimes inflamed by Civil War–era animosities, led to laws, quarantines, and other restrictions that limited the longhorns' viability as "cash on the hoof." In response to agitation from farmers for relief from the dreaded Texas disease, the Missouri assembly on December 15, 1855, made it illegal to bring diseased cattle from any other state into Missouri. Although this first quarantine law proved difficult to enforce, it still had enough teeth to create, however briefly, the first cattle town in Kansas. As some Texas herds proceeded northeast to Saint Louis, in violation of the law, a few veered west, just inside the eastern border of Kansas. Along the way they stopped at a small trading post nestled in the southeastern corner of Kansas, only a few miles north of Indian Territory and just west of the Missouri border. Founded by John J. Baxter, the stop offered Texas cowboys not only cool spring water but tobacco, flour, and a few other trade goods, as well as corrals to hold their cattle. Merely a shadow of later cow towns, Baxter Springs owed its momentary fame to the cows it sent to market but mostly to the ticks that came all the way from Africa. In ways that were not apparent at the time, the ticks created the location for cattle market towns and moved them gradually westward across Kansas.

In 1858 a new outbreak of Texas fever in Missouri killed $2,000 worth of cattle and exposed the weakness of the original law. As cattle drives continued to stream by Baxter Springs, area farmers formed new vigilance committees, which met Texas herds at gunpoint, forcing them to turn back. The local newspaper declared: "No one can for a moment blame the citizens of Missouri for adopting summary measures to protect their stock from the fearful ravages of Spanish fever."[44] For their part, Texans pointed out that the transmission mechanism of the disease was not known, that Texas cattle were being blamed for possessing mysterious and imaginary powers, and claimed that they were "victims of a scare" that "was caused by a sudden prejudice which had sprung up against Texas cattle."[45] The fear of Texas cattle spread after thousands of cattle died from Texas fever in 1858, and the Kansas legislature banned all cattle (not only those that showed signs of disease) from Texas, Arkansas, and the Indian Territory from entering into southeastern Kansas during the summer and fall driving months. Kansans also took enforcement into their own hands, forming rifle companies to meet Texas herds at the border. In several tense encounters, a few longhorns were shot, but human deaths between well-armed Texans and Kansans were avoided, at least for the moment.

On the eve of the Civil War, tensions were already running high all along the volatile border between South and North, and diseased cattle simply added to the violent prospects. As Northerners shut off the supply of Southern cattle, protecting their own livestock, the overtones of the impending sectional crisis were unavoidable. In 1859 the *Dallas Herald* reported: "Yesterday a drove of two thousand beef cattle passed through Dallas en route for the North, to feed our abolition neighbors. We hope the southern diet may agree with them." Three weeks later, the same paper remarked that the "great exodus of cattle northward . . . seems to have ceased."[46] This may have been merely a comment on the seasonal fluctuation during that summer, but it also served as a telling comment on what the Civil War would bring to the Texas cattle trade.

Cattle had always outnumbered people in the Lone Star state, usually by a ratio of at least four to one. Sparsely populated Spanish missions had recorded herds in the tens of thousands during the eighteenth century, while Stephen F. Austin noted in 1830 that cattle were "cheap and abundant" in his colony, numbering about twenty thousand, or four times the population of Anglo immigrants settled there.[47] By the time the Civil War began, Texas had a human population of six hundred thousand and a cattle population at least five times that: more than 3 million. It led the nation in quantity (if not quality) of commercial cattle. During the war, all Northern states saw cattle numbers decline due to the heavy wartime demand to feed the Union Army. Ohio, a mainstay of the midwestern cattle business, saw its cattle decrease by one-third. California, along with Oregon and Nevada, also saw drops in cattle numbers.[48] Southern states, which experienced the brunt of the war, experienced even larger declines in livestock. Because of the burden of feeding Confederate armies, Alabama, Georgia, and Virginia lost livestock due to the severity of fighting.[49] Everywhere cattle numbers were down, except in Texas. As young men left the ranches to join the Confederate Army, the cattle had less exposure than ever to human management and did what longhorns did best: survive and multiply. By war's end, their number may have approached 5 million.

Nowhere was this comparison between Texas and its neighbors more dramatic than in Indian Territory. By 1860 the Cherokee, Chickasaw, and Choctaw nations had developed a vibrant pastoral economy based on the practices of the open range, annual roundups, and livestock drives to market managed by horse-riding herders with whips and dogs. Mild winters and luxuriant grasses made cattle-raising a prosperous venture in Indian Territory, enough so that their herds numbered in the hundreds of thousands. Buyers came from midwestern markets and even the West Coast to purchase them. With a total human population in 1860 of fifty thousand, these native nations managed a cattle population of at least half a million. The Civil War changed all this, as rival armies moved through the region, taking cattle to feed themselves and leaving spoliation in their wake. Cattle that were not devastated by the war were stolen by thieves from both sides and then sold to hungry armies. In 1865 the Commissioner of Indian Affairs reported that "at least 300,000 head of cattle" had been "stolen from the Indian Territory, a country at one time rich in their cattle possessions, and now scarcely a head can be seen in a ride of 200 miles."[50] A Cherokee girl, six years old when the war started, remembered it as a time when soldiers robbed homes, killed hogs, and drove away cattle. Such, she concluded, were the "terrors of war." Another Cherokee recalled "the destroying hand of war" as responsible for the loss of abundant livestock. When the long drives from Texas through Indian Territory started in 1866, they went through not a virgin prairie of free grass, but a vacated prairie of Indian-owned grassland that the Civil War had transformed into, in the words of one native rancher, "a desert."[51]

With the supply of cattle drained all around, it seemed that Texas longhorns were in a unique position to dominate the cattle market. Texas congressman John A. Wilcox declared at the beginning of the war that his state possessed enough cattle to provide beef for the entire Confederate Army if only the Confederate Commissary would pay the expense of driving cattle east from Texas. The commissary partially obliged, and several prominent Texas cattlemen, including John Chisum and Oliver Loving, delivered herds of cattle to Louisiana and Mississippi early in the war. In 1862 New Orleans fell to Union forces, closing the market for many Texans. The loss of Vicksburg in 1863 ended the export of Texas cattle across the Mississippi, and for the last two years of the war there was virtually no market for Texas cattle. A few cattlemen took their cattle to Mexico, and a few Lone Star ranchers drove their beef cattle west to the Union forces in New Mexico, pioneering a cattle trail that became famous after the war as the Goodnight-Loving trail.[52] For the most part, however, the war closed markets for Texas cattle, called the young men who might have worked on ranches to battlefields, and drained the supply of cattle from competing states. While the young men fought, cattle were left to their own pursuits: herds wandered, cows multiplied, and calves were left unbranded.

When the soldiers came home from the war with worthless Confederate money in their pockets and looked at the impoverished Texas countryside, ranching represented one of the few avenues to prosperity. Land policy in Texas had always been generous toward homesteaders. As soon as it was independent of Mexico, the Lone Star Republic passed the first homestead law, allowing grants of one hundred sixty acres after only three years of residency, a more generous homesteading policy than the federal law passed in 1862. Moreover, unlike the federal law, which preferred the cultivation of land with a plow, Texas land laws anticipated that most of the semiarid plains of the state were not suitable for conventional farming and would be better suited to livestock grazing. Thus, with very little cash in hand, the enterprising Texan might begin a ranch. The real key to a prosperous ranch was owning the scarcest commodity around: water. A homestead claim built around a water source might control the grassland for thousands of surrounding acres. In later years the state sold its public land for a mere fifty cents an acre, a price so low that powerful ranchers were able to purchase and fence in thousands of acres of central and western Texas. As large ranches came to own much of the state during the 1880s, opportunities closed for start-ups, but during the first fifteen years or so after the Civil War, a generous land policy made the open range a reality and created the possibility of turning cattle into cash.[53]

For many Texans, the most disturbing obstacle to developing a cattle economy was the renewal of Comanche attacks during and after the Civil War. With so many would-be fighters away during the war, Comanches experienced a brief revival of their power and experimented with incorporating cattle into their own raiding and trading economy. As frontier counties lost population, settlers experienced a "great insecurity" along a line stretching some three hundred miles, from west of San Antonio all the way north to the Red River. As one observer lamented, "Instead of the western portion of

Texas expanding with new settlements and thriving villages, as it should be, the line of settlement is being contracted, on account of the frequent depredations of the Indians."[54] For their part, Comanches learned to eat beef for subsistence, substituting it for bison in some cases, and used captured longhorns, in addition to horses, to extend their trading influence in New Mexico and southwestern Texas. The longhorns' ability to travel long distances made them especially valuable for the Comanches. Although the fear of Indian raids may have been exaggerated along the Texas frontier, the loss of both human life and cattle was real enough to restrict the development of ranching and cattle trails to the eastern part of the state. It was not until after the Comanche defeat in the 1874 Red River War that ranchers, and cattle trails, could safely move into the central and western plains of Texas, Indian Territory, and Kansas.[55]

In the meantime, many of the ingredients that would make the long drives an attractive risk were in place. Longhorn cattle thrived in Texas, more numerous than the cattle in any other state. The cowboy system offered the labor and techniques for managing them on the long drives. The war had devastated the competition, leaving Texas in a position of unprecedented, if somewhat artificial, dominance. Yet obstacles still remained: at the edge of the Southwest, Texas was a long distance from urban markets, and ticks that accompanied Texas cattle were still lethal to other livestock. In 1866 the owners may have been eager to transform cattle into capital, but supply was still in search of demand.

2. How the Cattle Market Boomed and Busted

THE SPREAD OF THE CATTLE KINGDOM throughout the American West represented one of the great opportunities for plunder and profit in the Gilded Age. The Texas economy was in shambles, but an estimated 5 million to 6 million cows grazed on public lands, free for the taking by anyone with initiative and means. As one cowboy reminisced, "After the war a vast number of unclaimed cattle were running loose; they were the spoil of whoever could rope them."[1] While Union soldiers returned to farms with diminished herds and other Confederate soldiers retreated to devastated countrysides, Texas veterans went home to find thousands of unbranded, half-wild cattle roaming freely on the prairie.[2] Later generations remembered these as "the good old days of free range, when the grass was as free as the air" and a man with cattle "was monarch of all he surveyed."[3] In the aftermath of a war that left much of the South racked with poverty, southeastern Texas boasted of natural wealth ready for the taking. In report after report designed to boost economic development in the state, the *Texas Almanac* described the region as "a paradise of horses, sheep, and cattle."[4]

This Eden grew cattle without effort or expense, supported by forces seen and unseen. Texas land laws made it easy for war veterans and immigrants to homestead or purchase small acreages, offering a promised land for farmers and ranchers. Available land was considered open range—free for anyone to use. In these early years, even nature cooperated. The two decades after the Civil War provided more moisture than average, with generally mild winters.

Here in this land of plenty, a seemingly unlimited supply of unbranded cattle presented a unique entrepreneurial opportunity, a chance to get rich without any capital, especially if one was similarly unburdened by scruples or a keen sense of the law.[5]

The easiest method of cashing in on wild cattle was to round them up and drive them to the nearest port city. In the decade after the Civil War, Galveston and other Gulf Coast ports shipped thousands of longhorns each year by steamboat to markets in New Orleans and Havana. Smaller numbers of longhorns were moved by steamship up the Mississippi River to Illinois, where they were transferred to railroad cars and forwarded to stockyards throughout the Midwest. The *Texas Almanac* reported that four thousand head of cattle left Texas ports each month during 1867. The next year the total shipments nearly doubled. The *Almanac* encouraged ranchers, claiming that the best beef cattle could garner twenty-five dollars per head in the New Orleans market, a tidy return on a five-dollar steer.[6] But shipping costs cut into this profit, as would the inevitable loss of weight and sometimes loss of life for the longhorns during this cramped, stressful water journey.

The optimistic *Almanac* also exaggerated the price a longhorn could command in Illinois. Knowing that potential cattle purchasers would need to fatten the longhorns on pasture for several months before they would be "presentable," a local newspaper concluded, "They are the ugliest brutes we ever saw of the bovine species. With horns so long they can barely pass the car door, they are bully chaps for glue."[7] Other ranchers looked for profits in their longhorns by building "factories" to process their skin, horns, and bones. Until the business fizzled in the late 1870s, steamships crammed with barrels of tallow and stocked with hides of longhorns left the Gulf Coast of Texas bound for New Orleans or the East Coast. The *Texas Almanac* counted at least 205,000 hides leaving Texas ports in 1869.[8] Profits were lower for these disassembled longhorns, but the risks were few.

What would become the most popular route for changing cattle into cash offered the highest potential for earnings as well as the greatest risk: the long drive to Kansas railheads. Ranchers could gather their herd, hire a crew, purchase provisions, and drive their own cattle north, perhaps even combining animals with those from neighboring ranches for efficiency. Initially, this option also had the advantage of being open to all comers, or at least to those who had the wherewithal to gather a herd of wild or semiwild cattle. "Men of enterprise," as the chroniclers of the cattle kingdom called themselves, would risk trailing these large herds over hundreds of treacherous miles, bringing Texas ranchers into the national economy. These cattle entrepreneurs were a distinct species of Gilded Age capitalist, part David Crockett and part Horatio Alger: a thoroughly modern business man grafted onto a frontier folk hero.[9]

Gathering a Herd

The first step of the long drives was a centuries-old method of finding feral cattle: the cow hunt. Some hunts were organized by wealthy ranchers who hired anywhere from three to two dozen riders. One participant remembered hunts with crew of up to one hundred. Only men working together could catch, hold, and brand large numbers of these semiwild cattle. Animals were kept in temporary corrals held together by lariats while each one in turn was roped, held down, and branded, a process that necessitated numerous workers, each with a clear role. The postwar cattle surplus was so large that ranchers had to use hired hands to manage the vast herds, often engaging Mexican vaqueros and boys in their teens to do the work. Pay ranged from twenty to forty dollars per month, depending on the skill and equipment a laborer brought to the job. Will Hale, a young man at the time, recalled that his father "employed lots of Mexicans" to build his "great herd."[10]

Other cow hunts were community events without hired labor or much hierarchy, and these offered a possibility for individuals to amass their own collection. Lee Moore, later a trail driver and foreman of a Wyoming ranch, remembered of these early days: "Every man on this cow-hunt was a cattle-owner just home from the war. . . . They played [poker] for unbranded cattle, yearlings at fifty cents a head, so if anyone run out of cattle and had a little money, he could get a stack of yearlings."[11] These community hunts offered more opportunity for anyone to collect a herd, but they required pronounced self-reliance. On some cow hunts, herders were expected to bring along an extra horse and perhaps rawhide ropes. Every rider was expected to prepare his own "grub," supply his own mount, and provide his own *reata*. "Each man," one vaquero noted, "had a tin cup, some coffee, salt, perhaps some sugar, and either meal or a supply of corn bread." Cow hunters might supplement this diet with meat from cattle too wild to be branded.[12] For all of the cooperative elements of the cow hunts, Texas folklorist J. Frank Dobie suggests the Darwinian nature of this Gilded Age enterprise: "The open range was for the strong, for those who could hold as well as take."[13]

And take they did! Any unbranded cattle were considered fair game. One Texas cow herder, James G. Shaw, remembered the "poor soldiers" who returned from the war "barefooted, with little clothing and very much discouraged." Many of these men, Shaw recalled, spent the summer and fall of 1865 searching for cattle and claiming ownership of "anything that was not branded."[14] Texans had come to consider any unbranded calves "mavericks," probably named after Samuel A. Maverick, a rancher with a reputation for not branding all of his calves. When he sold his herd, the new owner claimed that any unbranded cow on the range was one of Maverick's and belonged to him. This fueled the idea that any "unmarked and unbranded calves" were mavericks and became the property of anyone who "found and branded them."[15]

Some cow hunters, however, were known to collect branded cattle—those already claimed as property—along with unbranded creatures. One trail hand remembered that "the maverick business" amounted to "the wholesale gathering of any and every ones cattle."[16] Some returning soldiers, Shaw observed, had "little respect for law," which they viewed as "an infringement upon their natural rights." He concluded that capturing stray calves, with or without brands, and slapping one's own brand on them amounted to a kind of "systematic thieving."[17] Texas cowboy Will S. James described these early years as a "general scramble as to who should get the greatest number, and on account of thousands of cattle having become wild and unruly because of neglect a very general license was granted, or rather taken, to kill and eat when one was hungry. . . . This, in after years, produced a regular harvest of thieves."[18]

During these early years stealing cattle became deeply ingrained in cattle culture. One widely circulated tale told of the Texas cattleman who invited a neighbor to dinner with a promise to feed him something he had never tasted before. When the neighbor arrived, he sat down for an ordinary-looking steak. The joke, of course, is that this beef was from his own herd, which he had never tasted because no Texas cattleman would eat his own cows when he could take one from his neighbor. Other stories, told with a wink and a nod, spread the lore that eating one's own beef would cause illness. Prominent rancher and trail driver Charles Goodnight reported that it was "a custom to kill everybody's beef but your own," which he blamed on the "lawless conditions" of early Reconstruction. He tells of a neighboring ranch woman who "would as leave eat one of her little children as one of her own beeves."[19]

In later years, cattle ranchers would popularize the term *rustling* as a description for stealing cattle and assert an official history that claimed honesty had been present all along. The National Live Stock Association, for instance, concludes that among ranchers "the cardinal rule is and has been from the beginning to guard a neighbor's property . . . and to see that it went back to him."[20] A very different account that circulated in the early days of trail driving may be closer to the truth: A group of cattlemen captured a thief who had run off with some of their cattle. After eating a final meal with him, they announced their intentions to hang him. For his final words, he did not deny his crime but simply asked for "the one of you who never stole a cow to step forward and put the noose around my head." The cattlemen responded with shocked silence and then laughter. In biblical fashion, as there was no one without sin, there was no one to cast stones, or in this case to brandish a noose.[21]

Regardless of ownership, there was no doubt that gathering a herd by means of a cow hunt required specialized skills and determined labor. Texas cowboys used a variety of techniques, many of them learned from Mexican vaqueros. The most straightforward was to lasso a cow and rope it to a tree until it tired out—effective but time consuming. Alternatively, groups of wild cattle might be surrounded at a watering place and herded into a pen, sometimes with the use of decoy cows—tame animals that mingled with the wilder ones and led them into the corral. This technique had limited success, as one cattle worker recalled: "After a hard day's hunt we headed towards camp with around a hundred head of the wildest and shaggiest bunch of scalawag steers that I have ever seen together. They ran and fought all the way, and out of the hundred we corralled only thirty-seven head." More resistant cattle might be "hog-tied" by roping their back feet together. For sheer excitement a cowboy might ride up behind a cow, grab its tail, twist it around his saddle horn, and jerk the animal to the ground. Some experienced cowhands could "tail" a cow with such force that they broke the animal's neck, although owners frowned on this practice, not so much for its brutality but because it resulted in one less cow for the herd.

Cruelty was part of standard practice. Even when broken "gently," one cattle hand recalled, "if the word *gently* can ever by applied to such a process—a grown animal is almost sure to be somewhat bruised. . . . The cow hunt was no place for members of the Humane Society. Nothing in the way of kindness would work on those old mossy horns." If all else failed, a technique to subdue a spirited steer was to shoot him through "the thick part of his horn." With proper aim, "the pain of the jar calmed the steer very promptly and he became manageable." Bad aim might kill the steer, and bad luck might ricochet the bullet back at the shooter. Truly unmanageable cows were eliminated. It was considered "an advantage to get rid of these outlaws at any price. They spoiled other cattle. They had to be either shot or driven off."[22] The cow that could not be reduced to property, subdued to human purposes, was a danger to the domesticated cattle, an "outlaw" that might steal them away, and was to be treated as such.

While cow hunts could be dangerous to cattle and horses, the danger appealed to some human participants. In one instance a cowboy rode out to rope a "big powerful steer, with horns long, well set for hooking and sharp as a lance." With the steer lassoed and the rope tied to the saddle horn, the large beast "jerked the horse down" trapping the rider's leg underneath. As the steer turned and charged, the now helpless man grabbed his revolver and shot the furious animal through the brain. The physical challenge and obvious danger of the cow hunt attracted "the young and adventurous,"[23] including returning soldiers as well as those too young to fight in the Civil War. Cow hunts offered a thrill that helped to entice young men into the life of the cattle drive, even if only for a summer. The mystique of the cowboy was beginning to take shape.

The relative equality of opportunity offered by cow hunts allowed for an aspiring rancher to put together a small herd of his own and trail it northward with animals from other herds. "It was the custom in those days," one rancher explained, for a trail herder "to take along cattle belonging to people they knew. . . . After driving the cattle up the trail to market, we then, on our return home, paid for cattle as the claimants appeared." This was done on trust and personal relationships, and many early drivers proudly remembered the days "when a man's word was as good as a gilt-edged note." In 1868 George Steen gathered his neighbor's cattle entirely on credit and even purchased supplies based solely on his spoken promise to pay.[24]

Within a few years the trail drives became more integrated into the national capitalist economy, and this older system of individuals with personal relationships gave way to professional contractors who worked according to business principles. They preferred larger herds, usually about twenty-five hundred or three thousand, a size that was small enough to control and large enough to maximize profits. Cow hunts were then replaced by more organized roundups, which had a chuck wagon, a boss, and specialized roles for each cowboy in the herding and branding process. Even the demographics of cattle herds became specialized. A cow hunt generally produced a herd of both sexes and mixed ages in which all were sent to market. The inclusion of cows of all ages caused problems on the trail, as some cattle were too feeble to be of value in the Kansas meat market. Professional drovers preferred to work only with steers, defined as mature neutered males, usually four years old. These "beeves" had the reputation of being better suited for long distances, even though they were more likely to stampede than a mixed herd of male, female, and young cattle. Nevertheless, standardized herds meant higher profits.

Whether gathered by cow hunt or by professional drover, a herd required a proper brand before hitting the trail. In addition to its ranch brand, they were given a road brand to mark them all as part of the same traveling herd. According to Texas law in 1871, all cattle driven in the northern part of the state had to have "a large and plain mark . . . which shall be branded on the left side of the back behind the shoulder." To brand these large, semi-domesticated creatures, cowhands bunched them in makeshift corrals while other workers heated the branding irons in a fire nearby. A cowboy or a vaquero would select a calf, throw a lasso over its head, and drag it toward the branding station. With a larger calf, a second lasso would catch the hind legs to stretch the animal while a third cowboy would grab either the tail or the belly of the calf and toss it to the ground. With the animal immobilized, another man placed the red hot ironing brand on its flank, being certain to burn through the hair and into the tender flesh, because a "hair brand" would not last through the season and could be altered by a "cattle entrepreneur" using a "running iron" to change the original brand. A cowboy, perhaps with his pocket knife, would cut the calf's ear with a distinctive mark, and another one would sever the male calf's testicles. With that the calf was released to scramble off and join the protection of the herd. The process required skilled ropers, "a good, clean knife, and a red-hot iron." Even so, the sizzle of cow flesh, the smell of burning hair, the sound of bawling calves, and the feel of constant heat and dust surely distressed some young workers. "Catching, throwing, and branding is hard work," one cowboy recalled. "The sun is hot, the corral full of dust from the cattle running round and round, and your clean suit is spoiled with blood and dirt." Yet the reward was clear. Every time the cowboy "slaps on the brand he seals a bit of property worth ten to fifteen dollars."[25]

Over time branding came to bear enormous symbolic significance. Branding livestock was an art as old as ancient Egypt and was associated with the medieval heraldic tradition of emblems and coats of arms that signified nobility. This association of nobility carried over into Texas, where unique brands have been protected by law since the 1830s. Brands, even road brands, could be elegant as well as functional and became almost sacred. Applying a brand properly—one that was neither a "hair brand," so shallow that next year's growth of hair would cover it, or a deep brand, one that penetrated so far into the flesh that the brand scabbed and smudged—was widely recognized as an admirable skill that brought status to the cowboy who possessed it. The ability to read brands quickly also became a badge of honor among cowboys. Since cattle gained another brand when sold to a new owner, over time they might carry a variety of markings, which led to the quip about cattle arriving in Kansas, "The critter don't amount to much, but sure carried a lot of reading material."[26] Cowboys even took pride in riding for a particular brand, as if it were a latter-day coat of arms. Yet it was not the man who applied the hot iron who became the owner of the animal. Rather, the brand claimed cattle for the rancher or professional drover who owned both the animals as chattel and the cowboys as labor. Despite the cattle herders' loyalty to the brand and their pride in its skillful application, it was the cattlemen who accumulated the capital, and cowboys, the rural proletariat, who worked for their wages.[27]

Searching for Markets

Optimism about lucrative markets in the North abounded in 1866. With livestock shortages driving up the price of beef throughout the country, the goal for Texas ranchers was, in the memorable phrase of historian Walter Prescott Webb, to "connect the four-dollar cow with a forty-dollar market."[28] Texans herded an estimated 260,000 cattle northward during this first year after the Civil War, but their optimism proved premature.[29]

There were a few success stories, like that of Missouri cattle trader J. D. Hunter. Born in Scotland, Hunter had joined the Colorado gold rush in 1859. When both his mining prospects and his health failed, he returned to Missouri. After several years, he thought he saw another gold rush in the form of Texas cattle. He purchased four hundred head and began trailing them toward the railhead in Sedalia, Missouri. Problems began when a local sheriff arrested Hunter and detained his herd, presumably for violating quarantine laws. Hunter cleverly persuaded the sheriff to join him at the local saloon, where he bought the lawman drinks until he was too inebriated to detain either Hunter or his cattle. He then moved his herd west into Indian Territory, where he rested them on the free grass of the Neutral Strip, a portion of Indian Territory just below the Kansas border. At last he drove them north again to a railhead in eastern Kansas. By stopping in Joliet, Illinois, long enough to fatten up his herd on bluestem prairie pasture, Hunter increased the value of the skinny longhorns enough to reap a profit of six thousand dollars. For the next five years he drove cattle north from Texas, sold them for a tidy profit, to either the Chicago market or government contractors, and became a prosperous cattle trader and later a livestock advisor to the railroads.[30] Presumably, success in the long drive required not only the cleverness to outwit a sheriff but also the determination and good fortune to find the best railroad access to markets. Hunter's shrewd realization that longhorns needed to be "beefed up" on prairie grasses before heading to the stockyards offered a preview of the pattern that would become so profitable in years to come.

Most of the long drives that year, attempting to move some quarter of a million cattle, were not as successful. Most were driven toward the railroad connection in Sedalia, Missouri, a route that was generally familiar to Texans as the Shawnee Trail, yet drovers encountered a wide variety of daunting obstacles. Coming face to face with densely thicketed forests in the Ozark Plateau or with flooding rivers, some turned back or sold their herds to local farmers. Texas herds also encountered significant opposition from Kansas and Missouri farmers afraid of Texas fever. One trail boss whose herd was turned back at the Kansas border declared that the state offered nothing but "sunshine, sunflowers, and sons-of-bitches."[31] Lingering Civil War animosities added to the tension, with former Union soldiers still leery of the ex-Confederates and their diseased cattle. Texans complained of "Jayhawkers" and "Red-legs," references to Civil War–era antislavery marauders, who acted like "armed mobs" composed of "soldiers mustered out of the Yankee army" and who were "nothing more than a bunch of cattle rustlers." Sometimes at gunpoint, Kansas and Missouri farmers stopped herds, charged high fees for the privilege of passing through pasture lands, or stampeded the longhorns. In this first year after the Civil War, all parties easily resorted to violence as, according to one Texan source, "the West was over-run by hordes of the most infamous scoundrels that ever encumbered the earth."[32] Given these difficulties, almost 40 percent of the longhorns that went up the trail did not reach their destination that year and spent the winter on pastures south of Kansas, in Indian Territory.

One widely circulated story illustrated for Texas cattlemen the injustice of their situation in 1866. J. M. Daugherty, a sixteen-year-old cowboy, acquired one thousand head of cattle, hired five cowboys, and set out for the rail connection in Sedalia, Missouri. After crossing the Red River into Indian Territory, they met a group of Cherokee Indians, who, in accordance with Cherokee law, demanded payment for crossing their lands. Daugherty refused and turned the herd east into Arkansas and then north toward Baxter Springs. As they approached, according to Daugherty, about fifteen or twenty Jayhawkers swooped down on him, shot his companion out of his saddle, stampeded the herd, and took him prisoner. These vigilante health inspectors, or "armed outlaws," depending on your point of view, tried and found Daugherty guilty of bringing cattle infested with Texas fever into the country. They threatened to hang him or whip him severely, but he claimed that he was ignorant of any laws about Texas fever, and they released him. He rejoined his crew, gathered the cattle, and with the help of a guide and stealthy nighttime herding, was able to get his cattle to market. He went on to become a significant Texas cattleman, while his story, sometimes augmented with an illustration of Daugherty being whipped, served to remind Texans of their role as innocent victims of Yankee prejudice.[33]

While connecting Texas cattle with the national market remained alluring but frustrating, the more successful drives in 1866 focused on western markets. Mining towns, the US Army, and reservation Indians proved the most reliable customers. Nelson Story led one of the largest and most exciting drives, starting near Fort Worth, Texas, and traveling all the way to the gold camps near Bozeman, in Montana Territory. With about one thousand longhorns and more than twenty well-armed cowboys, Story cursed Jayhawkers in Texas, violated army orders to stop in Wyoming, and fought with Lakota Sioux along the Bozeman Trail. Arriving in Bozeman at the coming of winter, Story sold his longhorns for at least ten times the purchase price and instantly became a leading cattleman, merchant, and banker in the new territory.[34] His were the first longhorns on the northern plains, but it would be more than a decade before the complete subjugation of the Lakota allowed for other drovers to venture along this trail.

One of the more famous of these early drives took place when twenty-year-old Charles Goodnight joined forces with the older Oliver Loving. Their crew included impoverished Confederate army veterans, one who had been dismissed from the Confederate Army for mental instability, and a former slave named Bose Ikard, who would become Goodnight's trusted companion. They took their combined herd west through a rugged desert, complete with quicksand, alkali water sources, and hostile Apaches and Comanches. Goodnight reasoned that the western trail would have two advantages: "a mining region would have more . . . money, and second, in that region there was good cattle country, so if I could not sell, I could hold."[35] He was right on both counts. In New Mexico they received as much as $60 per animal, paid for by the US Army for distribution as annuity payments to reservation Indians. Loving continued northward toward Denver, where emerging cattle king John Iliff bought the rest of the herd to be pastured on free grass in eastern Colorado. Goodnight returned to Texas carrying $12,000 in gold on his pack mule, an instant legend, and he gathered more herds for future trips. The path they traveled became known as the Goodnight-Loving Trail, and their success secured both men places in the lore of the western cattle industry.

Yet the image of Goodnight heading back over the treacherous trail to Texas with thousands of dollars in gold bulging out of his saddlebags emphasized the need for more secure financial transactions. It was one thing to turn cattle into capital, and gold was especially valuable after the collapse of Confederate currency, but it was quite another to have cattle turned into a safely transferable medium of exchange. Cattle country prided itself on its honest handshake agreements, and Goodnight's biographer declares that the partnership of Goodnight and Loving, agreed at a campfire "in the wilderness," was without paper or lawyers, and "yet its conditions bound its parties as strongly as the threads of life."[36] Other Texas cowmen also bought and sold cattle based on personal rather than paper relationships. Shanghai Pierce, for instance, who rose from poverty to become a legendary cattle trader, liked to arrive in a cow camp on horseback with a black employee carrying gold and silver on a pack animal. After Pierce spent a day or two selecting which cows to buy (rumor was that the portly Pierce preferred his cows large and fat, the better for profits but also mirroring his own body shape), the "Negro servant" poured out gold and silver from sacks to pay for them. Then "Shang" told stories until late into the evening. The whole ritual emphasized his personal power over others and his influence throughout the region.[37] Such arrangements reflected the moral integrity of the cattle buyers and demonstrated how some of them relied upon the sometimes dubious prospect that their reputations would guarantee their personal safety. But these word-and-a-handshake transactions could not sustain a cattle industry ready to supply a nation. Not until secure banking and credit were in place could Texas cattle be in a position to meet the nation's demand for beef.

In this first year after the Civil War, the experiment of herding longhorns over the long trail to midwestern markets had so discouraged Texas cattlemen that only an estimated thirty-five thousand cattle—scarcely more than one-tenth of the previous year's—crossed the Red River on their way to markets in 1867. That year six states—Colorado, Nebraska, Kansas, Missouri, Illinois, and Kentucky—passed new laws to keep out the disease-bearing Texas cattle. As a result, more longhorns were sent by steamship from Galveston to New Orleans or Havana than were herded northward. The revival of markets for hides, horns, and tallow meant that the scrawny longhorns were often worth more for their parts in Texas than for their beef potential in Kansas.[38] Those drovers who did attempt the long drive northward were desperate to find a trail west of Kansas farmers and east of the Apache and Comanche. More than anything, they needed access to railroads and secure financial arrangements. The lawless borderlands between Texas and Kansas, they complained, allowed "swindlers and confidence men" to pay with "worthless checks, bogus drafts, or other bottomless considerations from smooth and winsome strangers."[39] In a border country where cash was scarce and theft was a constant concern, prospective cattle buyers did not want to carry cash and so offered notes of sale that might or might not carry any value. If Texans were used to trusting the honesty of a face-to-face transaction with one another, this did not apply in the world of strangers, namely, Yankees and Jayhawk farmers. In the absence of systems of credit, banking, and stable law enforcement, the long drives made very little sense. For the first chaotic years after the Civil War, one report concluded, "the northern drives of cattle from Texas were not upon the whole profitable to the drovers." Joseph McCoy concluded that the drives of 1866 were a "great disaster to the Southern drover."[40] If the Texans were to turn their cattle into capital, they needed some law and order, an extension of the railroads, and some Yankee capitalist organization.

Making a Boom

The expansion of railroads was a key ingredient in the success of the long drives. It is not too much of an exaggeration to say that the drives that made the cowboy famous began simply as a long walk to the train station. In the eight years after the Civil War, the nation doubled its railroad mileage, with most of the growth spreading out into the Great Plains.[41] In particular, the Kansas Pacific and the Atchison, Topeka, and Santa Fe built lines through Central Kansas that offered the possibility of connecting the Texas herds with the stockyards of Kansas City and Chicago. A few other elements of Gilded Age business activity would be needed—entrepreneurial activity, political favoritism, novel financial arrangements, and even a bizarre advertising scheme—but more than anything else, railroads made the long cattle drives possible. Without railroads, the smoke-belching engine of modern life, the dusty trail of the pastoral era would have been an obscure footnote to history.

Yet the cattle drives still required new laws, and creative ways around the laws, for the new cattle economy to flourish. On February 26, 1867, the Kansas legislature passed a quarantine law representing a compromise between the Kansans who hoped to profit from the Texas cattle trade and those in the eastern third of the state, who demanded protection from Texas fever. Establishing a quarantine covering the eastern portion of the state, the new law prohibited Texas cattle from entering farming regions, but left large areas of the state open to longhorns. The Kansas Pacific had not yet built as far west as the quarantine line, so a cattle market could thrive only if the railroad was built westward. Yet many Kansans feared the idea of a cattle market in their state, viewing the longhorns, and their unruly Texas drovers, as an impediment to the civilizing project of spreading row-crop agriculture and building orderly towns with virtuous, church-going citizens. Farmers, in particular, feared that the cattle herds would trample their crops and infect their livestock. One letter to Kansas governor Samuel J. Crawford opposed the Texas cattle trade, claiming that, "as a mass, the settlers are against it. There are some fine herds of cattle in this part of Kansas, and now to have Texas fever break out among them would be bad. We are all afraid."[42]

If this fear was tinged with lingering Civil War animosities, the wariness was returned from the other side. It was Yankees, with their cold-fisted commerce, Texans contended, who had not yet learned the virtues of middle-class decency, order, and sobriety. In this sense, Texas fever was both a real issue and a stand-in for larger cultural differences. Nonetheless, a few Kansas towns pursued the cattle trade as an opportunity for economic development. Topeka, for instance, circulated an offer in Texas newspapers promising to have stockyard facilities and buyers ready for Texas herds in 1867. Later, Newton, Ellsworth, and Wichita briefly served as the destination for the long drive, while Dodge City became the premier link from trail to rail later in the

1870s. But it was Abilene that became the nation's first famous cow town, thanks to the strenuous labors of Joseph W. McCoy.

At age twenty-nine, McCoy brought youthful energy and an almost messianic enthusiasm for the project of connecting Texas cattle to Northern markets. A successful Illinois livestock trader, he had heard tales of the vast abundance of cattle, and he soon developed plans "to establish a market whereat [sic] the Southern drover and Northern buyer would meet upon equal footing." For McCoy, this was "an inspiration almost irresistible, rising superior to all other aspirations." His vision was about more than profit, although he worked plenty hard for that. He hoped to harness his and others' desire for financial success in a "great public good." His idealism about his mission led him to view anyone who interfered with the cattle trade as irrational or even subhuman. To refuse to participate in the cattle trade was, for McCoy, incomprehensibly brutish, an act of donkey stupidity."[43] Although impulsive and given to moments of wild speculation, he also had the respect of Illinois cattle buyers and earned the admiration of many Texas drovers. One friend called him "a man of advanced vision. He had what all men need but many lack—imagination." Another companion described McCoy as "a noble type of man, strong in character, with a large brain, but a visionary in much of his life work."[44]

Above all, McCoy was a market idealist. Where there was money to be made, prejudice would subside and legal barriers would melt away; the magic of the cattle marketplace, enabled by the railroad, would turn cattle into cash—or at least a reliable bank draft—and spread the smoothing balm of commercial prosperity throughout the nation. The key point was that selling a Southern resource—cattle—to a Northern market would bind together the nation's war wounds. He believed that commerce held the almost magical power to smooth over wartime animosities. McCoy, never one to miss an opportunity to make a grandiose claim for himself, later wrote that the cattle trade brought "an era of better feeling between Northern and Texas men by bringing them into contact with each other in commercial transactions."[45] Although the prosperity that McCoy envisioned for himself and others would prove more fleeting than he dreamed, the larger results for the nation proved more durable than anyone could have imagined.

McCoy scouted several Kansas towns that might serve as the railroad depot for longhorns, but those he approached had no interest in investing in stockyards or attracting Texas cattle. Junction City and Salina were farther west and more removed from settlements, but in those towns, as McCoy mockingly described himself, "The person making such propositions was apparently regarded as a monster threatening calamity and pestilence." He selected Abilene, in part because its poverty and obscurity made it anxious for a business opportunity. Located on the banks of Mud Creek, McCoy thought the location suited his needs because "the country was entirely unsettled, well watered, excellent grass, and nearly the entire area of country was adapted to holding cattle." The town itself, however, "was a small, dead place, consisting of about one dozen log huts, low small, rude affairs," most of them with sod roofs. Abilene also boasted a dry-goods store, a blacksmith, a hotel with six rooms, and of course a saloon, run by one Josiah Jones, "a corpulent, jolly, goodsouled, congenial old man of the backwoods pattern," meaning that he loved to hunt and fish and most especially to feed, trap, shoot, and sometimes sell to tourists the prairie dogs who lived near the town.[46]

For Abilene to become the destination for Texas cattle, McCoy had work to do. He first persuaded the Kansas Pacific Railroad to build a small side spur to accommodate the cattle traffic and to give him a small commission on all cattle shipped from this point. Although railroad officials may have been influenced by McCoy's persuasiveness, more likely they were convinced by the need to fill otherwise-empty eastbound trains with a paying cargo. Trains did a brisk business carrying people and supplies to Kansas towns but struggled to find passengers or cargo for the return trips. Cattle could fill that void. On June 18, 1867, McCoy purchased two hundred fifty acres in Abilene and began to construct stockyards, an office, a barn, and a three-story hotel known as the Drover's Cottage. Built to entertain eighty guests, the hotel was complete with Venetian blinds, plaster walls, a billiard room, and a bar. The establishment created the desired impression of luxury amidst a town of log cabins and sod roofs, where, in true frontier fashion, nearly everything and everyone came from somewhere else. With no trees nearby, the required lumber was freighted in over the railroad from Missouri, while workers from all over rushed to build the new boom town. Because Abilene lay sixty miles inside the state's quarantine line, McCoy had some political work to do as well. He visited Kansas governor Samuel Crawford and persuaded him to give his written blessing to the selection of Abilene, even if it did violate the law. The prospects of lucrative commerce, Crawford reasoned, trumped any rigid adherence to the letter of the law. Simultaneous with all of this activity, McCoy began his publicity campaign by hiring a friend from Illinois, W. W. Sugg, to ride south into Indian Territory and intercept any Texas drovers and persuade them to bring their herds to Abilene. Investments in construction, lobbying efforts, and advertising were all part of the plan.

By late summer cattle began to arrive in Abilene, and the first shipment of cattle packed into twenty railroad cars left on September 5, 1867. Altogether about thirty-five thousand head of cattle arrived that summer and fall, but only about twenty thousand were sent to market. Most were so lean that they sold for low prices, sometimes less than the costs of transportation. "Texas cattle beef then," McCoy admitted, "was not considered eatable and was as unsalable in the Eastern markets as would have been a shipment of prairie wolves."[47] Some of the low-quality beef was sent to reservation Indians, while the rest—about fifteen thousand—wintered on the prairie grasses west of Abilene. Altogether, Texas drovers and McCoy considered the inaugural year of the Abilene stock market a "failure," with Texas sellers unsatisfied with the price and Northern buyers unhappy with the product.[48] In the coming year McCoy doubled down on his investment. During the winter of 1867–68, he circulated a letter among Texas newspapers, businesses, and elected officials encouraging them to send more livestock to Abilene. Since he understood that Texas ranchers respected a face-to-face conversation more than impersonal communication, he sent two associates to travel the ranch country of Texas during the winter months, providing personal encouragement. McCoy also advertised extensively in newspapers that circulated in northern cattle markets, urging buyers to risk the chance of finding quality beef in Abilene during the coming season. By his count, McCoy spent $5,000 during the winter of 1867–68 in an attempt to bring buyer and seller together. The national market for Texas cattle did not just happen naturally; it had to be created.

The following year was more successful, with seventy-five thousand Longhorns arriving in Abilene. To ensure that cattle buyers would be present, McCoy advertised in a Saint Louis newspaper that "the best grazing cattle in the United States can be had in any number" in Abilene, a claim that ranks somewhere between an exaggeration and a flat-out lie. To make good on this claim, or at least to make certain that cattle would be there in numbers, McCoy sent his faithful rider, W. W. Sugg, to meet drovers and encourage them to resist the offers of rival rail towns. He also paid ten men the handsome sum of fifty dollars a month to encourage drovers to bring their herds to Abilene. In addition, he provided free lodging for some trail drivers in his hotel and for their horses in his livery stable. The pattern was clear. Northern cattle buyers could be influenced to come to Abilene through the impersonal medium of newspaper advertising, yet when McCoy wanted to persuade Southern cattle sellers, he turned to trusted personal connections augmented with financial incentives.

McCoy also relied on his personal charm, aided by monetary inducements, to entice local farmers to accept the invasion of the Texas herds. Fearing that the animals would trample their crops and Texas fever might devastate their livestock, some farmers near Abilene rode out to meet the first bunch of Texas cattle and drive them away. McCoy personally met with the farmers and persuaded them to sell their surplus crops to the trail crews. After a monotonous trail diet for two months, cowboys were eager to buy Kansas butter, eggs, corn, potatoes, and onions. With that the local opposition melted away. One leading farmer was supposed to have declared, "If I can make any money out of this cattle trade, then I am not afraid of 'Spanish fever;' but if I can't make any money, then I am d—d afraid of 'Spanish fever.'"[49] Ultimately, McCoy paid more than $3,000 in 1868 to local farmers to compensate them for damaged crops, and the next year posted a $20,000 bond against possible farm losses to cattle intrusions.[50] As McCoy noted, farmers near Abilene prospered by taking advantage of the opportunity to market their produce to the cattle crews. For McCoy, this was further confirmation of his belief in the healing powers of commerce, as if even crop-farming Cain and the livestock-herding Abel would get along if only they could both make money out of the deal.

A larger problem for Texas cattle in 1868 was a virulent outbreak of Texas fever in Illinois and Indiana, which killed about fifteen thousand domestic cattle and triggered a staunch resistance to Texas cattle drives all along the Missouri and Kansas border country. One observer noted, "Talk to a Missourian about moderation, when a drove of Texas cattle is coming, and he will call you a fool, while he coolly loads his gun."[51] A Kansas newspaper reported that Texas cattle fever was "causing much consternation throughout the country" and a "panic in the central meat markets."[52] Faced with the possibility of an Illinois quarantine on all Texas cattle, McCoy traveled the state legislature and argued that state laws regulating the movement of cattle were unconstitutional because only Congress had the right to regulate interstate commerce. To discriminate against some cattle based on "whether the cattle's horns were long or short" was to deny equal rights to all cattle owners. The national interest in a secure beef supply, McCoy reasoned, meant that federal supremacy should trump state sovereignty.[53] Strange as this argument may have sounded to Texas cattlemen, who only a few years earlier had gone to war for a state's right to discriminate based on skin color, federal supremacy over state laws now suited their financial interests. For McCoy, constitutional scruples were secondary to the logic of the cattle trade. McCoy had better success in Illinois in persuading the legislature to amend the quarantine law to allow cattle shipped from Abilene so long as they carried an easy-to-get certificate that they had wintered in Kansas. Although some Texas drovers lost money because the Texas fever epidemic scared away buyers, overall the year was profitable for the Abilene cattle trade.

All of this meant that Abilene had longhorns in great numbers, and sales moved briskly for the first half of the summer of 1868. But in August, with approximately twenty-five thousand longhorns grazing near the town, an outbreak of Texas fever frightened buyers so much that all sales ground to a halt and "distress ensued."[54] Desperate to attract buyers who would resuscitate the moribund market, McCoy engaged the power of spectacle. First, he sent a mix of Texas cowboys and Mexican vaqueros to the prairie west of Abilene, where they spent a week chasing and roping bison. With great difficulty, they loaded twenty-four of the hulking, shaggy beasts into a specially reinforced railroad car, but by the time the train arrived in Abilene, most of the bison were dead. To compensate for this deficit, McCoy added three wild horses and two elk into the mix, then painted the railroad car with a "flaming advertisement" of the Abilene cattle market and headed east. In Saint Louis, McCoy had the outfit put on a regular Wild West show, with wild animals and feats of riding and roping to attract large crowds. Both the Mexicans, dressed in black velvet and red sashes, and the Texans, sporting their distinctive wool shirts, red bandanas, and leather boots with large spurs, performed prodigious riding and roping stunts. Crowds were pleased, but more importantly, newspapers picked up the story. As it spread from one newspaper to another, the result was the nineteenth-century equivalent of an advertising campaign gone viral; McCoy's cattle market burst into life again. As a final touch, he invited some Illinois cattle traders to join him on a buffalo hunt in Kansas, after which they all stopped in Abilene, where several purchased cattle. If the dramatic spectacle injected new life into the Abilene cattle market, the buffalo were not so lucky. After the shows were over, they were killed and their skins sent to London for study.[55] The irony of using the soon-to-be-nearly-extinct buffalo to advertise longhorns, who would soon replace them on the prairies, was lost

Loading at Abilene. *Frank Leslie's Illustrated Newspaper*, August 19, 1871. Courtesy of the Library Company of Philadelphia

on the participants. Unintentionally, the spectacle served to emphasize the parallel fates of these iconic ruminants of the plains.

With these hard-won successes, McCoy made 1868 the take-off year for the long drive. Enough Texas drovers realized profits that word spread in Texas ranch country that Abilene was the place to go. During the next few years, the number of Texas cattle heading to market soared—over three hundred thousand in 1869 and 1870, with double that number in 1871. During these years Abilene became the "synonym for Texas cattle," and McCoy counted at least $3 million of cattle transactions each year. Before the Abilene boom was over, approximately 1.5 million cattle had shipped from the stockyards that McCoy built. He claimed that from any hill west of town, one could see up to fifty thousand head of cattle "at one view, grazing, herding and driving about like large columns of human beings."[56] Prices were good, with most of the lean Longhorns fetching $20 to $30 a head and a few selling at $40 each. Many Texans grew rich on longhorns and expected profits to continue. George Washington Littlefield, for instance, bought seven hundred Texas cattle on credit, combined them with six hundred of his own, and drove the herd to Abilene, selling them for a handsome price. This kind of speculation, using other peoples' money and gambling on high cattle prices, earned Littlefield a reputation as a successful cattleman. The boom also generated plenty of money in Texas cattle towns, which, newspapers noted, were "exceedingly flush" with money during the driving season, putting "thousands of dollars in the pockets" of local merchants.[57]

By 1869 the trail drives were increasingly the domain of professional trail drovers. These cattle entrepreneurs would often contract with a buyer in Kansas to deliver a certain number and kind of cattle, specifying age, sex, and condition of the animals, and then find the appropriate herds on Texas ranches. For a flat fee of one dollar or one dollar and a half per head, they would assume the costs of the trail drive, including hiring a trail boss and a crew of herders, collecting horses for the drive, and purchasing food and other supplies for the three-month drive. A herd of three thousand longhorns might yield, minus expenses, a profit of $2,000 for the trailing contractor. One successful trail driver claimed to earn between $3 and $4 per head after expenses. Other drovers purchased their own herds, often on credit, based on the speculation that cattle costing $4 to $6 in Texas might fetch $25 or even $40 in Abilene or other Kansas towns.[58]

One example of this professionalization of the trail driving business was James Ellison, a Texas farmer and Confederate Army veteran who borrowed funds and hired a few local farm boys to drive a small herd of 750 cattle to Abilene in 1869. He sold the herd to a representative from a Chicago slaughterhouse for a tidy profit and returned home by way of the Mississippi River with $9,000 cash in his pocket. Ellison gave up farming and became a professional trail driver, contracting to deliver thousands of cattle to Kansas over the next decade. Whether moving their own cattle or someone else's, these "hip-pocket businessmen" made tens of thousands of dollars for themselves in good years and accounted for more than half of the trail traffic to the Abilene stockyards. Eventually, professional drovers came to dominate the business, so that during the two decades of the long drive, probably not more than 15 percent of all cattle driven north traveled with the rancher who had raised them.[59]

Even inferior longhorns found markets in these years. If the Chicago stockyards were not interested, often there were government agents looking for cheap beef—up to fifty thousand head most years—to send to Indian reservations. Even though corruption was commonplace in these Indian contracts, and many people on the frontier, McCoy included, resented the government provision of beef to Indians, these contracts were crucial to the cattle trade because beef payments were a treaty obligation that went hand in hand with the subjugation of the Plains tribes. The "free grass" that longhorns fed on while walking north was, in fact, only available because the native inhabitants of that grassland had been conquered. Longhorns walked free because Indians did not. Added to this was the curious irony that the soldiers who conquered the Plains Indians also needed beef, and many of the government agents in Abilene were there to buy provisions for the army. In 1870 the US government purchased as many as fifty thousand longhorns, or one in six of those driven out of Texas that year. Additional markets for the low-quality longhorns were the thousands of men on work crews building the transcontinental railroad. Because most of these workers were Chinese, a racial rationale came into play yet again. The meat of longhorns, according to one contemporary Cheyenne, Wyoming, newspaper, was too stringy and tough for middle-class beefeaters but "was good enough for factory workers, reservation Indians, drunken and dissipated soldiers at the army posts, and the 'paddies' and 'chinks' who were the 'gandy-dancers' on the railroad construction crews."[60]

Still another option for skinny and "unmarketable" cattle was to hold them over the winter so they could fatten on prairie grasses. At first this was a desperate strategy, but over time this became a popular choice as Texas drovers learned that the buffalo grass and other bunch grasses of central and western Kansas, unlike the taller grass prairies to the east, stored nutrients during the fall that could be eaten during the winter. This made a sort of natural hay that would allow longhorns to graze all winter and add significant weight. Even if the winters were cold, as long as there was not too much snow, a Texas drover could move his herd west of Abilene, "finish" them on native grasses, and sell them in the spring for a profit. Some livestock traders even began to specialize in purchasing otherwise unmarketable longhorns—the young and the skinny—at low prices in the fall in the expectation of profits in the spring, courtesy of the nutritious bunch grasses of central Kansas. This strategy depended upon the free use of the public domain, but it did not take long before the grass around Abilene was eaten to stubble, the soil trampled, and nearby creeks crowded with herds of thirsty bovines. In this open access commons, water and grass were used and abused by the first takers.[61]

Managing a Bust

With markets seemingly ready to snap up any and all longhorns—fat and skinny, young and old, male and female—Texas drovers in 1871 pushed six hundred thousand cattle up the trail, an all-time record. But that year nothing went right. As farm settlements moved west, there were the usual complaints about Texas fever and calls for the strict enforcement of the quarantine line. One newspaper reported that a nearby "drove of Texas cattle" had "violated the law" and now caused "terrible consequences" to area farmers, who lost "a great number of their cattle by the Texas fever."[62] Other papers echoed the reports of perished livestock and called for enforcement of the law, noting that "every cattle owner should insist upon his right to preserve his cattle from the danger of taking the fever."[63] The mayor of Abilene circulated a petition, signed by four-fifths of the local residents, protesting the "evils of the trade" and calling for McCoy to move his stockyards elsewhere. For Kansas farmers, the cattle trade's evils included not only Texas fever but also violence, brothels, and the presence of large numbers of Texas cattlemen, "with their innumerable retinue of Mexicans, negroes and border ruffians."[64]

When railroads raised their freight rates and other towns started rival stockyards, Abilene lost its near monopoly. Meanwhile, a drop in beef prices in Chicago and elsewhere meant less demand that year. Buyers in Abilene bought more than one hundred ninety thousand head of cattle, but shipped only forty thousand.[65] The rest were left to winter in central Kansas, where even the weather refused to cooperate. The driving season was stormy, causing more stampedes than usual and leaving the grass "coarse, washy, and spongy," all of which meant that the longhorns were thinner and scragglier than usual. Unsold cattle were driven westward to winter on buffalo grass, only to find an overcrowded range. According to one account, "every vestige of grazing ground was occupied by cattle awaiting a market," and with only stubble left to eat, the "cattle shrunk visibly. . . . More than a quarter of a million head of cattle, thus insanely driven to a point where they were not wanted, and where there was no market for them, were put into winter quarters at the risk and expense of those who had been guilty of the blunder of driving them North."[66]

By winter, blunder turned into disaster. Freezing rain in Kansas, followed by three days of snow, encased the buffalo grass in several inches of ice. Unable to eat and frozen by the cold wind, according to one account, "the poor famished brutes drifted before the gale, and when, exhausted with their long fruitless tramp in search of food and warmth, they laid down to rest, they seldom rose again." As these "emaciated cattle perished by tens of thousands," cattlemen plunged into bankruptcy. When the thaw came, more than one hundred thousand dead cattle were skinned and the hides shipped east for the leather. Between two hundred fifty thousand and three hundred thousand Texas longhorns lay scattered starved and frozen along the Kansas landscape, and Texas cattlemen lost between $3 million and $6 million in livestock. Always a speculative business given to "violent and frequent fluctuations," McCoy concluded, the cattle market that winter was also a victim of "lack of information, poor judgment and poorer weather."[67] The next spring Kansas farmers threatened to fence their farms with the dead carcasses of Texas cattle that the cold winter had left strewn about the prairie.[68]

The next calamity could not be blamed on the weather. In 1872 Texas ranchers sent only three hundred thousand cattle to Kansas, about half the number from the previous year. The market temporarily recovered, enough to encourage cattlemen to send four hundred fifty thousand bovines up the trail in 1873, even though most of them were not in shape for sale to the slaughterhouse. Indeed, one writer thought that thousands of them were "so inferior that the northern ranchmen would not have wanted them at any price." Government contractors buying beef for reservation Indians and army posts "relieved the situation" to some extent, but even their demand was lower. Altogether, only half as many buyers were in Kansas in 1873 as in 1872. Unable to sell their herds, many drovers spent their last dollars or borrowed money to feed their herds through the fall and winter, in hopes of improved prices the following summer.[69]

Then, on September 18, 1873, the financial firm of Jay Cooke and Company triggered a national disaster when it found itself unable to make payments on its loans for the construction of the Northern Pacific Railroad. Within days, banks across the country were calling in their loans; within a month the nation's financial system was paralyzed. Built on railroad expansion, the Kansas cattle market was devastated by the failure to finance further construction. The "Panic of '73," as it became known, burst the bubble of the cattle market as rapidly and cruelly as it did any other sector of the economy. Hundreds of thousands of longhorns, with scarcely enough meat on them to be sold in the boom years, now could not find a buyer on any terms. One writer described the "feeling of horror" as banks demanded payment on their loans, and over-extended Texas ranchers and cattle contractors lost millions of dollars. Some cattlemen cut their losses and sold their longhorns "for their hides, horns and hoofs and for the tallow they would produce, the flesh being thrown away as superfluous." Other cattlemen borrowed even more money—total indebtedness of cattle drovers in Abilene reached $1.5 million—to pay for the expense of shipping their cattle to the Chicago stockyards themselves, only to lose even more when they learned that the sale price of the longhorns was so low that it could not even cover shipping costs. According to McCoy, "money was lost as fast and completely as if a bonfire had been made of it. . . . To a man whose sympathies ran with cattle men, it was like attending a funeral of friends daily."[70]

The first great cattle boom was over. With only a few years of good profits, what one sympathetic writer called "the spasmodic and alluring boom" from 1868 to 1871, some Texans were beginning to realize that they had "built castles in the air, and dreamed of large prices and prompt payments." Despite the widespread stories of longhorns fetching $40 in Kansas markets, there was a growing recognition that the nation's demand for beef was not as large or as constant as Texas cowmen imagined. Some were coming to grips with the reality that their beloved longhorns, for all the emotional attachment and regional pride that Texans felt for them, were to the beef markets of the Midwest a "rough and nearly worthless stock," which rewarded cattle drovers neither for their "work or their speculation."

It is surprising how much this word, *speculation*, is used in the early accounts of the cattle trails. The long trail always had a chimeric quality about it, pursuing the mirage of the $40 cow even if it was only occasionally real. In the best of circumstances, cattle owners, contractors, and trail drivers could make large profits, but this was more the product of effective, or lucky, speculation than hard work. Hard work was necessary, but not always sufficient and certainly not always rewarded. Even the irrepressible McCoy considered the twin disasters of the winter of '71 and the panic of '73 to be the end of the trail. In his 1874 memoirs, he regarded it as "effectively settled" that "no more stock cattle are needed or wanted from Texas in the Northern states."[71]

Later writers have used naturalizing metaphors to describe the long march of the longhorns as an inevitable process. Water metaphors are especially common: Texas at the end of the Civil War was a "reservoir" of longhorns until the "dam burst" and "rivers of longhorns" surged northward to feed the insatiable national demand for beef.[72] Yet the accounts of the trail drivers at the time reflect none of this sense of inevitability. Their experience was tentative, speculative, full of hard work and hope that the end of the trail might lead to fantastic profits. Sometimes it did, but their memories were also haunted by herds of unsold cattle and trails of frozen carcasses in the snow-covered Kansas prairie.

3. How to Organize the Largest, Longest Cattle Drive Ever

Driving cattle for long distances to markets was not a new enterprise. Scottish Highlanders drove cattle along established roads to London, Australian herders pushed their cattle great distances through the outback to coastal port cities, and the British settlements in North America had a long history of driving cattle from the pastures of Pennsylvania and the backwoods of the Carolinas to Charleston, Baltimore, and Philadelphia. There were regular drives of cattle from Ohio and Indiana to Chicago. Texas cattle were routinely pushed north to New Orleans and south to Mexico. In that sense, the postwar cattle drives out of Texas were nothing new. But earlier drives had used established routes with regular stops offering fenced areas, feed for the cattle, and raunchy taverns with entertainment, drinks, a meal, perhaps even a bed. The herders on those drives traveled on foot or on horseback and used dogs to manage the modest-sized herds of mostly tame animals.

The post–Civil War cattle drives, in contrast, traversed vast distances of treeless plains with enormous herds of only partially domesticated cattle. This required greater organization, control, and hierarchy among both men and beasts. Although the legend of the trail drive glorifies the freedom of the experience, in the words of the famous driver Charles Goodnight, "the most successful drives were always systematically ordered."[1] Popular representations of the cattle drives celebrate them as a refuge from modern society, but the long drives required the same centralizing and ordering impulses common throughout industrial America.

Gathering the Herders

With a herd of up to three thousand cattle collected and branded, a trail drover next had to put together a crew of ten or twelve herders, acquire forty horses, and purchase food and other provisions. Crew selection began with hiring a trail boss, usually a more experienced ranch hand, who would manage the entire outfit for the three months of trail life. Some smaller ranchers might serve as their own trail boss, but after a few years most drives were organized by entrepreneurs who contracted with ranchers to deliver their cattle to Kansas. These trailing contractors organized large operations and usually hired an experienced hand to boss the herd. This crucial job earned as much as $100 per month, sometimes more, with bonuses, for bringing in a herd with minimal losses.

The long drive was no place for democracy, and the foreman was a very busy and benevolent autocrat. According to drover William Poage, "He must see that there are enough provisions, as short grub does more towards dissatisfying a cowboy than anything else. He must assign each man to his proper duty. He must be the first up in the morning to wake the men. He must ride ahead to see that there is water at the proper distance. He must know where to stop for noon. He must count the cattle at intervals to see that none have been lost. He must settle all the differences among his men."[2] Riding ahead of the herd, the foreman chose the pace and direction for each day's drive to avoid other herds and overgrazed trails. The trail boss made all decisions for the group down to mundane daily details. Neither unruly animals nor rebellious cowboys were tolerated for long. Yet a competent trail boss commanded great respect and "was worth an awful lot of money to an outfit," Teddy Blue Abbott explained, because "your profit all depends on moving them along quiet and easy."[3] Just as Teddy Blue's "wild cattle" needed to be handled with "kid gloves," so a good foreman earned respect by exercising a firm, gentle, and generous hand over independent-minded cowboys. J. T. Lytle, for instance, had a reputation for provisioning trail drives well, a reputation that allowed him to hire the best trail riders.[4]

For most trail drives, the trailing contractor also provided enough horses for the journey: three or four for each cowboy, who would need spare mounts for the long days and nights. While some cowboys might bring their own favorite horse, the rigors of the trail were too exhausting for only one animal. The traveling horse herd, known as the *remuda*, traveled with the cattle herd and required the constant care of a wrangler, who might be an older hand and earn as much as fifty dollars per month or a younger boy, who would receive considerably less. At the end of the drive, the horses could be sold to Kansas ranches, and a few trail contractors turned this into a tidy side business. Since a cowboy on foot violated both self-esteem and practical necessity, the management's control of the *remuda* meant that the labor force remained dependent on the larger operation for the duration of the drive. In stylized popular images of this era, the trusty horse is always the cowboy's best friend, but the reality was that most horses were used as a piece of machinery—ridden hard and sold or discarded when no longer needed.

A final innovation for the long drive was the chuck wagon, which was unknown in earlier trail drives or cow hunts but which, by the 1870s, was standard equipment. Charles Goodnight is credited with being the first cattle drover to use a chuck wagon, a special reinforced wagon carrying food and provisions for the traveling crew. A centralized chuck wagon made good sense for drives that lasted weeks instead of days. It allowed for a cook's work table and a sourdough jar, making sourdough biscuits a familiar staple of the trail.[5] It also introduced the specialized position of cook to the society of the cattle trail, freeing the herders of this task but simultaneously making them more reliant on the camp cook and the trail boss. Prior to this, cattle herders typically carried their own food and supplies, as much as a week's rations, in a "wallet," or pack, behind their saddle. This might have been inconvenient, but carrying one's own sustenance also gave each worker the independence to leave the drive if conditions became too rough. The status of cooks varied tremendously in the world of the trail. Cooks might earn as much as seventy dollars per month, ranking second only to the trail boss in wages. Some cooks were respected older ranch hands with bodies that could no longer withstand the long days in the saddle. Others were Mexicans or African Americans, whose position was subordinate to that of herders. Whatever the status of the cook and his chuck wagon, this innovative way of feeding cowboys for the long trail forced hands to rely on the organization of the boss and crew for their basic survival.

Three thousand cattle also required from ten to twelve herders, who were usually hired from the local itinerant labor pool. Experienced ranch hands were reluctant to give up their regular job to join the rigors of trail life, so the vast majority of riders were young, some barely twelve years old. This mostly adolescent labor force was properly called cow*boys*. Historians estimate that the total number of herders for the long drives from 1866 and 1885 was no more than thirty thousand and perhaps as low as twelve thousand.[6] Most were from Texas or the South, many of them farmhands or soldiers back from the war. At least a few were orphans who found in the trail boss a surrogate father. Some were drawn to the long drive by the cowboys' outsider social status, the romance of an adventurous trip, or the freedom of the horseback ride across the prairie. One young cowboy earned "a taste of the life" from three years of cow hunts and, upon hearing neighbors tell their trail stories, "decided at once that this was the life for [him]." His father reluctantly agreed, but not before the young man promised that "if [he] was going to be a cowman that [he] would be 'an honest one.'"[7] Cattleman Ike T. Pryor spent his childhood as a poor farmhand near Austin and felt bored and trapped by his monthly wage of fifteen dollars. Sensing the adventure of each passing trail herd, the nineteen-year-old Pryor told his farm boss, "You can take your plow and go to hell" and resolved to find a job that involved riding horseback after cows. His first trip to Kansas nearly doubled his monthly wages and set him on a new career path. Pryor fell in love with the romance of trail, became a trail boss, and eventually a professional drover and wealthy cattleman.

Yet Pryor's story is atypical. Most trail riders, however captivated they were by the first trip up the trail, did not repeat the experience. While a handful of well-known drovers specialized in repeated trips up the trail, the vast majority of cowboys went on only one long drive. Many saw this as an initiation experience into the world of cowboys, and having proven their mettle, decided that there was no reason to repeat the rigors of the trail. Only a few were able to turn riding herd into an opportunity for social advancement. Most rode for twenty or thirty dollars per month, felt proud that the journey validated their status as "a real graduated cowboy," and were happy to remember a romanticized view of their coming-of-age experience. One trail veteran remembered the journey more realistically, "I went up the trail twice and drove drag both times, did all the hard work, got all the 'cussin,' but had the good luck never to get fired."[8]

Despite the widespread prejudice against them, vaqueros, freed slaves, and native workers also were drawn to the mystique of going up the trail. Hispanic and African American trail herders did not leave behind romanticized reminiscences of their journeys as their Anglo counterparts did, so they are harder to find in the documentary record of the period, just as they are less visible in the popular Western films of the trail. George Saunders, founder of the Old Time Trail Drivers' Association, the old-timers who acted as the official repository of trail memories, once casually estimated that one-third of the men who went up the trail were Hispanic or African American. Yet when he proposed that his organization collect the personal narratives of trail drivers, he was only interested in "the white trail drivers . . . who ought to be members of our association."[9] More recently historians have contested his one-third estimate on the evidence that census records show a much smaller percentage of African American ranch workers, but there is simply no firm evidence to validate or discredit the one-third estimate for transient trail workers who might not show up on the census.[10]

There is widespread agreement, however, that Texas cowboys learned their skills from *vaqueros*, as evidenced by the techniques and terminology of *rodeo, remuda, la reata,* and *lazo*. Trail drivers hired vaqueros because of their skill on horseback and because they would work for less pay than whites, and yet there is not much surviving evidence that vaqueros rode the trail to Kansas in large numbers. This may be because of the intense prejudice against them in northern cattle towns, where they were not admitted to saloons or brothels, even when those businesses admitted blacks. Moreover, the trail drives took place in a context of increasing violence directed against Mexican Americans in Texas, including harassment by Texas Rangers and some two hundred vigilante lynchings.[11] There are far more references in trail narratives to African Americans, who had demonstrated their expertise in riding and roping during the time of slavery. Some slaves in Texas and other Southern states had been entrusted to work with cattle before the Civil War, and the end of slavery encouraged many more to make the transition from farm worker to cattle herder. Wages ranged from ten to fifteen dollars per month for black riders, lower than their white counterparts but higher than farmhand wages for freed slaves. Moreover, the allure of equestrian freedom and adventure proved as strong or stronger for former slaves as for rural whites.[12]

As elsewhere in nineteenth-century America, blacks faced discrimination in hiring and on the trail. Despite this prejudice, blacks as well as Hispanics were often hired because they were paid less and could be tasked with the most difficult and dangerous jobs, such as being first to ride a rambunctious horse or test the current of a dangerous river crossing. Some were hired as the horse wrangler of the *remuda*, usually considered the lowest status job on the trail. In some outfits the job of cook was reserved for African Americans, presumably because most cowboys considered this a subordinate position. They were rarely hired as foremen or allowed to build up their own herds.[13] Nevertheless, many black trail riders earned respect for their skills and formed long-term relationships with their white trail bosses. A few even became famous. Bose Ikard rode for years with the legendary Charles Goodnight and became his trusted confidante; Addison Jones (widely known as "Nigger Add") formed a lifelong partnership with respected cattleman George W. Littlefield; "Nigger Jim" Kelly earned a reputation as a top hand and a gunfighter with the Print Olive outfit; and Bill Pickett transformed his trail-riding exploits into a career in the rodeo, eventually becoming the first black entry into the National Cowboy Hall of Fame. Yet as these offensive nicknames suggest, these relationships were paternalistic and often just plain ugly.

The best-known black cowboys, as the above examples suggest, were respected for their fidelity to famous white trail drivers rather than for their independent prowess, as if they needed a well-known white boss to validate their faithful service. They also had to accept the commonplace use of the racial epithet *Nigger* as first word of their name. According to Teddy Blue Abbott, trail drivers from Texas (he was born in England and raised in Nebraska) "was mostly hard on Mexicans and niggers, because being from Texas they was born and raised with that intense hatred of a Mexican, and being Southerners, free niggers was poison to them."[14] Because of such widespread racism, most African American cowboys learned to keep a low profile and practice habits of deference to white authority. This pattern of deference is what allowed an unknown white cowboy to describe the famous Bill Pickett as "a good nigger that don't get smart."[15]

If African Americans were present but rendered subordinate and virtually mute on the cattle drives, the Indian presence—except as antagonists—was nearly invisible in Anglo accounts of the trail. The Old Time Trail Drivers' Association collected no accounts of self-identified Indians, nor are there any in other sources.[16] Yet in the sense that the Hispanic vaqueros were largely Indian by inheritance and culture, an Indian inheritance was present every time a cowboy threw his lasso, tied it to his pommel, or gathered a horse from the *remuda*. In a more immediate sense, the native people of Indian Territory participated in the trail drives by trading with drovers for food and sometimes providing labor at river crossings or other stress points. The natives' pre–Civil

War experience with cattle ranching gave them necessary experience, and one Wyoming cattle rancher in the 1870s claimed that Indian herders were "the best in the world."[17] On his 1866 journey, for example, George Duffield complained about Indians but also hired twenty skilled Indian riders to assist him in getting his herd across the Arkansas River.[18] Duffield was not alone. Despite the exaggerated fears of Indian depredations, cooperation was more common than fighting. Contractors such as Duffield hired temporary help from the Five Civilized Tribes, who offered many workers experienced in working with cattle, especially at river crossings or sometimes to assist in rounding up after a stampede.[19] In a stark contrast to the stereotype created by fictional Westerns, the actual labor force along the trail consisted not of John Wayne figures, but largely of the very young, Mexicans, African Americans, and sometimes American Indians.

The world of the cattle herder is usually perceived as a "lonely, all male culture,"[20] and this was generally, but not always, the case. Texas cattle culture was known to have women laborers, even if this violated nineteenth-century expectations for gender roles. A popular account from the time described frontier Texas women who, "by the absolute necessity of out-door work, had been rendered . . . very coarse and masculine in character. All the ordinary labors of men, such as digging and herding cattle, were performed by them. We saw one of them lasso a wild looking mustang on the prairie, and vaulting on his back, canter away in search of her cows, without saddle or bridle." To emphasize the repugnance of this transgression of traditional domestic roles for women, the authors commented, "The condition of the children must be yet, for many years, barbarous and deplorable."[21] Enslaved women more easily crossed gender barriers, presumably because they were expected to perform hard labor, as evidenced by the popular story of Henrietta Williams Foster, better known as Aunt Rittie. She earned respect working with male cowboys in the 1850s, according to one report: "She worked cattle bareback with the men and she would go out in the cow camps with the different cow crowds. . . . She rode sidesaddle and bareback on her white horse. She wore those old white dresses and rode astraddle. She could throw calves and do anything a man could do and maybe better."[22] Yet this female expertise in the world of horses and cattle had the weight of nineteenth-century cultural mores against it. Not only were proper Victorian women not supposed to work in the male domain, but doctors at the time advised that riding astraddle—while necessary for control when chasing, turning, or roping cattle—would damage women's most important asset: their reproductive organs.

Nevertheless, a few women went up the trail along with the men. How many went disguised as men is unknown, but there is at least one story that suggests this was known to happen. One trail outfit lost hands along the way and so hired a "kid" from the nearest town who worked with the crew for four months. Near the end of the trip she revealed herself by returning to the cow camp dressed as "a lady." Her explanation to the astonished trail crew was that she had caught the allure of trail life from her father's stories. I determined, she said, "that when I was grown I was going up the trail if I had to run off." Disguised in her brother's clothes and boots, she found a job with the trail crew and, judging by the men's surprise at her revelation, worked the disguise without detection for the duration of the trip. The story ends with her departing for home on a train, good feelings all around, and the remark, "She was a perfect lady."[23] No one knows how many more "perfect ladies" spent time on the trail masquerading as men.

A few other women went on the cattle trail without disguise. On a drive to Kansas in 1868, Jack Bailey kept a daily diary of a trip with women and children following along in wagons. They slept in tents, and women performed the usual chores expected of their gender: cooking, washing, and caring for children. Bailey notes that the women were afraid of storms and stampedes and that once a baby fell out of the wagon, but was unhurt.[24] In 1873 Margaret Borland supervised a trip to the Kansas cattle markets after her husband died and left her with nearly ten thousand cattle. She hired her nephew for a trail boss while her teenage sons went along as hired hands. Her timing was unfortunate, however, as she arrived in Wichita during July of 1873, when the cattle market was low. Unable to sell her scrawny longhorns in a market glutted with beef, she died of what the local newspaper called "congestion of the brain" or "trail driving fever," which had been "superinduced by her long, tedious journey and over-taxation of the brain." Another paper concluded, "This may show that cattle driving is not exactly suited to the female sex."[25]

Other women on the cattle trail followed more acceptable feminine roles. Amanda Nite Burks rode along with her husband on the trail to Kansas in 1871. She traveled in a buggy along with Nick, a former slave, who prepared her meals, set up her tent every evening, and generally attended to her needs. Once Mrs. Burks accidentally started a prairie fire that spread fifty miles;

later, when investigators came to identify the source of the fire, they said nothing when they learned that a woman had started it. Another time she got lost looking for wild plums and flowers along a creek bottom. Although this slowed the herd, the cowboys treated her chivalrously, as if to protect this innocent yet vulnerable example of womanhood. In keeping with this sentimentalized view of her femininity, the Old Time Trail Drivers' Association later declared her a "cattle queen" and gave her honorary membership and a place in their collection of storied trail drivers.[26] Mary Taylor Bunton exploited this Victorian sensibility of innocent and emotional womanhood to persuade her husband to take her with him up the trail even though he had decided taking a woman along was "neither a safe [n]or a sane thing to do." Employing what she called "a woman's weapon—tears," she won the argument and traveled in a wagon along with the herd. Decorating her hair and her horse's bridle with wildflowers led the cowboys to call her "the cowboys' beautiful queen of flowers."[27] She once wore riding pants and rode astraddle her horse, which greatly surprised everyone, but for the most part she seems to have reinforced more than challenged the conventional cultural norms of domesticity.

Perhaps the most famous of all women to ride the trail was Hattie Cluck, who accompanied her husband as he trailed a herd to Abilene in 1871. Hattie, who had three children under age six and was pregnant with another, went along because she reasoned that "there was nothing else to do with me and the babies but to take us with him." The trip proved uneventful and she apparently played no special role, although once a group of would-be robbers approached the herd and were chased away by the armed trail crew. Yet her story grew in the twentieth century, when she convinced newspaper reporters and the Old Time Trail Drivers' Association that she was "the first white woman to go over the trail." In another interview she claimed that her group found the ashes of a wagon presumably burned by Indians. In an attempt to link her experience with the famous Little Bighorn battle, which happened five years later and more than a thousand miles away, she saw this as "clearly a forerunner of the famous Custer massacre that took place a few years earlier." Later embellishments added a picture of her holding a gun and her claim to have skirmished with Indians: "I had to load the guns for the men and keep handing them out." Later she claimed to have organized this fictional fight with Indians as well as to have supervised the cattle herd across the Red River while fearful cowboys watched and followed her orders. Before she died, this "queen of the Chisholm Trail" was alleged to be a crack shot with the courage of Joan of Arc, able to scare away bandits merely with her regal appearance and shotgun.[28] For Hattie Cluck, the older she got, the better she was. Her climb to legendary status, however, reveals not only the longing of the imagination in later years but also the very real limits that standards of Victorian womanhood placed on the actual cattle drives.

Driving the Cattle

With the herd road branded and the crew hired, cattle and men started moving north along the "old cattle trail," or sometimes the "long and lonesome cattle trail." For the first few days, the herders pressed the cattle to walk as much as twenty miles in order to push them away from their customary ranges and break them into a trail routine. After several days or a week, the herd adopted a slower pace, of eight to twelve miles each day. Then both cattle and cowboys settled into a daily routine. By sunup the cook had prepared a breakfast of sourdough biscuits, beans, and coffee thick enough to float a horseshoe. While the cook with his chuck wagon and the wrangler with his *remuda* of horses went ahead, the "men ate, saddled and fell into place as soon as possible." The "waddies," as seasonal cow herders were sometimes called, roused the herd from its nighttime "bedding grounds" and into a leisurely walk northward. By eleven o'clock or noon the herd had walked four or five miles and would stop for rest and grazing while the cowboys took turns eating—usually the same fare as breakfast. Afternoons featured another four to five hours of steady walking to the arranged meeting place, where the cook had prepared camp in a location with water and grass. While the cattle grazed and settled for the night, the men ate their evening meal of biscuits, beans, and coffee. During the night they alternated sleeping and riding two-hour shifts guarding the cattle. During the first two weeks, or whenever the trail boss anticipated danger, the guard was doubled. By dawn the first cowboys rode out to relieve the last night shift, and the routine began again.[29]

While on the trail both cattle and men settled into a social hierarchy. Within a week or two the herd was "trail broke" and would fall into a predictable line. McCoy noted, "Certain cattle will take the lead, and others will select certain places in the line, and certain ones bring up the rear, and the same cattle can be seen at their post, marching along like a column of soldiers, every day during the entire journey." Initially the herd might be bunched together, with perhaps as many as fifty or more walking abreast. As the herd became "trail broke" it would spread into a long, sinewy line, perhaps as few as four or five abreast, which, depending on the size of the herd, might snake along the prairie for a mile or more, creating what McCoy called, again using a military metaphor, "a very beautiful sight, inspiring the drover with enthusiasm akin to that enkindled in the breast of the military hero by the sight of marching columns of men."[30] Lead cattle could make or break a successful drive. If lead steers were amenable to speed, direction, and river crossings, the rest of the herd would usually follow. At the rear were the "weak and lazy" animals, which needed to be "pushed" to keep up. In between, cattle traveled in pairs or small groups. Heifers usually had a following of males, and sometimes "muleys," or hornless cattle, gathered together. These "traveling partners" helped the waddies control the herd and find any missing animals after a storm or stampede. Every morning, according to one trail veteran, "You string them out along the trail, and take a count, or look that all the bulls and other animals with distinguishing marks show up present to the roll-call, and move off on another day's expedition."[31]

The herders also had distinct positions and functioned with military precision. While the trail boss rode in advance, two experienced riders rode at the head of the herd, or point, to provide direction and speed. As the herd thickened toward the middle, swing riders appeared one on each side, followed at a distance by flank riders. At the rear, where the herd was thickest and the cattle were poor, weak, or wounded, came the drag riders. These positions indicated "cowboy rank," with the youngest "tenderfeet" at the drag and the trail veterans on point, at "the post of honor." These social positions were observed not only at work in pay but at meal times and in sleeping order as well.[32] In a smooth-running operation, every person and every cow knew his place. Teddy Blue Abbott explained, "At noon you would see the men throw them off the trail, and half the crew would go to dinner while the other half would graze them onto water. No orders were given; every man knew his place and what to do." This was not a society of equals, and the drags suffered the most. Abbott remembered seeing drags after a day's ride "with the dust half an inch deep on their hats and thick as fur in their eyebrows and mustaches, and if you shook their head or tapped their cheek, it would fall off them in showers. . . . They would go to a water barrel at the end of the day and rinse their mouths and cough and spit and bring up that black stuff out of their throats. But you couldn't get it up out of your lungs."[33]

Col. O. W. Wheeler's Herd, en Route for Kansas Pacific Railway, in 1867.

As Abbott suggests, the measure of a well-ordered cattle drive was precision operations socialized into a daily routine that required no verbal instructions. When communication was needed, it was usually in the form of hand signals. The trail boss would signal directions from a high spot to the point riders, who would send hand signals down the line from flank to swing to drag. "Trail hands were well disciplined and governed entirely by signals," Goodnight explained. "A column of cattle would march either slower or faster, according to the distance the side men ride from the line."[34] The width of the herd was also controlled by hand signals. If the herd was too bunched together, "the heat from so many moving cattle was terrific." If the herd was too thinned out, gaps between the cattle would cause the cattle to trot to fill the spaces. Either extreme caused cattle to lose weight, and therefore value. If the herd was bunched, the point riders would increase the pace while the flank and swing riders would "squeeze them down" by riding closer. If the herd was too strung out, the point riders would slow the pace and the drag would increase it. As the herd came off the trail at noon, the foreman could give a hand signal to split the herd with half on each side of the trail. Over time the cattle became "gentler" and more accustomed to these instructions, just as the cowboys learned to recognize a mere hand signal or change of a horse's direction.

At its most efficient, the system had a kind of beauty, as McCoy recognized: "columns" of cattle "marching" northward in military formation, "everything in its place and moving on" as if this were a natural process, guided only by handlers who worked with unspoken orders in a pattern so socially ingrained that it effortlessly maintained the hierarchy of men and animals.[35]

The success of a cattle drive was often attributed to the skill of the trail boss, but it might have had more to do with the nature of the animals. Longhorns had evolved not only horns but also longer legs and lighter bodies than other cattle, which made them less desirable for beef but more suited for trail conditions. The very traits that made longhorns especially good on the trail—their ability to fend for themselves, their rangy physique, which enabled them to cover miles easily, and their ability to travel long distances without water—made them difficult to control. Yet they could walk long distances with minimal handling and had a reputation for not losing weight. Charles Goodnight, who made his rugged reputation by working with partially wild longhorns, claimed that "as trail cattle their equal has never been known and never will be. Their hoofs are superior to those of any other cattle. In stampedes they hold together better. . . . They can go farther without water and endure more suffering than others. . . . I have never handled any cattle on the trail which space themselves out on the march as well as they do. . . . They have at least double the endurance." Perhaps most importantly for Goodnight, longhorns could "be handled on the trail for less expense" because it did "not require as much skill and patience to handle them" as it did for other breeds of cattle.[36]

For all of their vaunted independence, longhorns possessed a most useful herd mentality. They spaced themselves, traveled in pairs, and followed lead steers "by instinct," Goodnight believed, and cooperative lead steers had more value than "a hundred hands," especially at crisis points such as stampedes or river crossings. They were so crucial that professional drovers cultivated them for use on multiple trips. The most famous one, Blue the Bell Ox, or Old Blue, helped make Charles Goodnight famous. Blue led so many of Goodnight's herds that he earned the reputation of knowing "the way to Dodge City better than hundreds of cowboys." In time, this lead steer learned to exercise "the privileges of individuality." He "would walk right into camp among the pots and pans and eat pieces of bread, meat, dried apples—anything the cook would give him or the boys could steal from the cook. He became a great pet."[37] Needless to say, Blue, the pet animal with economic utility and individual personality, did not go to the slaughterhouse along with the thousands of longhorns he led up the trail.

Of course, not all longhorns were as cooperative in their precision march northward. Noncooperation came in various forms. Trail cattle were often reluctant, petulant, or simply slow to follow the will of the waddies. They would express their own resolve in their slowness to move or their unwillingness to cross rivers. Most frightening of all for the waddies was the stampede, the sudden and seemingly uncontrolled mass flight of the herd. Goodnight noted that "the whole herd started instantly, jarring the earth like an earthquake." Teddy Blue Abbott described a "low rumbling noise along the ground," which alerted all of the herders to the life-threatening possibility that a herd of longhorns might be coming straight at you.[38] Stampedes figured so large in the collective memory of the trail drives in part because of the terror they induced, but also because of their frequency.

As a prey species, cattle are motivated by fear of the unknown or of new surroundings. They have distance vision for scanning the horizon as well as sensitive hearing, although they cannot quickly focus on close objects or easily locate the source of a noise. Thus they are especially frightened by the novelty of sudden nearby movements or unexpected sounds. Modern livestock science has detected a hormonal change in frightened cattle that heightens their sensitivities and, most disturbingly for those who want to sell them, causes weight loss. As a species celebrated for their wildness, longhorns were more likely to stampede than domesticated breeds because wild species of grazing animals have a higher sensitivity to sound and sight, a stronger flight reaction, and a tendency to flee for greater distances.[39] Thunder, lightning, or even a strong rain activated the fear senses. But so did any sudden movement by people, from lighting a match to snapping a blanket. Even a rain slicker flapping in the wind could trigger a reaction. The many stampede stories of the trail herders are testimony to the longhorns' biological imperative to behave as would any self-respecting grazing species when placed in a constantly changing situation. They quite literally would not be "cowed" into submission.

Some of the wildest longhorns resisted all attempts to be tamed, gentled, or controlled; folklorist J. Frank Dobie called these cattle "outlaws . . . who made their reputations in fierce, hardy, persistent, resourceful, daring efforts to maintain freedom. They refused to be 'dumb driven cattle.' Unlike the orthodox ox, they knew not their masters and would not be led to the slaughter block." Living wild in the brush or on the open range, these outlaws might be ignored or shot; if they were captured and became part of the herd, their fate was the same as that of most outlaws in the West—they were either subdued or killed. In the week or two before the herd was "trail broke," they would "prowl up one side of the herd and down another" without any identifiable social group. If they socialized into the group structure of the herd, they might find a place at the drag. Here they would be pushed and abused as necessary to force them to keep the pace. These wilder longhorns were also more likely to stampede, and some foremen found it "economical" to kill the stampede leaders rather than allow for repeated demonstrations of longhorn rebellion.[40]

Longhorn biology interfered in another way with trail life. Herds came in two types: "beeves," the beef herds made up of mature four-year-old steers that would bring a good price at the Kansas meat market, and mixed herds consisting of steers, cows, and yearlings. Many drovers preferred beeves not only for the better price but also because they could walk at a steadier pace than the mixed herds. Yet beeves were harder to find and collect from Texas ranches, and they had a reputation for being more likely to stampede. Mixed herds created a different problem, as they frequently included pregnant cows, which bore calves along the trail. Since a newborn could not keep up with the herd on a day's drive, and a mother would attempt to stay with her new calf, the trail herders usually removed the newborns from the herd every morning and shot them. "We killed hundreds of newborn calves on the bed grounds," Charles Goodnight recalled. "I always hated to kill the innocent things, but as they were never counted in on the sale of cattle the loss of them was nothing financially. In our outfit we had a nigger named Jim Fowler. . . . Every morning I'd give Jim a six-shooter and tell him to kill the calves dropped during the night. One morning he said he wished I'd get somebody else to do the killing." When Goodnight insisted that "it has to be done," Jim stayed with his grisly task.

Another trail driver remembered the deeply disturbing experience: "It was customary to kill the young calves found on the bed ground. I had a pistol and it was my duty to murder the innocents each morning while their pitiful mothers were ruthlessly driven on. It looked hard, but circumstances demanded the sacrifice, and being the executioner so disgusted me with six-shooters that I have never owned—much less used one from that time to this." If the newborns were not removed immediately, the mother would form an attachment and spend the next days and nights milling through the herd looking for her calf. This not only slowed the herd but bothered the crew, as the calfless mothers "would bawl all night long, and then all day, until their voices became mere ghosts of voices." To avoid being haunted by these voices, some outfits took along a wagon "for the purpose of saving the calves, but it did not pay."[41] When near a settlement, the calves could be sold or traded to nearby farmers, but most of the time they were shot as "an act of mercy."[42] In a business that existed for the purpose of taking cattle to the slaughterhouse and was accustomed to cruel treatment of animals, it is striking that herders were haunted by the voices of mothers looking for their calves and that some were emotionally stricken by the daily slaughter of "innocent" newborns. On a ranch such newborns would be protected, for financial if not for sentimental value, but on the trail there was no room for sentiment, as the demands of economy trumped the emotional lives of both cattle and men.

Driving Through Texas

Most herds started in southern Texas and could spend one or two months negotiating through five hundred or so miles among the towns and farms of Texas. This leg of the trail was far different from the long and lonesome trail farther north that formed the stuff of most memories. Hundreds of feeder trails from all over south Texas funneled north to the cities of San Antonio or Austin, and from there past Waco and to Fort Worth. John Fletcher recalled that before starting up the trail near Indianola, the crew went for a swim in the warm waters of the Gulf and then held a "grand stag dance" with some Mexican guitar pickers, "while festive cowboys danced waltzes in the warm embrace of another wearing spurs, leather leggings, and broad-brimmed sombreros." During the first week on the trail the cattle stampeded twice, once because a woman waved her bonnet and spooked the herd and another when the herd was bedded down in a "thickly settled region" on a lane surrounded by farmers' fences. Another stampede in crowded country required the hiring of additional labor to round up the missing cattle. Controlling a herd without losing any cows in the dense oak thickets and brush country of south Texas also proved difficult.[43]

As the herd moved north of San Antonio, there was more open grazing country, but there was also more competition for this grass as more herds joined the main thoroughfare. As drovers turned their herds from the main path to find grazing land, they frequently encountered landowners who charged a fee for water and grass. Towns offered opportunities as well as obstacles. Farmers might trade for eggs or fresh vegetables in order to provide some variation in the otherwise monotonous trail diet, and sometimes towns provided extra labor for river crossings or recovering lost cattle. Larger towns, such as San Antonio or Austin, offered a chance for resupplying as well as the possibility of entertainment in the saloons or dance halls. Yet most of the time there was nothing "to break the monotony or hush the humdrum" of dull days in the saddle. One trail driver reminisced that "water was scarce, herds plentiful, and dust more so."[44] When excitement did come, it was often in the disastrous form of stampedes, which could cause injury or even death to cattle, horses, and men. The spring weather in Texas could be just as wild as the longhorns. On April 22, not far from Austin, a "terrible rain" started in the afternoon and lasted all night, leaving the cowboys "near freezing" while some of their horses and a few of their cattle died from the exposure. In 1868 lightning killed a young cowhand near Dallas and burned three others so badly that they returned home. Hailstorms scared the cattle and left bruises on men and horses. Heavy spring rains flooded the east-flowing Texas rivers—the Colorado near Austin and the Brazos near Waco—and made them difficult and dangerous to cross.[45]

As herds from many different starting points fed into the main cattle thoroughfare, they all funneled through Fort Worth, the last notable town on "the old cattle trail" before Kansas. A quiet town of about five hundred souls in 1870, Fort Worth leveraged its position as the last store on the cattle trail to develop into a bustling town of more than six thousand a decade later. By this point most herds had been traveling for a month and had covered some two hundred fifty miles; a herd that started near the Rio Grande had been eating trail dust for two months and had walked more than five hundred miles. A few exhausted trail drivers sold their herds to northern buyers or other drovers who continued northward. Grocery stores sent solicitors to greet the cowboys with gifts, including whiskey and cigars, encouraging them to stay in town for more shopping. Foremen and camp cooks stocked up on supplies while cattle and men rested.

After Fort Worth the cattle trail continued north for perhaps a hundred miles across mostly open prairies to the Red River, the boundary between Texas and Indian Territory. For John Fletcher, leaving the Texas settlements behind was a moment of excitement. "The prospect of entering an uninhabited wilderness was a source of great joy to the cowboys," he remembered, with a touch of exaggeration. "Civilization and cattle trailing were not congenial, and we had been greatly annoyed in the settled districts of Texas. Depending entirely on free grass for forage for our cattle and horses, we had constantly come in collision with the farmers, who wanted the grass for their domestic animals." For Fletcher, the "wilderness" ahead meant an easier access to what he considered to be an open-grazing commons. Not all trail drivers agreed. Mindful that town residents could provide occasional trailing assistance as well as emotional solace, some lamented the "few settlements on the way" and "were all joyful again" when they reached Kansas.[46]

After leaving the settlements behind, the tenor of the trip changed in another way, too, at least for some. Many trail foremen forbade their crews to carry handguns for fear that, if used, the noise would scare the cattle into stampeding. Because even a six-shooter was cumbersome and heavy to wear, many trail hands kept their pistols, if they owned one, wrapped in their blankets and took them out only if they felt threatened. Moreover, in 1871 the Texas legislature passed a law making it illegal for anyone to carry a concealed weapon, either a pistol or a knife, "on or about his person, saddle, or in his saddle bags." The law did not apply, however, to "frontier counties," which were judged to be in danger of Indian attack. Although there are no firm numbers on this, it seems possible that after Fort Worth, or perhaps after crossing the Red River into Indian Territory, some cowboys stuck a six-shooter in their belt or strapped on a pistol and holster for the first time. John Fletcher recalled that as his herd approached the Red River, they were in a border county and "were told that we could wear side arms without fear of arrest, so every cowpuncher who had a six-shooter buckled it on just to enjoy the privilege of carrying a weapon."[47] Contrary to the popular image, not all of these cattle herders owned a gun, and those who did only wore them when they were far from populated areas.

At the northern border of Texas, herds gathered for the perilous crossing of the Red River. With its steep south bank and intermittent quicksand, this river could only be traversed with extreme care. If rain had swollen it, many a trail driver opted to wait for the floodwaters to subside. One seasoned cowboy arrived at the Red River Station, a small trading post, to find "a dozen herds scattered over the country," all waiting for the river to recede. Suddenly a lightning bolt struck very close to him, killing nine cows and knocking the man's horse to the ground and stampeding the cattle. Another driver recalled arriving at the Red River Station only to find the same thing: the river high and several herds already waiting to cross. While in camp, "we killed a fat yearling—I won't say whose it was," and feasted on half the animal, leaving the rest hanging. When a panther came into camp for the meat, one of the cowboys shot at it. The noise, of course, triggered a general stampede, and it was all hands on horseback for several days to find the cattle.[48]

Once on the other side of the Red River, the herds were in Indian Territory, which elicited a variety of emotions from the cowboys. Some felt the allure of buffalo, antelope, and other wild animals, which gave the open prairies a sense of frontier adventure. Others, trained by decades of hostility toward Indians in Texas, felt the exaggerated fear of Indian attack and rode close to each other for mutual protection. Forgetting that they were passing through Indian Territory, land that legally belonged to the Choctaw, Chickasaw, Seminole, Creek, or Cherokees, John Fletcher gushed his excitement at the prospects ahead, "The country ahead was then a wilderness, without a human habitation in view of the Chisholm Trail to the line of Kansas, nearly three hundred miles away by the meanderings of our route."[49]

Beyond the Red River

While it may have felt like a wilderness to some, the herders in Indian Territory had joined a carefully measured and mapped route. The cow path from Texas to Abilene had many names: the Great Texas Cattle Trail, McCoy's Trail, or the Abilene Trail. While in Indian Territory this route followed a path that had been used by buffalo herds and native peoples for centuries but that became associated in the 1860s with Jesse Chisholm, a well-known trader who frequented the route. Over time Texas cattle drovers applied Chisholm's name to the entire trail. Although he never trailed a large herd of longhorns along the route that bore his name, Chisholm's life reflects the Anglo-American backwoods origins of cow drives. Jesse Chisholm's grandfather had herded livestock in Scotland before moving to South Carolina, where his son continued herding and married a Cherokee woman. Their son, Jesse, moved west with the backwoods cattle trade, spoke several languages, and roamed freely along the borders between peoples and states. In 1864 he took several wagons loaded with trade goods into Indian Territory and returned the following spring with cattle, buffalo robes, and furs. After the war, many

Texas cattle herds followed Chisholm's trail through Indian Territory, and it became so popular that the Kansas Pacific Railroad published five editions of a detailed, annotated guidebook, "denoting camping grounds, wood, water, grass, and other important facts, together with which is given a map of the country traversed by the Trail, obtained from reliable authorities, showing all streams, trading posts, etc." The guidebook included descriptions of high rolling prairies, water sources, and good camping grounds, which were conveniently located every ten to fifteen miles. Its careful description of physical landmarks makes it possible even today to trace the path of the cattle herds through what is now Oklahoma.[50]

As the guidebook made clear, this was no track through a pathless wilderness. Rather, it was a well-traveled route that required only the ability to follow the ruts made by previous herds. One trail driver described it as being as much as one or two miles wide, while a newspaper writer remembered it as "a chocolate band amid the green prairies, uniting the north and south. As the marching hooves wore it down and the wind blew and the waters washed the earth away, it became lower than the surrounding country and was flanked by little banks of sand drifted there by the wind. Bleaching skulls and skeletons of weary brutes that had perished on the journey gleamed along its borders."[51] Located about one hundred thirty miles west of the old Shawnee Trail, which took cattle to Missouri or Baxter Springs, this was, McCoy bragged, "more direct, has more prairie, less timber, more small streams and less large ones, and altogether better grass and fewer flies—no civilized Indian tax or wild Indian disturbances—than any other route yet driven over, and is also much shorter in distance because direct from Red river to Kansas." It was, McCoy bragged, "so plain, a fool could not fail to keep in it."[52]

Because it coursed through Indian Territory, the various Indian nations did indeed attempt to collect a toll from the passing herds. During the 1870s the Creeks, the Cherokees, and the Chickasaws passed a tax for all cattle crossing their land. Because the Indian prairies were level, well-watered, and luxuriant in grass growth, many drovers slowed their herds in order to allow the cattle to gain weight. The Chickasaws responded with a set of guidelines that regulated grazing and the speed and direction for herds entering its territory. However, none of these legal mechanisms could be enforced. Lacking adequate policing powers themselves, the Indians were forced to rely on federal troops, which were scattered sparsely across the territory and somewhat reluctant to enforce the law against Texas trail drivers.[53] Without the support of adequate police, some Indian groups simply liberated a few head of cattle from the passing herds as a payment for the use of their grasslands. When remote from settlements or army posts, they approached herds with a request for beef. If the request was not honored, they could threaten or actually stampede the herd, creating the opportunity for Indian riders to collect wandering cows or be hired to assist in gathering the herd. These instances rarely escalated to violence, but they did provide many a trail driver with a story of menacing Indians. Some trail bosses thought it best to minimize conflict by acceding to Indian requests, usually by offering a few drag yearlings of little value or offering fewer cattle than the Indians requested. Others took pride in standing up to the threat of what they termed "Indian thievery." When members of the Osage nation asked for a "steer or two" for the privilege of grazing on their lands, one trail driver refused, and when the Indians threatened to stampede the cattle, he "pointed to our Winchesters" and chased them away. Another trail driver refused a Kiowa demand for six cows while passing through his country and threatened to kill the Kiowa representative. They settled on two steers.[54]

These stories were usually told in a manner that emphasized the strength of the Texas drivers who defeated the Indian requests with Winchesters and superior wit. Yet these encounters were more complicated than the Texans preferred to remember. One story that illustrates this complexity comes from a drover who started in Texas without much money and ran out of flour while in Indian Territory. He traded a ten-dollar gold piece for a sack of flour, leaving both participants satisfied with the deal. Yet almost immediately this cooperative moment in his narrative is overcome by "trouble with Indians," when one Indian man tries to make off with some of the outfit's horses. The Texas trail driver makes good by catching him and threatening to shoot him, but ultimately releasing him.[55] As long as Texas trail drivers successfully defined the verdant prairies of Indian Territory as an open commons, they viewed the Indians as thieves. Federal law, however, defined Indian Territory as the property of sovereign nations, making the true larcenists those who insisted on fattening their cattle on grass belonging to others, but refused to pay.

The Chisholm Trail through Indian Territory, about two hundred fifty miles, or four to five weeks of travel, gave the Texas cowboys plenty of opportunities for adventure and romance, providing fodder for many a cowboy legend. John Fletcher romanticized this portion of the trip: "The Indian Territory was the cowpuncher's paradise. Now we would have no more lanes, no more obstructing fences, but one grand expanse of free grass." We were, he continued, "in a wilderness now, free from all the restraints and annoyances of civilization. . . . Now that we were in the Nation, where there was no pistol law and nobody to enforce any law. . . . We marched on now, armed to the teeth for savage foes and wild animals."[56] Indians loomed much larger in the imaginations of these Texas trail hands than the actual Indians they met, and a few trail accounts note that the writer saw his "first Indian" while in the Territory. Many others saw their first buffalo and noted their first chance to hunt, or for the more adventurous, to rope a buffalo. Occasionally trail crews reported eating a buffalo, but they did not like the taste. More often they chased, killed, or roped buffalo because this "afforded great sport." In this paradise of open prairies, unbridled freedom, abundant game, and unrestricted guns, as one trail hand noted, it was a great amusement to hunt big game, but "as for chasing Indians, that was out of the question, for at that time they were under the watchful care of government agents and, as Uncle Sam was trying to tame his Indians, we quietly passed them by."[57] Indians played multiple roles in this cowboy paradise: as a toll-demanding "threat," as an imaginary fear keeping adrenalin levels high and ammunition stockpiled, and as a dehumanized creature who, save for the paternalistic federal government, could be hunted as big game.

For some the Chisholm Trail through Indian Territory offered less romance and dealt out very real hardships. Spring to summer weather on the southern plains could turn deadly at any moment. Sol West and his entire outfit were caught in an April blizzard that left over a foot of snow, sleet, and ice on the ground near the aptly named Hell Roaring Creek. His entire *remuda* of sixty-eight horses froze to death during the night, leaving him to trade steers for horses with a nearby farmer, a cattle crew coming along the trail, and some Indians.[58] On July Fourth one year later a storm brought wind and hail big enough to kill some of the cattle and leave the cowboys "nearly froze to death," with "knots and scars all over our hands and backs." And of course lightning storms could kill a mounted cowboy—the tallest spot on an open prairie—and cause a stampede. One driver described a variety of types of lightning, "It commenced like flash lightning, then came forked lightning, then chain lightning, followed by the peculiar blue lightning. After that show it developed into ball lightning, which rolled along the ground. . . . The air smelled of burning Sulphur; you could see it on the horns of the cattle, the ears of our horses and the brim of our hats. It grew so warm we thought we might burn up with it."[59] Another veteran trail driver experienced lightning that "flashed so continuously and so bright we could see everything plainly and smell burning brimstone all the time."[60]

Apparently, even in this paradise there were moments when it looked and smelled like hell. These storms could also bring floods of biblical proportions, creating more perilous river crossings. The main river crossings along this part of the Chisholm Trail—the Washita and the North and South forks of the Canadian—were relatively easy for cattle and horses to swim most of the spring and summer months, but a rainstorm could quickly turn a routine river crossing into a perilous adventure. Swift currents could wash away cattle, horses, and men, all of whom had to swim for their lives, while an improvised raft might ferry the chuck wagon and equipment across. One driver remembered waiting in the rain for eight days on the Washita River as the "hardest time of the trip. For six nights I slept only about one and a half hours and never pulled off my slicker and boots."[61]

For most trail hands, however, these moments of adventure and danger stood out in their memories in the way that an exceptional experience crowds out the mundane. During peak years the trail was crowded, which could be useful when one crew assisted another at river crossings or in rounding up cattle scattered from a stampede. But it also required trail bosses to veer from the trail each night in order to find grass for grazing and bedding grounds. One trail boss crested the ridge into the Washita River Valley and, seeing that "the whole face of the country was alive with herds," turned his cattle five miles to the side for a different ford of the Washita River. More common was to find multiple herds crossing the river at the same place, often on the same day, as the herders assisted each other in the dangerous task. Some herds traveled in tandem for long stretches of the trail, checking in on each other and sharing stories and supplies.[62] Cooperation more than competition marked the routine of trail life.

After months on the trail, the daily routine settled into long periods of boredom punctuated by moments of extreme danger. One driver recalled that his trail experience was characterized by "many stampedes, sleepless nights, gyp water and poor chuck."[63] Bill Poage remembered a drive that got caught in a bitter cold storm that froze some cattle and stampeded the rest. Although it was their job to pursue the stampeded cattle, about half of the crew "got lost and were found next morning warmly snugged up in the chuck wagon." Surveying the field of frozen cattle the next morning, Poage reported, "All the romance was taken out of the boys."[64] Another remembered the "wonderful experience on this trip in the stampede, high water, hailstorms, thunder and lightning which played on the horns of the cattle and on my horse's ears. We suffered from cold and hunger and often slept on wet blankets and wore wet clothing for several days and nights at a time, but it was all in the game, and we were compensated for the unpleasant things by the sport of roping buffalo and seeing sights we had never seen before."[65] This combination of misery and romance appealed to many of the trail drivers, at least in their memories, but perhaps the most telling comment about trail life comes from one of the romantics, Teddy Blue Abbott. He pronounced the worst hardship of trail life to be loss of sleep and admitted that sometimes he would sit in his saddle sound asleep for a few minutes. The solution, he found and his crew learned, was "to rub tobacco juice in our eyes to stay awake. It was rubbing them with fire."[66]

Fire in the eyes and bolts from the heavens interrupted a trail life that otherwise suffered from stifling boredom. When trail drivers reminisced, their stories were thick with Indian troubles, stampedes, buffalo chases, and other novelties. More telling reports come from the much rarer genre of personal diaries. These scant journals tell a story of loneliness and unrelenting tedium, with only scattered moments of adrenaline-pumping, life-threatening adventures. George Duffield's 1866 cattle trip diary is full of gloomy days and dark nights, miserable rain storms and unruly cow hands. He complained of fever, hard shakes, various pains, fatigue, and loneliness.[67] Jack Bailey frequently noted that there was grumbling in camp, "Bosses all mad at Boys. Boys all mad at Bosses. . . . No grass, no water, no nothing." Beautiful days and scenic countryside mixed with dreadful days and extreme hardship. Illness was a theme, as Bailey suffered from rheumatism, a pain in the side (which he diagnosed as pleurisy), fever, and life-threatening pneumonia. One fatigued night he wrote, "Bunked for the night. Let the cattle rip. I wouldent herd to night for the herd."[68] Medical care was limited; perhaps the cook would have a few herbal remedies for various ailments, but more likely the best advice was not to get sick. And there was no cure for the thing that ailed Duffield and Bailey the most: loneliness. Only when they came to settlements did they cheer up, and only at trail's end did they find rest and comfort. Both Duffield and Bailey were older men, and very likely trail life was more suited to those with the vitality of youth. Yet even that youthful vigor could be sapped, according to Joe McCoy, who noted that trail life was unnecessarily "routine and dull" because of a monotonous and unhealthy diet and the lack of "a hundred comforts, not to say luxuries," such as tents, blankets, cooking utensils, and clean water. All of these, he reasoned, were readily available for minimal expense. In direct contrast to the mythological cowboy, McCoy found the real cattle herder at the end of the trail to be "sallow and unhealthy, deteriorates in manhood until he often becomes . . . capable of any contemptible thing; no wonder he should be half-civilized only."[69]

The truth for many of those young adventurers who went up the trail is captured in another account, which describes "the trip that was once so exciting and thick with adventure has come to be an unspeakably cheerless and tiresome thing. . . . Day after day, the slow, dull drive continues, each day so like every other that soon all reckoning of its place in the week is lost." The trail herders were "adrift on these great, vague and melancholy prairies," experiencing "a continual torturing heartache and sense of exile." Under these conditions, the writer continued, "the most ignorant and indifferent of herders—and perhaps even the worn and bewildered cattle, also—catch a glimpse of this feeling" of gloom. Soon "depression comes upon the entire outfit . . . , daily conversation dwindles into monosyllables, every man draws into his shell . . . and there he remains taciturn and brooding."[70] This account contains the eerie suggestion that the cowboy's legendary silence, the strong silent type of so many twentieth-century movies, comes from trail-induced loneliness and depression. The daily monotony left the waddies so isolated from each other that the evening campfire was reduced to chores and monosyllables. Even the longhorns, in this version, were rendered mute on their long march to the slaughterhouse. Fortunately for the cowboys, if not for the longhorns, there was an end in sight. As the herders crossed the border from Indian Country into Kansas their spirits picked up. The cowboys and the longhorns approached their very different fortunes at the end of the trail.

4. How Kansas Survived the Longhorn Invasion

One May morning in 1877 the farmers of Ellis County, Kansas, only recently arrived from Russia, awoke to find their unfenced wheat fields trampled by a herd of long-horned Texas cattle. The animals had apparently stampeded during a storm the previous night and wandered several miles. The farmers had already herded the cattle into their fenced enclosures by the time the trail boss, Mike Dalton, arrived. As he pleaded for the release of his herd, the local constable arrested him for violating the state's quarantine law. The local court fined him a sum nearly equal to the value of the herd and used part of it to compensate the farmers for the damage to their crops. The *Dodge City Times* mistakenly identified the farmers as Mennonites, probably in an attempt to humiliate the Texas drovers even further. How insulting, the newspaper implied, to have ones cattle corralled by a group of pacifists. In any case, the newspaper reasoned, the farmers had combined with the state's quarantine law to form "a barrier through which not a hoof of Texas cattle can be driven."[1]

The Cow and the Plow

These Russian-German farmers were part of a much larger migration that brought more than a million people to Kansas in the years after the Civil War. Originally from Germany, the farmers had spent more than a century on the Russian steppes, where they had learned to grow hard winter wheat, a seed that they planted in Kansas with spectacular results. While early homesteaders in eastern Kansas had mostly grown corn, a familiar crop, the new hard winter wheat soon replaced corn as the preferred crop, especially as farmers pushed westward into the drier parts of the state. Attracted by the Homestead Act's promise of free land and recruited by the Atchison, Topeka, and Santa Fe Railroad, tens of thousands of farmers moved to Kansas every year during the 1870s. Kansas law protected domestic livestock from the prospect of Texas fever with a "quarantine line," sometimes referred to as a "deadline," which banned Texas cattle from the eastern, agricultural parts of the state. This line drifted steadily westward until eventually the entire state was quarantined against Texas cattle. Yet the law was not evenly enforced. Farmers and ranchers complained to the governor that Texas cattle were "retarding the growth and prosperity" of the region. Petitions coming to the governor's office over the next decade demonstrate repeated frustration with the difficulty of enforcing the quarantine line as ticks from Texas cattle continued to cause devastating outbreaks of disease.[2]

Motivated by fear of Texas fever as well as by the prospect of thundering herds destroying crops, the farmers had sound economic reasons for opposing the trail drives. But their hostility was about more than money. Kansas farmers aspired to build a society of churches, schools, and respectable middle-class families, in the face of a cattle trade that brought with it transient Texas cowboys who "were swearing, drinking and doing as much as they please."[3] Moreover, as one newspaper noted in 1867, Texas cowboys appeared to be unapologetically Confederate: "Every man of them unquestionably was in the Rebel Army. Some of them have not yet worn out all of their distinctive gray clothing."[4] Although the newspaper exaggerated, it reveals the lingering Civil War animosities that were still very much alive in the world of cattle drives. By Teddy Blue Abbott's reckoning, the trail herders were still "bitter" from the Civil War, and as a matter of pride could not allow themselves to be bossed by a "Yankee."[5] In addition, the African American cowboys and Hispanic vaqueros herding alongside the ex-Confederates were no more welcome, indeed sometimes less welcome, than their white counterparts.

Yet not all Kansans responded with hostility to the invasion of the longhorns and the Texas cowboys who drove them. Aspiring merchants and other community boosters eyed the cattle trade as an opportunity both to build personal fortunes and to elevate the status of their towns. Kansas was thus caught in a tension between a fear of ticks, trampled crops, and loose morals, on the one hand, and a desire for profits, on the other. Agriculturalists argued that a county of family farms producing a steady wheat crop provided a more durable economic base than the fleeting cattle trade, but the lure of fame for one's town and fortune for one's purse led settlements to compete for the privilege of becoming the link between trail drive and railroad. The result was a series of ephemeral cattle towns that loom large in the legend of the West, although they struggled in their brief existence to combine effective cattle centers with the larger project of spreading agricultural civilization on the moving frontier. These *cow towns*, to use the mildly derogatory term for the series of settlements that handled the Texas cattle trade, grew up where the cattle trails met the railroads and ultimately connected the cattle ranges of Texas with the meatpacking facilities in Chicago. Beginning with Abilene and moving south and west to Ellsworth, Newton, Wichita, and most famously, Dodge City, these towns were notorious for their prostitution, saloons, gambling, and violence. The Russian-German cattle capture in Ellis County was then not merely an isolated incident, but a moment in a conflict between two cultures—the cow and the plow.

Agricultural settlement in Kansas in 1870 was largely limited to the populated eastern third of the state, east of where Wichita now sits, where more than ten persons per square mile lived. West of Wichita, where the climate was drier and long-stem bluegrass gave way to shorter buffalo grasses, there were fewer than two persons per square mile. Later ecologists and historians would mark this border, approximately the 98th meridian, as the boundary between prairie and Great Plains, the land where conventional agriculture requiring more than twenty inches of rain per year gave way to innovative dryland techniques and newer crops that could prosper with less than twenty inches. But lines on the map were not always obvious on the ground, and as Kansas farmers moved westward during the two decades after the Civil War, they created a variety of problems for those Texas herders who tried to follow the quarantine "deadline."

It was not immediately obvious to most Texas drovers that the state which welcomed their business would in time prove a more serious obstacle than stampedes, storms, Indians, or river crossings. Some, however, remarked on the changes they perceived as soon as they left Indian Territory and crossed into what they considered to be "civilized" Kansas. One trail driver noted, "We crossed over the line into Kansas, and now and then we could see a little 14 X 16 box house where some farmer had located his pre-emption, and near it would be a few acres in a field, but no trees, fences or other improvements. These squatters were not very friendly toward Texas cowboys." Another remarked, with a similar mix of wonder and condescension, that the prairies were filling up with "grangers, who lived in dugouts, a square hole in the ground, or on the side of a bluff. . . . Each granger had taken up about 160 acres of land, part of which was cultivated." Lacking fences, these homesteaders plowed furrows around the edge of their claim, which trail drivers were supposed to understand as a marker to keep herds away. This did not always work, and sometimes herds found their way into corn or wheat fields and on at least one occasion actually trampled on top of the grassy roof of a sod dugout house and fell into a man's bedroom.[6]

A few herders welcomed Kansas because it signified the end of the "wilderness" of Indian Territory. One Texan found in Caldwell, the first Kansas town along the Chisholm Trail, "a tent full of trail supplies, so we stocked up."[7] This marked the first opportunity to buy provisions since Fort Worth, making it a vital stop for herds short of coffee, flour, or other foodstuffs. Detailed maps of the Chisholm Trail compiled in the early twentieth century contain several notations of stores and farms that served as short-lived supply depots.[8] Mrs. Amanda Burks, one of the few women who accompanied a herd up the trail, appreciated the site of "two Yankees who called themselves farmers" who sold vegetables to the Texas crew.[9] One Kansas farm woman recalled cowboys as "very kind and courteous in their primitive way." She especially remembered how they would come to her house for well water in a glass, a marked improvement on the trail habit of getting water from rivers, ponds, or buffalo wallows and drinking from "their hat or boot, or getting down and drinking like a horse." The cowboys appreciated her kindness, and she concluded that they were "creatures of feeling and quite a large degree of refinement."[10]

More common, however, was deep-seated hostility between Texas herders and Yankee farmers. One trail boss, accurately foretelling that it would be farmers rather than Indians who would end the days of the cowboys, remembered fewer troubles with toll-collecting Indians, who could be "pacified," than with "grangers," who "displayed a degree of animosity toward the trail drivers that was almost unbearable."[11] Trail boss Bill Poage thought that Kansas settlers "were far more troublesome than ever were the Indians. . . . The boys took delight in doing everything they could to provoke the settlers. The settlers paid us back, with interest, by harassing us in every way they could think of."[12] Another trail boss recounted the story of being "enraged" while encountering signs to keep cattle away from water and pastures protected by plowed furrows. Despite being confronted with "bare-footed, bare-headed" farmers, he allowed his thirsty herd to run to the protected watering grounds. Arrested the next morning, he was forced to pay a fine of $130, as if he were "one of the worst criminals on earth."[13] Other trail bosses complained of being "skinned" by a "colony of grangers" who charged $50 for inspecting herds for contagious diseases or of being met with angry "nesters" with shotguns attempting to keep Texas fever away from their domestic livestock.[14] One notoriously aggressive trail driver, Print Olive, known for running a "gun outfit," would deliberately cross plowed furrows in order to antagonize "sodbusters" who were protecting their crops and water supplies. When controversy erupted, they would send in "Olive's bad nigger . . . and that big black boy with his gun would sure tell them punkin rollers where to head in at."

As Teddy Blue Abbott remembered, it was always the Kansas farmers who provoked the conflict. There was, he remembered, "no love lost between settlers and cowboys. Those jayhawkers would take up a claim right where the herds watered and charge us for water. They would plant a crop alongside the trail . . . and come out cussing and waving a shotgun and yelling for damages. And the cattle had been coming along there when they were still raising punkins in Illinois."[15] For Abbott and other drovers, the trail had prior rights, and all attempts to limit it were a devious assault on the natural freedoms of the open range. In contrast, the Kansas farmers assumed the rights of homesteaders and viewed the Texas cattle as noxious intruders. The age-old conflict between livestock and row crop agriculture, animated by Civil War animosities, played out in central Kansas.

Given this constant skirmishing, the Chisholm Trail in Kansas did not stay in one place for more than a few years. The trail that Jesse Chisholm personally traveled came north from Indian Territory only as far as the Wichita settlement on the Arkansas River, near his ranch and trading post. To establish a trail all the way to Abilene, in 1868 Joseph McCoy sent a survey crew "to straighten and shorten" the path through Kansas from the Arkansas River crossing directly to Abilene. The crew laid out camping spots where grass and water were abundant and marked the new trail extension with earthen blocks of sod and "a full supply of sign-boards."[16] The new editions of the Kansas Pacific's *Guide Map of the Great Texas Cattle Trail* updated Texas drivers on how to avoid farmers, find stores and watering places, and most important of all, locate the "extensive range" and "large stock yards" that waited at the end of the trail.[17] A Kansas writer recalled, "The Chisholm Trail—over which came all this living, bawling sinuous, snake-like hegira of cattle—was a wide, dusty roadway from which every vestige of grass" had been trampled under thousands of longhorn hooves. Another much later recalled running barefoot through the fields and finding the trail by "locating where cow chips were most plentiful."[18] For the busy years between 1868 and 1871, even a directionally challenged Texan could find his way from Texas to the Abilene cattle market; all one had to do was read the guidebook, follow the brown, rutted, dusty path through the green prairie, and turn northeast at the big sign post.

While trail drivers were always searching for new acreages of green grass near the trail, they were also hemmed in and pushed westward by laws that held livestock owners responsible for crops destroyed by their animals. In 1872, Dickinson County and Sedgwick County, home of Abilene and Wichita, passed herd laws which established that the owners of free-ranging livestock were liable for all damages caused to property owners. Designed to protect farmers' crops and gardens from Texas cattle, the laws were popular in part because local ranchers complained that trail herds stole local cattle and incorporated them into their passing herds. There was also a concern that farmers and ranchers who wanted to improve their breeding stock could not do so as long as the prairies teamed with "ravenous slab-sided carpet-baggers from Texas."[19] This forced trail drivers to stay west of cattle towns, with the result that these grasslands were filled with so many herds that "the whole prairie was covered with cattle for many miles around."[20] During late summer and early fall, the height of the season, one observer described seeing so many cattle that they were "covering the land like a swarm of locusts."[21] When demand was high, prospective cattle buyers had to ride as far as twenty miles or more out to meet and make deals with the trail herders.

Abilene's Glory

All cattle towns required sponsors. They came into existence not because of natural advantages or unseen economic forces, but rather because of the hard work of specific individuals. Abilene emerged because of the persistence and deep pockets of Joe McCoy, but it was always in constant competition with nearby villages, all vying to make their settlement into the region's hot spot for business and culture. Each of them hoped that commerce in cattle would bring the sustainable economic growth and urban vitality to transform

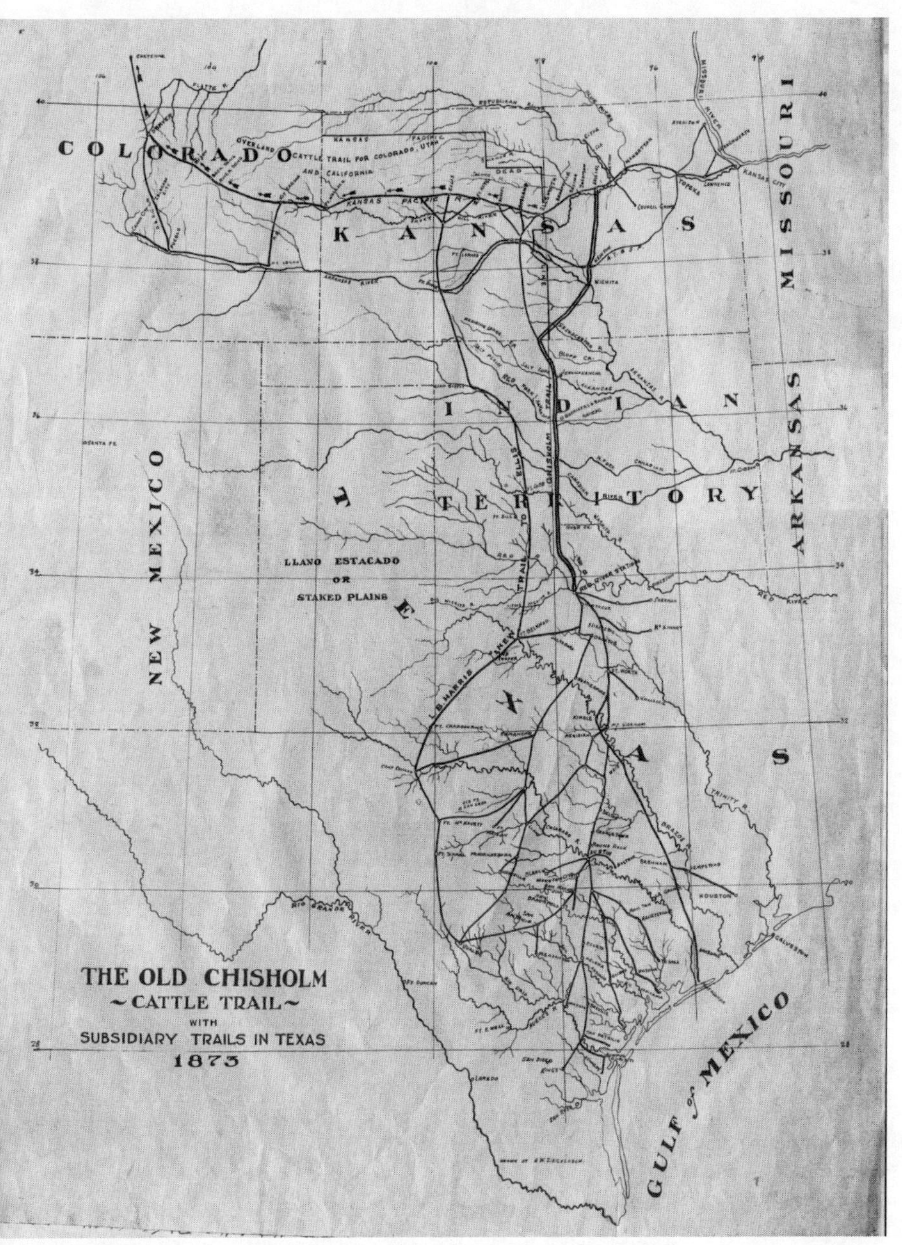

The Old Chisholm Cattle Trail, 1875 map. Courtesy of the Kansas State Historical Society

it into the region's hub.[22] When J. B. Edwards arrived in Abilene to work as a bookkeeper for McCoy, he found it abuzz with excitement. As he remembered, "no one thought of anything but Texas cattle, selling goods and liquor to the cow men, & gambling and prostitution."[23]

During the go-go years of 1868 to 1870, the Abilene cattle market could yield fantastic profits for some trail drivers. Mark Withers, of Lockhart, Texas, put together a herd of 600 steers valued at less than $10 each and trailed them to pasturage twelve miles west of Abilene, where in time he sold them to an Illinois firm for $28 each, earning nearly ten thousand dollars after expenses.[24] Another Texas drover the next year trailed a herd of 750 mixed cattle north and returned home with "$9,000 cash, which was quite a lot of money in those days."[25] Perhaps no Texas cattleman profited more in the Abilene cattle market than Rev. George Webb Slaughter, the circuit-riding preacher who wore a pistol in the pulpit as protection from Indian attack. Between 1868 and 1870 he sold nearly 5,000 cattle in Kansas, for which he was paid well over $200,000. In 1869 J. H. Baker trailed 480 along with Slaughter's herd of over 2,000 and reaped just over $4,000 for his efforts.[26] Even J. M. Daugherty, who famously nearly lost his herd and his life in 1866, recovered with several successful drives, including one to Kansas in 1868 that established him as a successful trail driver and rancher.[27] Reports of trail drivers pocketing several thousands of dollars for their three- to four-month journey were so common that, according to one later account, "the very name of 'Abilene' will revive stirring memories in the minds of many of the old-time cattlemen."[28]

During these profitable years, cattle buyers in Abilene were plentiful and represented a number of possible destinations for the Texas longhorns. Because the national supply of beef was still depressed from the Civil War, representatives from meatpacking houses in Chicago and, to a lesser extent, Kansas City, were present to purchase cattle for direct shipment to the slaughter facilities. A careful statistical analysis of profits during the two decades of the long drives shows that the last few years of the 1860s were the most profitable years of the entire period, largely because of the direct demand in Chicago for beef.[29] Many longhorns were sold at Abilene to be loaded on railroad cars and sent to the Midwest, where they would fatten up on corn before their final journey to the slaughterhouse. After wintering on Illinois corn, they could fetch as much as 25 percent more in Chicago.[30] Still another group of buyers purchased cattle for stocking the northern ranges of the Great Plains. But in Abilene in 1870, the greatest profits were in the direct meat market, where a

Abilene in Its Glory. Illustration by Topeka artist Henry Worall and printed in W. G. McCoy's *Historic Sketches of the Cattle Trade of the West and Southwest*. Courtesy of the Kansas State Historical Society

nine-hundred-pound steer, valued in Texas at $11–$14, might sell for double that amount and bring in an additional $10 in Chicago.[31] McCoy claimed that at the peak of the Abilene market, a Texas drover might clear a profit of $15 to $25 per head. The total profits of the cattle business amounted to more than $3 million dollars annually.[32]

Yet cattle prices were notoriously fickle, and both buyers and sellers who pocketed large sums in 1870 were vulnerable to market vicissitudes in the years to come. Texas trail drivers required funds to pay their cowhands, purchase supplies, and pay for personal expenses in Abilene while waiting to sell their herds. As markets dipped in 1871 and collapsed in the Panic of 1873, many drovers were forced to sell at a loss simply to pay off their debts. As one Kansas journalist noted, "To sell or not to sell, that's the important question. . . . So sacrifices are made, and cattle men, as well as cattle, are slaughtered every day." Cattle buyers in Abilene were subject to monopolistic railroad freight rates as well as prices that could drop precipitously even in the few days between purchases in Abilene and delivery in Chicago. Because of this the cattle business could be something of a crapshoot and, in this sense, had more in common with gambling than with a more traditional business. Like other forms of gambling, it could be addictive, as Joseph McCoy noted: "Few men, after beginning, are ever willing to quit the business of stock trading and shipping. . . . Bankruptcy and financial ruin is the only means that will put a stop to his operations."[33] McCoy, who made tens of thousands of dollars in the cattle market and lost still more, could have been speaking of himself when he wrote that many were "anxious to plunge into the inviting waters of speculation, only in turn to be swallowed up in the inevitable maelstrom of ruin."[34]

The only people to get rich in the cattle business were a few large-scale drovers, some shrewd cattle buyers, and the local merchants of cowboy clothing, alcohol, prostitution, and gambling. The basic purpose of cattle towns was to purchase longhorns at a good price and then relieve the Texans of as much of their money as possible. Like any other western boom town, the real money in Abilene was not in the cattle market itself but in providing services for those who bought and sold cattle. A scant quarter mile from McCoy's elaborate Drovers' Cottage, the headquarters for all serious buyers and sellers, were the stockyards, "almost constantly a scene of great activity. . . . Constant whooping and yelling by the men loading the cattle into cars could be heard, a cloud of dust or a foot or two of mud according to whether it was dry or wet weather was to be found in the yards."[35] Nearby were grocery stores, two saloons, a small schoolhouse, and a Baptist church. Within two years there were more saloons, hotels, and a second church, all near what was known as "Texas Street." Every day buyers left town with cash in their pockets to purchase cattle from approaching Texas herds, and every morning throughout the summer and fall more cattle, prodded along by men on horseback, filled the stockyards.

If stockyards and saloons were the obvious sights of the Abilene boom, the institution that made it all possible was banking. In 1870 the First National Bank of Kansas City opened a branch in Abilene and processed $900,000 worth of stock transactions in the first two months. Exchanges of cattle for cash routinely ranged from $1,000 to $20,000, with a few transactions as high as $50,000 or even $100,000. Banks allowed these sums to be transferred securely and safely, as opposed to the older customs of famed Texans such as "Shanghai" Pierce or Charles Goodnight, who bought and sold cattle with gold. Banks profited by collecting a small percentage from the large amounts that they processed, as well as by lending money to cash-strapped cattle drovers. Trail drivers sometimes needed financing while they waited for a better price. Banks provided this ready cash, to the extent that McCoy estimated that drovers were $1.5 million in debt during the panic of 1873. As one observer noted, "A fabulous interest is paid for cash, and banks are as fat a thing as gold mines."[36] For the banking enterprise, it was the old promise coming true: cattle were indeed being transformed into capital.

Another can't-miss enterprise in Abilene was groceries, which sold better than any other merchandise. Just as cattle buyers regularly traveled in search of herds for purchase, enterprising grocers rode south toward the herds to solicit orders from trail crews. Sometimes cattle bosses from Texas arrived early in Abilene, traveling separately from their herds, and purchased groceries to greet their incoming trail crews and feed them while the herd grazed on nearby grasslands awaiting sale. For the months on the trail, cowboys ate almost exclusively a diet of sourdough biscuits, beans perhaps cooked with bacon or salt pork, sprinkled with an occasional mix of dried fruit or fresh game. Although they were driving cattle to the slaughterhouse, they rarely had beef from one of their own herd for fear of cutting into profits. McCoy, noting this trail diet, thought that a "feast of vegetables he wants and must have, or scurvy would ensue. Onions and potatoes are his favorites, but any kind of vegetables will disappear in haste when put within his reach." The farmers surrounding Abilene could realize high prices for any "bushel of grain, peck of vegetables, pound of butter, or dozen of eggs that they could possibly produce."[37] Cowboys, it seemed, missed their vegetables and were willing to pay good money for them. Cattle town grocers responded happily by selling them tens of thousands of dollars' worth of produce brought in by the railroad from eastern farms. Texas cowboys traded longhorn beef for eastern vegetables, and Abilene grocers profited.

Almost as much as fresh food, the trail herders longed for a clean change of clothing. It was in the Kansas clothing store that the cowboy began to acquire his accustomed look. When the waddies left Texas, especially in the early years, there was great variety in their appearance. "Home-made clothing was the rule of this period," according to an early source. The "working costume" of the trail rider included a broad-brimmed straw or felt hat, loose-fitting flannel shirts with pockets for carrying the "fixings" for hand-rolling a cigarette, durable pants, which would be tucked into narrow-toed, high-heeled boots. The boots were awkward for walking, but ideal for staying in stirrups. Covering pants and boots would be calf or goat skin chaps, with the hair on the outside. On the trail, cowboys usually also wore large spurs on the boots, a large bandana for covering the face from dust, and perhaps a revolver tucked into the belt.[38] After three months on the trail in these clothes, the cowboys were ready to spend sixty to ninety dollars on new clothes in Abilene. Flush with their paychecks, according to McCoy, the herders went straight to the barber shop for a shave and trim of their three-month growth of hair and beard, then to a clothing store, "and the cow-boy emerges a new man, in outward appearance, everything being new, not excepting the hat and boots, with star decorations about the tops."[39] Beaver felt or wool hats replaced straw ones, and leather chaps replaced calf skin. In time hats made by John Stetson in Texas and fancy boots made in Kansas became essential to the cowboys image of themselves.

Becoming this "new man," which involved replacing homemade and worn-out clothes with gaudy manufactured clothing, became almost a rite of passage for the newly arrived herders, as if it were an outward symbol that they had been "up the trail" and were now graduated into full-fledged cowboys. One cowboy recalled that after Abilene, they were "all dressed up in a new suit, boots and hat, the rig-out costing about $30, and when we reached home we were 'somebody come' sure enough." Another recalled arriving back in San Antonio at the end of the trailing season "rigged out with a pair of high-heeled boots and striped breeches," but poor enough that he had to borrow money to get back to the ranch, where he spent the winter working and "telling about the big things I had seen up North."[40] Over time this enthusiasm for new "cowboy" clothing became an important statement of identity for herders at the end of the trail. Charley Siringo reported spending most of his first month's wages on a "pair of star topped boots" and a "fancy pistol." Before heading home after his long drive, Teddy Blue Abbott bought red- and blue-topped boots decorated with stars and crescents, ten-dollar pants, a fancy shirt, and a twelve-dollar Stetson hat. "Lord, I was proud of these clothes," he remembered, "I thought I was dressed right for the first time in my life."[41]

The equipment list expanded to include much more than apparel. One trail driver recalled a costume including $14 boots, large spurs, leather leggings, and a Colt six-shooter and a Winchester rifle. "This was the first time in my life that I had been rigged out, and you bet I was proud."[42] A full outfit for the well-dressed cowboy might include not only firearms but also a saddle and saddle blankets, quirts, reins, and braided ropes—all presumably tools of

Cowboys Dressed for Photograph. Courtesy of the Kansas State Historical Society

the trade. A proper cowboy outfit cost at least $100, and might run as high as $500 or more, depending on the expense of the saddle.[43] For a character type that became famous for individualism, this cowboy outfit quickly became a uniform. The leather boots, saddles, and reins were store bought and replaced earlier homemade versions, while the fancy flannel shirts, denim pants, and firearms were manufactured in factories and mills outside of Texas, as if to emphasize the trail herders' dependence on the national market. Moreover, despite the view of this clothing and equipment as a practical necessity, because it was usually purchased at trails' end suggests that it was more important for image than for work. As one historian concludes, "Cowboys spent earnings on costume, on show, on what might be called personal performance."[44] Because sometimes a trip to the clothiers was followed by a visit at a photography studio, these cowboys in their freshly manufactured garb, not the day-to-day work clothes of the trail, became the standard for cowboy fashion. This posed image became their statement to the larger society, the manufactured picture of independence and self-reliance that came from making a trip up the trail.

To take advantage of cowboys who were willing to spend one-third of their trail wages on new clothing, in 1870 Jacob Karatofsky opened the Great Western Store, selling a variety of "Dry Goods, Clothing, Boots, Shoes, Hats, Caps, and Gents' Furnishing Goods." He also stocked some fancy dresses, presumably appealing to the expensive tastes of the Abilene prostitutes. Thomas C. McInerney specialized in making boots for the Texans—two-inch heels decorated with red tops and a Lone Star. Selling at between $12 and $20, these boots were so popular that during the summer and fall cattle season McInerney hired as many as fifteen workers to help him satisfy demand. Mayer Goldsoll, a recent immigrant from Russia, opened an Abilene branch of his Old Reliable House, specializing in clothing, boots, watches, and guns and ammunition. All of these merchants were successful enough in Abilene that they moved with the cattle trade to Ellsworth and then Wichita. Business was so brisk during the season that store owners hired as many as five sales clerks and sometimes had monthly purchases totaling $30,000.[45]

Trail-weary travelers were also eager for the comfort of a hotel room, which formed another means for Kansas entrepreneurs to keep cattle money in Abilene. McCoy's Drovers' Cottage was the first and largest of the hotels, featuring 100 rooms in three stories, a laundry, a dining room, and a large covered porch. Built for leisure as well as business, the Drovers' Cottage became the Abilene home for both buyers from Illinois and sellers from Texas, causing some to remark that the building exemplified a form of post–Civil War reconciliation. Buyers might come early and stay the entire season, while some Texas cattle owners would travel north by river and rail ahead of their crews and spend weeks living at ease waiting for their herds to arrive. Comfortable accommodations were widely recognized as an essential feature of any would-be cattle town, as crucial as a railroad connection, banking facilities, trail accessibility, and nearby grazing lands. Wichita, Caldwell, Dodge City, and even tiny Newton all boasted of luxurious hotels, some of which included "stock registers" in their lobbies, a kind of bulletin board where cattle owners left their names, local addresses, and a description of the herd they wished to sell.[46] If a luxurious hotel was mandatory for buyers and sellers, most trail cowboys stayed at simpler hotels or boardinghouses while in town. For half of the year, these places were always busy, putting profits from cattle into the pockets of Kansas businessmen.

As with other boom towns in the American West, Abilene found a great many ways to relieve cowboys of their cash in what can loosely be called the entertainment industry. As McCoy recognized, "No sooner had it become a conceded fact that Abilene, as a cattle depot, was a success, then trades' people from all points came to the village" and employed "every possible device for obtaining money in both an honest and [a] dishonest manner." Gamblers, prostitutes, and saloonkeepers quickly realized that cowboys flush with cash formed a market ready to be exploited. Cowboys, and some cattle owners, were only too happy to oblige. As McCoy noted, "When the herd is sold and delivered to the purchaser, a day of rejoicing to the cow-boy has come, for then he can go free and have a jolly time; and it is a jolly time they have."[47] As a local newspaper put it, with a different spin on the notion of the Great Plains as an ocean of grass, the cowboys were like "a cargo of sea-worn sailors coming into port, they must have—when released—some kind of entertainment. In the absence of something better, they at once fall into liquor and gambling saloons at hand."[48] Like sailors home from the sea, these trail-weary workers sought a release, a spree of pleasure after months of hardship. They sought what had been denied on the trail: alcohol and the companionship of women. They gambled, drank, and whored openly for all to see, as if these activities were a rite of passage into the public manhood that was their due.

One trail driver found Abilene a "wide open town" and said it "did not take the gamblers there long to relieve me of all the money I possessed." Another noted that "it had been a long time since we had seen a house or a woman, they were good to look at." After a night gambling and dancing, this cowboy lost his money and his "girl." Another trail driver sold his cattle and profited $8,000 in cash, but "any old trail driver who found himself rich in Abilene, Kansas, in 1871, knows the rest." As many of the early trail drivers reported, they left Abilene nearly broke.[49] The frequency of cowboys reporting with an enthusiasm bordering on pride at the loss of all their earnings suggests that, to the extent that going up the trail was a rite of passage, getting fleeced in Abilene completed the experience. In this way cowboys reflected their Southern culture of honor, which valued physical courage, masculinity, and public displays of wealth. What better way to demonstrate that the culture of honor mattered more than a few months' wages than to drink, gamble, and consort with women in conspicuous ways. One cattle seller was reported to have lost $30,000 in a short stint on the gambling tables in Abilene. A resident noted that if anyone had tried to steal this much from the Texan he would have been "bored full of holes in the twinkling of an eye," but to lose this much in a game of cards was perfectly acceptable. The beauty of the Abilene entertainment industry was that no theft was necessary; the Texans were willingly and even joyfully separated from their pay, as if to prove that some things were more valuable than mere money.[50]

The saloon was the central establishment for cattle town entertainment and the first stop for freshly cleaned and clothed trail herders. At its peak in 1871, Abilene supported eleven saloons, ranging from the ornate Alamo to back-alley joints peddling watered down whiskey. The Alamo, the most famous of many Texas-themed businesses, featured three glass doors opening onto a large room with brass fixtures on a long bar. Large nudes painted in the style of the Renaissance graced three walls, while mirrors on the back wall created the feeling of spacious luxury. The notes from a small orchestra completed the atmosphere, even if the gambling tables that filled the room spoke to the true intentions of the establishment. Enter here, the Alamo said, and leave the dreary trail behind. Relax, enjoy, and leave your money behind as well. Saloons dispensed alcohol and comradery and introduced weary cowboys to a variety of pleasures to reward them for the privations of the trail. Gambling tables offered the excitement of risk-taking of small and large amounts in games of faro, monte, or poker. Some saloons sponsored professional gamblers, taking a portion of their winnings, while others encouraged itinerant independent gamblers. In either case, gamblers flocked to the cattle towns during the summer and fall cattle season, then left town just as quickly.

Most saloonkeepers could also direct the cowboys to a back room or nearby brothel where they could buy sex, a market that flourished in every town where cattle were sold. Most prostitutes were young; the most common ages were from seventeen to twenty-three, although a few were as young as thirteen and as old as forty. Most were white, but they came from many countries and backgrounds. No doubt some came by choice, others out of desperation, and a few appear to have been abducted. Just as saloons used names such as *Alamo* or *Lone Star* to appeal to the Texans, prostitutes often took on fictive Southern names, such as Hattie or Minnie, with the last name of Lee, presumably to appeal to their ex-Confederate customers. Nicknames such as "Mary Magdalene," "*nymph du prairie*," "sporting woman," or "soiled dove" rendered most women of the demimonde anonymous in newspapers or other historical records. One exception comes from an Ellsworth census worker who attempted humor, it seems, by listing, in red ink, the presumably real names of *Libby Thompson*, *Harriet Parmenter*, and *Ettie Baldwin*, with their occupations described as "diddles," "does horizontal work," and "squirms in the dark."[51]

Beginning in 1871, Abilene boasted of a related source of entertainment, the dance hall. Here men of all classes, from respectable cattle buyers and sellers to the lowliest herder, could dance with a woman for the cost of a drink for himself and his dance partner. Since many if not most of the dance hall women were also prostitutes, for more money he might purchase sex after a few dances. Authorities generally took a lenient approach to alleged abuses in dance halls, as when George and Mag Woods, owners of the Caldwell Red Light Dance House, and their sex worker employee, Lizzie Palmer, were arrested for resisting arrest and obstructing the law. Their attorney, who had apparently spent the previous night attending the dance house, delivered a defense in the form of a handwritten poem, which the judge accepted and then dismissed the case. Whether for companionship or sex, dance hall women worked for the owners and helped to ensure that many a Texas cowboy left his hard-earned wages in Kansas.[52]

For the few years that the cattle trade boomed in Abilene and elsewhere, these entertainment industries worked themselves into the fabric of the town. Not only did they support one another, with bartenders recommending prostitutes and gamblers, but together they became vital to the town's economy. Saloons arranged their tables so that gamblers were always visible from the street, and a few became recognized as prominent businessmen. Since the buying and selling of cattle represented a risk-taking enterprise, those who dealt cards and played the odds could in some sense be seen as pursuing the same goal—taking risks to acquire capital. For their part, prostitutes—the most vulnerable members of the entertainment industry—often protected themselves by aligning with a prominent gambler, businessman, banker, or saloon owner. Abilene and subsequent cattle towns generally

"Dance-House." Illustration by Topeka artist Henry Worall and printed in W. G. McCoy's *Historic Sketches of the Cattle Trade of the West and Southwest.* Courtesy of the Kansas State Historical Society

took a tolerant attitude toward gambling and prostitution and used the law creatively to turn this entertainment industry into a source of tax revenue. When Abilene passed ordinances prohibiting gambling and prostitution, the local law enforcement began fining the violators at the rate of five or ten dollars per month, collected on a regular basis. Court records indicate that in some cases prostitutes were charged a "fine" on the same day each month, then left alone until the same day of the next. In Abilene, Wichita, and later Dodge City, these "fines" in effect legalized, regulated, and taxed gambling and prostitution. Revenue raised in this way paid for police protection in the dangerous districts of town and allowed cattle towns to solicit other businesses by advertising that the municipality charged little or nothing by way of taxes. Prostitution and gambling in effect subsidized the development of other, more respectable enterprises.[53]

As the countryside surrounding Abilene filled with farmers, the cattle market became increasingly less viable. By 1871, the peak year for the cattle drives, with more than six thousand cattle and thousands of cowboys flooding into Kansas, the town claimed a year-round population of one thousand, with two schools and five churches. Before the trail season, the town newspaper vigorously debated the merits of the cattle trade, with advocates pointing to the financial benefits, and opponents charging that it benefitted only a few merchants. "These thousands of cattle that are annually pouring in on us," one town leader wrote, "retard the development of our county by deterring settlement and cultivation." As if to reinforce the point, there were a large number of conflicts that season, including several that nearly came to violence. Longhorns trampled corn crops and ate preciously guarded pastures while Texans either ignored the farmers or, in one instance, told them to "go to hell." Twice farmers defended their corn crops with guns, only to be met with greater force by numerous armed cowboys. Only timely intervention from nearby friends prevented bloodshed between the desperate farmers and the brash cowboys.[54]

At the same time, social pressure was building against the "evils" of gambling and prostitution. The local newspaper ran stories claiming that "men and boys are falling from virtue and honor almost daily" because of exposure to prostitutes in the streets. Articles threatened that the "respectable" citizens of the county would take vigilante action if necessary to rid the town of brothels and gamblers. McCoy, elected mayor in 1871, understood that gambling and prostitution were a necessary part of attracting the cattle drives to Abilene, so he attempted a compromise by moving all of the brothels outside of city land. McCoys Addition, as it was called, "did not fully satisfy good people," however, since many prostitutes frequented their usual places of business in the center of town. As one resident remembered, "the genuine good citizen together with his wife, rose in open rebellion and demanded the town be made safe for their wives and daughters to go to the stores, post office or elsewhere in the town without being insulted and outraged by prostitutes who[,] often drunk, were everywhere."[55] A "fallen women" in person, the argument suggested, was an intolerable assault on the morality of anyone who came into contact with her.

Combined moral and economic arguments gave life to the forces in Abilene that viewed the cattle trade as an obstacle to their vision of a decent and prosperous civilization. In February 1872 they circulated a manifesto, complete with fifty-two signatures from leading citizens (all male), requesting that Texas cattle drovers take their herds elsewhere during the coming season, "as the inhabitants of Dickinson [County] will no longer submit to the evils of the trade." Supporting documents referred to "the great curse of the county, the Texas cattle trade and its concomitants."[56] Just to be sure, they mailed copies to a number of Texas newspapers. In 1872 the Kansas legislature reinforced the state's quarantine law and passed legislation authorizing counties to pass herd laws that further restricted the routes cattle drives could take, all of which made cattle trailing more difficult. Dickinson County, home to Abilene, promptly passed an ordinance requiring herds to be fenced or controlled at night and to be kept out of all cropland. These restrictions ended Abilene's four seasons as a cattle town. For McCoy, it was a bitter end to his dream. "Its glory has departed from it, and so have the cattle," he wrote, "and the streets that were once filled with life and animation, are growing up in grass."[57]

Abilene's Successors

Abilene's glory had departed, and so too had both Joe McCoy and his famous Drovers' Cottage. This architectural symbol of the cattle trade was taken apart and shipped west to Ellsworth, the next cattle town on the Kansas Pacific, and McCoy moved south to supervise the building of stockyards in the new cattle markets at Newton and Wichita.

In some ways Ellsworth seemed like the logical successor to Abilene, located some sixty miles west along the Kansas Pacific Railway and for the moment, at least, ahead of the westward-moving agricultural frontier. In 1871, enough drovers steered toward Ellsworth that they shipped more than twenty-eight thousand head, or 18 percent of the total transported on the Kansas Pacific that year. By the next year the town boasted the entire infrastructure necessary to facilitate the Texas cattle trade. Its stockyards were among the largest in Kansas, and the Kansas Pacific could reasonably claim that they had more stock cars and more experience than the competition. For hotels, Ellsworth had not only the reconstructed Drovers Cottage but also the elegant Ellsworth Dining Club, including a twelve-foot-wide sidewalk made of limestone to replace to usual boardwalk. Jacob Karatofsky moved his clothing business to town, and a bank opened to cater to "merchants, stock dealers, and the Texas cattle trade." According to one observer, the streets of Ellsworth took on the appearance of "a town in California in its early days when gambling flourished and vice was at a premium." Professional gamblers and honest homesteaders mingled with "the tall, long-haired Texas herder, with his heavy jingling spurs and pair of six-shooters; the dirty, greasy Mexicans . . . , the keen stock buyers; the wealthy Texas drovers; deadbeats; cappers; pickpockets; horse thieves; a cavalry of Texas ponies; and scores of demimonde."[58] In addition to the usual entertainment industry, Ellsworth added horse races. It was, a newspaper reporter added, "thoroughly revolutionized and to-day is the Abilene of last year." Another journalist accurately summarized the town's situation: "Ellsworth has her cattle trade, the same that rendered Abilene so famous, and wherever that is there will be money."[59]

Yet Ellsworth's run at the money proved even more fleeting than Abilene's. Its cattle trade peaked in 1872, at forty thousand shipped from the Kansas Pacific stockyards, with another twenty-five thousand wintering nearby on the prairie grasses. The railroad attempted to boost sales by publishing a new version of its *Guide Map of the Great Texas Cattle Trail*, with the trail straightened and adjusted westward but still pointing to the "old reliable" Kansas Pacific. Nevertheless, the Kansas Pacific steadily lost ground as a cattle shipping point to its upstart competitor, the Atchison, Topeka and Santa Fe railroad. Kansas already had a transcontinental railroad in search of cargo, the Kansas Pacific, so the new Santa Fe's ability to solicit livestock trade was crucial to its hopes of turning a profit. Historian Richard White describes Kansas as the epicenter of railroad overbuilding in the West, with five different lines, which, by 1890, provided Kansas with more miles of railroads than New York and four times the mileage per person as New England. This excess capacity, White concludes, made the Atchison, Topeka and Santa Fe "an utterly unnecessary road over most of its route."[60] Cutting a southwesterly course through the state, it carried freight and passengers west and sometimes carried would-be Kansas farmers back east after their homesteads had failed.

One feature of the railroad freight business, however, revealed just how dependent frontier settlers were on the national market: most freight trains rumbled west carrying lumber, agricultural implements, flour, groceries, and clothing but rattled eastward mostly empty. Manufactured goods flowed to the hinterland, without much in return. The overbuilt railroads courted the cattle trade offering cheap freight costs. For as long as the Kansas Pacific had a monopoly, it charged $6 or $7 per head, or $120 or $140 per railroad car carrying twenty longhorns. With competition from the Atchison, Topeka and Santa Fe, the rate on both lines dropped to approximately $2 per head, or $20 per car.[61] The exuberance of investors to build railroads through Kansas in advance of demand thus lowered shipping costs for Texas drovers significantly.

The Atchison, Topeka, and Santa Fe also called into life a series of ephemeral cattle towns modeled on Abilene. The first of the Santa Fe cattle towns was Newton, which in the spring of 1871 consisted of several tents and a few buildings lining a single street, surrounded by miles of bluestem tallgrass to the east and shorter switch grasses and buffalo grass to the west. Within weeks of the railroad's arrival, there was a construction boom. Joe McCoy came from Abilene to supervise the stockyards and sent word to the herds that Newton was open for business. By August, when the Texas herds began arriving, the town had over a thousand residents and a nearly complete range of cow-town services. Indeed, it seems that Newton was a cattle market before it was a town. Lumber, groceries, dry goods, gamblers, and prostitutes all arrived by train to meet the needs of the Texas cowboys. Some twenty-seven saloons, which could be built for as little as $400 and might yield profits of $100 per night, dominated the construction boom. Their names—*Alamo, Lone Star, Texas*—were once again designed to appeal to their Southern clientele. Boardinghouses and gambling halls were plentiful. Brothels and dance halls were clustered just outside of town in a district known as Hide Park. But the most profitable business in Newton, as in Abilene, was groceries, with wagon loads of fresh vegetables from nearby farmers and trainloads of produce from afar selling for as much as $700 in a day.[62] During the summer and fall of 1871 an estimated forty thousand head of cattle were shipped from Newton, marking it as a proper rival for Ellsworth that season.

Newton's moment as a cattle trading center lasted only one season, however, as it was beset with a variety of problems. Because it was a cattle market more than a town, and in fact had not yet been incorporated so as to have properly elected officials and regular law enforcement, Newton experienced more violence than other cow towns. The county provided two constables and a deputy, but this was clearly inadequate. Most infamous was the "General Massacre" of August 20, when eleven people died in a gunfight. This level of violence offended even some trail drivers, one of whom called Newton "one of the worst towns I ever saw," containing "every element of meanness on earth."[63] The Topeka newspaper reported that there was "considerable talk" of asking for federal troops to occupy the town and restore order. As with other cattle towns, its active demimonde and loud dance halls gave it the reputation of "the wickedest city in the West" and suggested to more respectable settlers that "hell had broke loose." In 1871 Newton had no churches, and there was, according to the nearest newspaper in Topeka, "no place in the world where religious and church influence [was] more needed." Yet ultimately it was not these sensationalized features of Newton that cut short its career as a cattle market. More important for the trade was the lack of banking facilities and the absence of a "good hotel," of the sort that would provide comfort for the "gentlemen" who bought and sold cattle.[64] The ultimate factor in undoing Newton's cattle market, however, was simply that the Atchison, Topeka, and Santa Fe built a spur line south to Wichita, which was both closer to the Chisholm Trail and possessed an aggressive business community. The railroad birthed the cattle market in Newton and killed it just as quickly.

No town in Kansas pursued the cattle business more fervently than Wichita. The little town where the Little Arkansas River joins the larger Arkansas River had certain geographical advantages to be sure. Located eighty-five miles south of Abilene and thirty miles south of Newton, it reduced the travel time from Texas to a railhead by a week or more. The site had been home to the Wichita Indians, who settled there in 1864 as refugees from the Civil War violence in Indian Territory. It was also the site of Jesse Chisholm's trading post, his starting point as he marked out a trail south into Indian Territory, which so many now followed north. Until 1876, Wichita was also just southwest of the state's quarantine line. The early merchants of the town were so anxious to corral the cattle trade that, upon hearing that the trail might bypass them in favor of Ellsworth, they sent four men, the "Four Horseman" in local legend, to ride through the night to intercept the herds and direct them to Wichita. When sweet reason and knowledge of local geography failed to persuade one trail boss to turn the herd toward Wichita, one of the town leaders took the foreman aside and "used an argument in the way of a handsome consideration that proved more potent than words." A hard night's ride and a substantial bribe demonstrated not only the town's eagerness for the cattle trade but also the truth of Wichita merchant and horseman James Mead's dictum: "Cities are not the result of chance, nor do they make themselves."[65]

By 1871 Texas drovers were beginning to notice the effort made by this new town. "Wichita has made enormous progress since I was here a year ago," wrote one. "It begins to assume the appearance of a city."[66] It lacked the critical railroad connection until local business leaders persuaded county residents to float $200,000 in bonds, to persuade the Atchison, Topeka and Santa Fe to build a spur line south from its main line. In 1870 and 1871 the city made itself known as cattle friendly by establishing a fund to compensate farmers whose crops had been damaged by longhorns and by getting word out to Texas drovers that the town had established a corridor that passed near

Wichita, "to allow you to drive your cattle unmolested, and we are ready and willing to protect you."[67] With the railroad expected to arrive in the spring of 1872, the town prepared for the upcoming season by hiring Joe McCoy to travel through states in the upper Midwest to encourage cattle buyers to do their business in Wichita. Meanwhile, they also paid $400 to James Bryden, a native of Scotland, well-known in Texas for his years as a rancher, to follow the Chisholm Trail southward to tell drovers of the new market in Wichita. The town's business and civic leaders also spent $250 from municipal funds to make Douglas Avenue, the main street of the town, "a thoroughfare for Texas cattle en route through the city." Altogether, Wichita spent $4,000 of municipal funds in one year to compensate farmers, advertise to cattle buyers and sellers, and build facilities in town. Of all the cattle towns in Kansas, Wichita proved the most successful by far in using tax money aggressively to recruit and nurture the cattle trade, helping to make it profitable, as if it were almost a form of public enterprise.[68]

Convinced that capturing the cattle trade would transform the town into the region's leading metropolis, Wichita's civic and business leaders invested funds to build an "immense stock yards," measuring three hundred by three hundred fifty feet, which could hold twenty-five hundred cattle and load ten railway cars per hour. They also spent $28,000 to build the first bridge over the Arkansas River, "one of the best investments Wichita has ever made," the newspaper claimed. Most herds swam the river, but during floods the bridge, which could hold two hundred cattle at one time, allowed the trade to continue without interruption. In 1873 town officials spent $200 a month to employ the well-known Texas cattleman Abel "Shanghai" Pierce to supervise the stockyards. His imposing bulk and commanding voice must have been a welcome sight for many Texas drovers. For an equal salary, town officials also hired a full-time writer tasked with spreading positive publicity about the cattle business. The town also issued scrip as legal tender to help cope with the shortage of cash, which was endemic in cattle towns. These certificates were accepted at full value in Wichita businesses and could later be redeemed with funds from the city treasury. Private individuals contributed to the cattle trade infrastructure by establishing two banks and a three-story Douglas Avenue Hotel, which, at a cost of $12,000, could cater to the elegant tastes of transient cattle buyers and sellers.[69]

The results were quite lucrative in Wichita for a few years. In 1872 the Wichita stockyards shipped eighty thousand cattle, making it the largest cattle market in Kansas and justifying its boast that it was "the best shipping point in the West for Texas cattle."[70] According to one observer,

> the railroad yards, cattle pens, and stockyards covering many acres, were the throbbing pulsating heart of great activity. Cars were constantly shunted to ever-building sidings by snorting engines, their crew directed by gesticulating brake-men, hastily loaded with wild-eyed, bawling cattle and moved out to make room for others. . . . Cowboys on tough ponies loping hither and yon, yelling, cursing and swinging ropes, everything apparently in wild confusion, but the constant stream of cattle moving in regular order into the great pens, up the chutes and into the gaping cars, was evidence that an efficient system prevailed.[71]

During the cattle season, Wichita was, the local paper bragged, "the livest and fastest town . . . in Kansas. . . . All is excitement, stir, and activity."[72] With a population of two thousand residents and hundreds of seasonal arrivals from the cattle drives, all sorts of businesses were booming. During 1872 one grocery company grossed $100,000 in sales, much of it in bulk, as advance agents went south along the trail and solicited trail crew orders. Another grocer sold 190 tons of foodstuffs to trail-weary herders in just one month. On the streets of Wichita vendors sold buffalo tongues and tenderloins, as well as choice cuts of meat from deer and antelope. The Douglas Avenue Hotel housed 1,260 guests that season, and three other hotels combined for 19,410 guests as cattle sellers from Texas and cattle buyers from northern markets bought rooms for months at a time.[73] Wichita's two banks claimed up to $40,000 in transactions a day and in excess of $900,000 for the season.[74] By 1872 the Texas cattle trade was becoming more professional as Texas ranchers sent thousands of cattle up the trail and then traveled to Wichita to cultivate potential buyers. The magnitude of the Wichita cattle trade is indicated by one Texas rancher who sold seven thousand head of cattle for $210,000 in one sale, and by the tens of thousands of longhorns on the prairies south and west of Wichita waiting for the best buyers. All of this lent some truth to the local newspapers claim, "There is probably more money in circulation at Wichita than in any other town of three times its size in Kansas."[75]

With so much money in circulation, Wichita entrepreneurs employed all of the usual methods of relieving Texas herders of their earnings. Saloons dotted the urban landscape; by one count there were forty-five alcohol-dispensing establishments in the town, not counting the ramshackle hole-in-the-wall variety. Brothels and dance halls were restricted to the Delano District, on the west side of the river, so as to segregate the ruffian entertainment from the respectable businesses. Even so, the city council boasted that, along with superior pasturage, fine hotels, and banking services, the city offered "houses of amusement of an excellent character."[76] These places, designed to amuse Texas herders, included a bordello owned by Bessie and James Earp, brother of the not-yet famous Wyatt Earp, and a dance hall owned by Joe Lowe, who had killed a man in Newton for making what Joe considered to be an improper advance on his wife, Rowdy Kate. In this "unique as well as interesting" place, one reporter wrote, "the Texan with mammoth spurs . . . and a broad-brimmed sombrero," his eyes "lit up with excitement, liquor, and lust," danced with "painted and jeweled courtesans" while whiskey flowed and gamblers played poker in the corners of the hall. The dance music competed with the clank of poker chips and the shouting of frenzied debauchery. Based on this lethal but profitable brew of alcohol, sex, and gambling, Rowdy Joe could take in more than $100 in one night.[77] Wichita also featured a race track, where Texas ponies could race Wichita mares with more than $1,000 in bets changing hands. At one race, there were "one thousand men present, besides five carriage loads of soiled doves."[78]

Those carriage loads of soiled doves at public races presented visible evidence of a major problem for all cattle towns: how to separate cowboys from their money without being exposed to their unsavory habits. The towns catered to the Texas herders by offering unfettered access to pleasures that had been denied on the trail, yet they also required order and restraint so that business could prosper. Wichita's civic leaders tolerated prostitution and other popular if not entirely respectable activities as a necessary inducement. Saloons were licensed for significant fees, while gambling and prostitution were illegal but in practice regularized and fined, providing an important source of municipal income. Technically illegal, gambling and prostitution were thus woven into the financial and social fabric of the cattle towns during the boom years.[79] Nevertheless, respectable citizens rankled when sex workers plied their trade publicly, and gamblers were the most visible features of many saloons. Some respectable Wichita residents complained when prostitutes bathed nude in the Arkansas River during daylight hours. Even the saloons could be troublesome to some residents, such as one who worried that Wichita's forty-five saloons might inhibit the town's growth because some people "will not feel like emigrating to a land flowing so bountifully with whiskey, and whose chief attraction is Texas cattle without limit."[80]

The Trouble with Cowboys

The Texas habit that troubled residents most of all, however, was shooting pistols into the air and sometimes at other people. Stories circulated at the time, and of course ever since, of Texas cowboys walking through town with jangling spurs attached to their high-heeled boots and six-shooters strapped to their hips. Historian Robert Dykstra argues that violence in cattle towns has been exaggerated and become part of the sensationalized image of the cowboy character. In his careful count, five Kansas cow towns between 1870 and 1885 experienced only forty-five homicide victims, including nine cowboys, nine gamblers, six police officers, and a scattering of others not necessarily connected with the cattle trade. Of the six police officers killed, two were felled by "friendly fire" from other officers, including Abilene's James "Wild Bill" Hickok, who famously shot his deputy just as he showed up to help. Dykstra found no instances of anything resembling a movie-style shootout; instead, less than a third of the victims returned fire, and a good many of them were unarmed. Other historians have disputed these numbers, noting that Dykstra included only homicides committed within the city limits and did not include Newton, whose career as a cattle center was so brief. It seems fair to conclude that the image of daily shoot-outs or gunfire every night was exaggerated, but the cow towns did experience homicidal outbursts during their boom years.[81]

In some ways it mattered more *who* was killed than *how many* were killed. A certain level of violence might be tolerated as a regrettable but necessary cost of doing business with Texas cattle drovers, especially if the victims were other cowboys, gamblers, prostitutes, or other transients with little status in the community. On the other hand, Wichita citizens were outraged when a Texas cowboy shot a black construction worker on Main Street several days after they had argued. For the Texas herder, shooting a black laborer for arguing with him in public might have seemed a legitimate response for the perceived challenge to his honor and authority, but Wichita residents did not see it that way. In vain they sent a posse after the shooter and gave the victim an honorable funeral. As a journalist said of the incident, "Drunken roughs, thieves and confidence men might indulge in the periodical pastime of sending each other . . . to their eternal reckoning without disturbing perceptibly the sentiment that sustains and enforces the law, but when a man who earns his bread by honest work is shot down in broad day light on our principal thoroughfare, be he black or white, the result is widely different."[82] The brazen murder of a sober citizen suggested that any and all residents could be vulnerable to random acts of violence, that Texas guns and tempers could not be contained to the saloons and dance halls.

Cattle towns attempted to control violence in the same way that they sought to regulate the social evils of gambling and prostitution. Beginning with Abilene in 1870, every cattle town passed a series of municipal ordinances that banned disorderly conduct, public drunkenness, vagrancy, discharging firearms in town, and carrying concealed weapons in town. Combined with Texas's 1871 ban on carrying weapons in public, these laws meant that gun control was widespread in the world of a cowboy. Despite the cowboys' reputation for wielding pistols at all times, the public display of weapons was banned both in his Texas home and his Kansas destination. Yet, as with other municipal ordinances in cattle towns, these gun-control laws were designed to regulate, not eliminate, the problem. Just as gambling and prostitution were illegal but widely practiced, so the goal was to have guns turned in to police headquarters, where they would be kept for the duration of the cattle herders' in-town spree. Since these were misdemeanors, routine violators could be fined a few dollars. Arresting cowboys who refused or forgot to turn in their guns became an important way for the towns to pay for law enforcement salaries.[83]

Enforcement of gun control ordinances proved difficult but not impossible. It was not, as legend would have it, the lone heroic sheriff who stood down the evildoers with nerve and a quick draw. Although Wild Bill Hickok was the most famous sheriff of Abilene, he spent most of his time in gambling halls and achieved notoriety primarily for killing his assistant. Wyatt Earp worked for the Wichita police and later in Dodge City, where he was joined by another well-known gunslinger, William Barclay "Bat" Masterson. Yet the only sheriff who made a noticeable impression on Texas herders' compliance with gun-control laws was Abilene's Thomas Smith, who enforced the law with his fists rather than his gun. As the story goes, Smith knocked senseless two well-known desperadoes, "Big Hank" and "Wyoming Frank," for refusing to give up their revolvers. The saloon crowd, stunned into silent admiration for the sheriff's "nerviness," then followed the lead of the saloon proprietor who stepped forward and said, "Here is my gun. I reckon I'll not need it so long as you are marshal of this town." According to one account, "No guns thereafter were worn on the streets of Abilene."[84]

As appealing as the story of the lone hero is, it was in fact the machinery of a police force that wore down the herders and forced a modest amount of compliance. Police in cattle towns usually worked in pairs, sometimes in groups of five. During the cattle season they were busy regulating the guns, tempers, and abuses of Texas herders, but the winter months would find the police, even those gun-wielding sheriffs made famous by twentieth-century movies and television, such as Wild Bill Hickok, Wyatt Earp, or Bat Masterson, cleaning the city streets of dead animals and repairing sidewalks. The cattle trade business dictated that judges be lenient and use considerable discretion in convicting for misdemeanors such as drunkenness and carrying a deadly weapon in town, so as to ensure a steady stream of municipal income from fines and court costs and to protect the town's reputation as friendly to the Texas cattle trade.

Overall, however, the violence was not easily tamed. One trail driver remembered that during his trip to Abilene "we found the town was full of all sorts of desperate characters, and I remember one day one of these bad men rode his horse into a saloon, pulled his gun on the bartenders, and all quit business. When he came out several others began to shoot up the town."[85] Other times cowboys would ride into stores and place their orders for merchandise while still in the saddle. Cowboys in Abilene were notoriously reluctant to give up their firearms; when the municipal ordinances went into effect prohibiting carrying guns, the law was not immediately enforced. When the town made signs announcing the new law, cowboys "made targets of them, and as they rode around whooping and howling they took shots at these proclamations that gravely forbade any one carrying firearms within the town's limits."[86] Apparently the Western penchant for shooting up signs, presumably as a show of resistance to authority, and the occasional riding-a-horse-into-the-saloon (which still happens now and then) had their origins in Abilene. So too did the jail break scene replicated in many Western movies. Cowboys first tore down the Abilene jail facility as it was being built, forcing construction to finish under armed guard. The first prisoner was a black camp cook who became thoroughly inebriated and then shot out a street lamp. Showing their loyalty to their cook, the rest of the trail crew gleefully chased away the guards, shot off the locks, and freed the prisoner before shooting holes in a municipal office on their way out of town.[87] Freed from restraint, aggression became the "War-Path," as one newspaper reported, so that "no man's life or property was safe from the murderous intent and lawless invasions of Texans."[88]

This sort of violent shenanigans assumed a vital role in the life, as well as the later mythology, of the cowboy figure for a host of reasons. The act of gathering longhorns and forcing them on a long march up the trail necessarily requires a certain amount of violence toward the beasts. Cow hunts for longhorns in the brush, roping and branding, and even methods of "pushing" or driving cattle required a measure of cruelty. Because these longhorns represented mobile property, there was always a possibility that they might need to be protected with the force of arms. Added to this was the experience of Texans on the ragged edges of a prolonged and often bloody borderland, topped with a good measure of Civil War animosity. The violent culture of the cowboy harkened to an earlier honor culture developed in the British Isles and carried to Texas through the American backcountry, one that valued public displays of masculinity, physical courage, sensitivity to insult, and a readiness to fight in defense of reputation or property.[89] In addition, the police force in cattle towns was composed mostly of Northerners, many of them ex-Union soldiers. Hickok, for example, known for his gun fighting and his gambling, was raised by abolitionist parents and fought for the Union during the war. No wonder that his most infamous killing in Abilene was of Phil Coe, a popular Texas gunfighter and gambler. Although Hickok shot Coe while Coe was employed as a police officer, the fight was fueled by sectional animosities and tensions between two professional gamblers. The Texans saw the police force as bureaucratic agents of the urban, commercial North, while they considered themselves offspring of their antebellum society, based on family relationships and personal honor. As Teddy Blue Abbott pointed out, most lawmen were Northerners, and no self-respecting herder could return to Texas followed by the words, "He let a Yankee lock him up."[90] To surrender to the lawman was to lose the war again.

Yet there was comparatively little violence on the trail. The spasms of violence, sometimes coming as almost joyous outbursts, were mostly a feature of the cowboy in the Kansas towns, not the cow herder on the trail. Since gunshots would cause stampedes, trail bosses discouraged the use of guns, and many did not allow their men to carry guns except during unusually dangerous periods. John Arnot, who spent sixty years as a Texas cattleman, said that he never saw gunplay and that during the long drives most cowboys kept their six-shooters wrapped in their blankets; they were too cumbersome and heavy to wear. D. W. Barton, who led a drive from Texas to Dodge City, urged cowboys not to carry guns "except where absolutely necessary." Many leading Texas cattlemen, including John Chisum and Shanghai Pierce, conspicuously refrained from carrying firearms for fear that merely carrying a gun would be provocative. As Murdo Mackenzie explained, "I thought the matter over and decided that if I did carry a gun, I wouldn't last long. If anyone picked a fight with me and it came to shooting, he would get me first. For me to tote a six-shooter would be a provocation and an excuse to others."[91] Branch Isbell, who took several trips up the trail, learned to dislike guns because of his unpleasant experience of killing the unwanted newborn calves every morning on the trail, and he had an "aversion to habitual pistol toting." On a later trip, when cattle thieves stole part of his herd, he, "by being unarmed and innocent—while feeling scared—got them down to a parley," which resulted in most of his cattle being returned.[92]

It was in comparison to the trail that the cattle towns appeared so violent. In fact, Kansas cattle towns were violent even in comparison with Texas cattle shipping towns, such as Fort Worth, where, according to one account, "disorder . . . was incidental and not dominant."[93] Only the Kansas cattle towns—at the end of the three-month trail of dust and drudgery—achieved notoriety for their violence. The cowboys' gun violence was part of the "spree" at the end of the trail, the moment of decadent indulgence in pleasures that had been denied during the harsh discipline of the trail. Because the trail demanded sixteen to twenty hours each day of constant readiness, almost all trail crews did not allow alcohol for the duration of the trip, and it was expected that cowboys would get drunk when they got to town. Because cowboys endured three months or longer in an all-male society, it was tolerated that cowboys would pay for the company of dance hall girls and prostitutes. Cowboys valued their reputation for independence, yet for months they had been following the demands of longhorns and the dictates of a trail boss. When the trail was over, an outlet for manly assertiveness in a spree of violence made just as much sense as the excuses for binge drinking and commercial sex. The cowboy as gunfighter came not so much from the cattle trail but from the cattle towns, not from the cattle herder at work but the cowboy at play.

Ultimately, violence proved difficult to contain because it was so much a part of the lethal brew of alcohol, gambling, and prostitution. Serving alcohol was necessary to attract business, yet it increased the likelihood of violent outbursts. According to Joe McCoy, the trail life of the cowboy left him so dispirited that "an affront, or a slight, real or imaginary, is cause sufficient for him . . . to deal out death in unbroken doses to such as may be in range of his pistols, . . . his anger and bad whiskey urge him on to deeds of blood and death."[94] J. B. Edwards said of the Texas herder in Abilene that when he "got too much tanglefoot aboard, he was extremely liable under the least provocation" to grab his revolver and shoot "in the air, at anything."[95] Gambling also contained an ever-present threat of violence. Accusations of cheating might at any moment lead to gunplay, with victims both intended and accidental. It was the rare gambler who died of natural causes. Ben Thompson, a notorious gambler and gunfighter in several cow towns, accurately predicted his own violent death: "Sooner or later, however prosperous a gambler may be, he meets with an untimely death. . . . Every time a man sits down to a card game to gamble he takes his life in his hands and lays it between him and his adversary."[96]

Prostitution was perhaps the most violent of all activities in the cattle towns. The young women might make as much as five dollars per night compared to one or two dollars per day for domestic occupations, and a few achieved respectability through marriage or successful businesses. The threat of violent abuse, however, was an everyday reality for those caught in a labor market with few options for women who needed to support themselves. Male drunkenness, fighting, and beating were normal; gunshots were the occasional punctuation to this "dreary and bleak" world.[97] Sex workers quickly found that paying for protection, either from pimps or the police, consumed most of their earnings, and few were able to survive long enough to accumulate any savings at all. "Soiled doves" were sometimes seen as so morally compromised that they deserved whatever fate came their way, and cattle town newspapers treated violence against them as a cause for mockery or jest. For protection, prostitutes sometimes aligned themselves with well-known gamblers or law enforcement officers. Wichita's Wyatt Earp, while on the police force, no doubt ensured the safety not only of Bessie and James Earp, who ran the family bordello, but also of sex workers Sallie, Eva, Kate, and Minnie, all of whom, when arrested every month, followed the usual practice of claiming the last name of their patron, Earp. Their monthly fines, as well as their fictive kinship, helped to ensure their protection. Since fines for prostitution constituted one-quarter of all fines paid in Wichita, this de facto tax no doubt paid part of Wyatt's salary. Similarly in Abilene, the brothel district required a regular "detail of police" to maintain order. Rumor had it that any fatalities were kept secret.[98] Violence was not the exception for cattle town cowboys; it was built into everything they did at trail's end.

5. How the Trails Died and the Cowboy Lived On

By 1876 there were good reasons to think that the days of the long cattle drives were over. The panic of 1873 had triggered a recession in cattle prices that led to a precipitous drop in the number of animals sent to Kansas markets and to a steady decline in the number of buyers waiting for them. New railroad lines now stretched into Texas, allowing ranchers to transport cattle directly to Kansas City or Chicago by train rather than by trail. At the same time, many Texas ranchers were rejecting trail-hearty longhorns in favor of shorthorn cattle, Herefords, and other beefy breeds, which brought higher prices at the slaughterhouse. Furthermore, new refrigeration technology on trains and ships allowed ranchers to slaughter cattle in Texas and send packaged beef directly to markets in the eastern US and even in England. The days of the longhorn—so good on the trail but too much hide and horns to make good beef—were apparently numbered. When Kansas moved the quarantine line westward once again in 1876, it sounded the death knell for the Chisholm Trail and effectively ended Wichita's days as a cow town. No less a figure than Joe McCoy, the man whom many Texans credited with making the Kansas cattle markets possible, wrote that there was no longer any reason for Texans to drive their cattle northward. In 1876 the *San Antonio Express* agreed and predicted the end of the long drives.[1]

The Cattle Bonanza

Yet the cattle trail refused to die. Surprisingly, Texans sent almost as many cattle up the trail in the decade after 1876 as they had in the decade before. They blazed new trails, swinging to western Kansas, clear of quarantine lines, and heading northward into Nebraska, Wyoming, Montana, and the Dakotas. These trails may have increased the distance and usually doubled the time spent on the trail, but they also promised abundant free grass, which could make a cattleman rich. The almost mythical attraction of these northern grasslands was illustrated in a story that circulated during the 1870s of a trader freighting a load of supplies through Wyoming. Caught in a severe fall snowstorm, he realized his oxen could not make it through the blizzard and abandoned them to their wintry death as he made for a safe camp. Returning the next spring, he expected to find the bleached bones of his oxen but discovered them sleek and fat from feeding on prairie grasses all winter. The moral was clear: untended Texas cattle could thrive in the lush grassland of the northern ranges with no additional feed. Never mind that this story originated as a tall tale and circulated mostly among those all-too-eager to believe. It was an apocryphal story that provided an origin myth for the hope that Texas longhorns could find a new home on the northern plains.[2]

The kernel of truth in this story, as Texas cattlemen were learning and northern ranchers already knew, was that the grasses of the northern Great Plains held their nutritional value even during the severe winters of that region. The dominant short-grass species, blue gramma grass and buffalo grass, grew to only six or twelve inches tall, but sent down roots from three to six feet into the soil. With most of their nutrient matter underground, they survived drought, cold, and grazing. In fact, they depended on grazing animals as one strategy for seed dispersal. Because of the dry climate and grasses' high protein content, the autumn frost did not wilt the plants but rather cured them into natural hay that stayed edible and nutritious all winter long. Although winters on the northern plains could be long, with sustained periods of subzero temperatures, Richard Grant, Conrad Kohrs, and a few others had proven a decade earlier that cattle could survive in western Montana's sheltered mountain valleys. Cattle trickled into the northern plains during the 1870s, with cattle numbers in Wyoming topping half a million by 1880. Ranchers quickly realized that longhorns grazing on the northern grasses added more weight than cattle wintered in Texas. Especially when crossed with the meatier Durham and Hereford breeds, Texas longhorns wintering one or two seasons in Wyoming might gain three hundred to four hundred pounds and fetch a considerably higher price than if they had remained in Texas. Even the Chicago livestock market recognized the value of beef raised on the shortgrass prairies of the northern range and began, during the 1870s, to pay more for cattle wintered in Wyoming or Montana.[3]

A series of mild winters and rising beef prices in the late 1870s helped make this prospect of plump cattle raised on free grass seem like a reality. Moreover, the increasing experience and greater professionalism of trail drivers by the late 1870s drove down both the costs and the risks of the long drive. It was, Ike T. Pryor of San Antonio wrote, "reduced to almost a science, and large numbers of cattle were moved at the minimum cost." At a time when shipping a Texas longhorn by rail might cost three dollars or more per head, Pryor calculated that he could send a herd of three thousand cattle from South Texas to Montana at less than one dollar each.[4] Rail travel for longhorns had other problems as well. A multiday journey was stressful enough to cause longhorns to lose weight, but not long enough for them to lose the ticks that caused Texas fever. Thus they arrived in cattle stockyards emaciated and yet still capable of spreading a lethal outbreak of Texas fever. A well-managed drive followed by a winter in the north, in contrast, allowed longhorns to add weight and lose the ticks that made them dangerous.

For Texas cattlemen this was all a natural process, part of an orderly succession from buffalo to cow. Nature's bounty had provided them with "a pasturage upon which the plentiful buffalo had lived and flourished for ages" and now "might be profitably utilized in grazing cattle."[5] By the 1880s the potential profits of long drives to this grassland paradise created an economic boom similar to a gold rush. Everyone wanted in on the action. Cattle, it appeared, could be readied for market at almost no expense in capital or resources and very little in labor.[6] Profits seemed inevitable. For cattle promoters this new "beef bonanza" would be the greatest moneymaker of all, creating "golden visions in a blaze of glory."[7] Cowboys were willing to ride this longer trail north, and cattle speculators invested more than ever. The promise of success wiped out all memory of failure.

There were several prerequisites, however, before cowboys could follow their long-horned bovine companions into the northern grasslands and embrace their moment of glory. Without railroads to take them to market, cattle roaming the northern ranges had very little value. Not until the Union Pacific railroad through Cheyenne connected ranges in northern Colorado and southern Wyoming with the urban markets of the East did a few adventurous Montana ranchers collect herds and trail them south. Regional newspapers promoted the image of the limitless potential of the northern ranges, while the Union Pacific pushed the notion that in the nation's "great Pastoral Belt" cattle could thrive "upon the plains without hay, grain, or artificial shelter."[8] This railroad artery was only part of the solution for cattle growers, however. There were still two important obstacles. Cattle numbers in Wyoming grew, but large parts of Wyoming, Montana, the Dakotas, and Nebraska still belonged not to cattle but to buffalo, not to cowboys but to Indians. Railroads helped bring an end to both the bison and their horse-mounted Indian hunters.

At the end of the Civil War, an estimated 6 million to 15 million bison grazed the southern plains, while a smaller herd roamed the northern grasslands. As explorer Stephen Long had noted, these "immense herds of bison" were so thick that they obscured "the verdant plain."[9] Buffalo may have been in decline, but they were still the dominant ruminant of the Plains. As long as the large herds of bison could blacken the plains, eating grass wherever they went, cattle could not be the top bovine. Charles Goodnight, while trailing cattle on his western route to New Mexico, met herds of migrating buffalo that stampeded and scattered his own smaller and more domesticated bovines.[10]

The annihilation of at least 4 million to 5 million bison between 1871 and 1874 dramatically altered this dynamic, with railroads playing a crucial role. As the leading nineteenth-century bison scientist observed, "as soon as railroads crossed the buffalo country, the slaughter began."[11] Towns famous for their cattle markets, especially Dodge City, Kansas, and Miles City, Montana, spent their first few years as notable shipment points for buffalo hides before shifting to cattle. A new industrial tanning process, which turned green buffalo hides into leather for shoes and machine belts, created a strong demand for bison skins. Throw into the mix "an unlimited supply of new and marvelously accurate breech-loading rifles," notably the 0.50 caliber Sharps rifle, and the result was "a wild rush of hunters . . . eager to destroy as many head as possible in the shortest time." This was not sport hunting; it had none of the adventure of chasing down a buffalo from horseback that had thrilled earlier adventurers. This was industrial slaughter. Applying "business-like principles," teams of four or five, usually one hunter and several skinners, financed by local merchants, spread over the Plains. Finding a spot downwind of the herd, a good hunter might make a "stand" by shooting the lead bull first and then killing the rest while they milled about. The heavy rifles were accurate to several hundreds of yards, far longer than the bison's vision, and could be fired every thirty to sixty seconds. A good hunter averaged 25 bison killed per day, and some "stands" decimated more than 100 bison in a few hours.[12] This rapid-fire operation was fast but amazingly inefficient: less than half of the dead bison actually yielded a hide for market, leaving millions of bison to rot under the prairie sun. "The air was foul with sickening stench," wrote Richard Irving Dodge, "and the vast plain which only a short twelve months before teemed with animal life, was a dead, solitary, putrid desert." Even the air "was offensive from the stench of putrefying carcasses."[13] By 1874 the buffalo in Kansas and Texas were all but gone. A decade later there were virtually no bison left on the northern plains, eliminating the competition for nutritious prairie grasses.

The second cattle boom could only gather momentum once the Lakota Sioux and the Northern Cheyenne had been subjugated. The Great Sioux War of 1876–77, made famous by the Battle of the Little Bighorn, ended with Crazy Horse dead, Sitting Bull in exile, and the Cheyenne and Lakota people confined to reservations. The loss of autonomy for these plains peoples cleared a path for Texas longhorns, whose numbers in Wyoming tripled in the three years after Crazy Horse surrendered.[14] Moreover, the simultaneous demise of bison and native self-sufficiency created a market for longhorns. Having been stripped of their subsistence, reservation Indians now depended on federal annuity payments, which meant that federal agents were eager to buy cattle from Texas. Other government employees—the army that dispossessed the Indians, for example—also needed to be fed. The result was that government livestock buyers purchased from fifty thousand to sixty thousand longhorns each year during the 1870s.[15] The whole market had a cruel symmetry about it: buffalo hunters annihilated a species and impoverished indigenous people, the army forced them onto reservations, and Texas cowboys rode in to feed them all.

Although cowboys often talked as if Indians were their sworn enemies, in stark market terms the cowboys needed the Indians, especially the impoverished, reservation Indians whose food source had been systematically destroyed. A bonus for Texas drovers was that prejudice against Indians and general disregard for the welfare of soldiers meant that tough, stringy longhorn beef, the sort that could not be sold for middle-class consumption, was acceptable. Government beef purchasers often bailed out drovers who otherwise could find no buyers, even though drovers sometimes broke these contracts when a better offer appeared.[16] Just as the federal government provided some of the first paper currency for the cattle towns of the plains in the form of money orders written by Indian agents and army supply officers, now the contracts to feed reservation Indians stimulated a growing market. The contracts for the recently defeated Sioux proved especially lucrative, with one estimate placing annual profits to the cattlemen at $117, 500. With Indian agents purchasing about one of every six cattle driven up the trail during the late 1870s, these well-paid federal contracts promoted the expansion of ranching in the northern plains and provided the foundation for a number of large cattle enterprises.[17] Courtesy of the federal government, many Texas cowboys rode into this second cattle boom by providing inferior beef to reservation Indians and the army that had conquered them.

To meet the demands of this "beef bonanza," the cattle trail grew longer, up to fifteen hundred miles, or more than twice the distance of the earlier drives, and moved farther west. Dubbed the Western Trail, this route might take up to six months if it started south of the Brazos and ended near Wyoming's Powder River or Montana's Yellowstone River. For Texas cowboys, the new trail offered a similar experience to the older Chisholm Trail, but there were a few new wrinkles in this more westerly route. T. J. Burkett described his "long and tiresome journey in the direction of the north star." Gathering a herd in central Texas, he bought provisions in Fort Worth and trailed north to Doan's Store, the last stop in Texas, where he crossed the Red River into Indian Territory, "a paradise for the long horn." The tedium of the journey was interrupted by moments of life-threatening danger: "Hour by hour, step by step and day by day we pursued our way, not knowing the hardships that were in store for us," including the usual thunderstorms, stampedes, sleepless nights, and long days of rounding up scattered longhorns. Burkett's crew met the famous Comanche leader Quannah Parker, who asked for a cow to help feed the five hundred people camped with him near the trail. They sent him a young steer, as did nearly every passing herd. According to Burkett, "Hundreds of cowboys knew Quannah Parker, and he had scores of friends among the white people."

Dodge City, the last and most famous of the Kansas cow towns, offered both an opportunity and a danger. Burkett combined his cattle with another herd to make a larger, more efficient group of 3,350 cattle, allowing them to reduce labor costs because "all of the scrub employees" were sent home. When Burkett's trail boss sent several of the cowboys into Dodge City for much-needed supplies, they began "to 'tank up' on mean whiskey and proceeded to shoot up the town." They left in a hurry, but the marshal managed to shoot and kill one of the hands. After attending to the funeral, the group headed north into Nebraska, where, "for a distance of 75 miles we did not see a stick of timber." They heard stories of winter time temperatures of 30 degrees below zero and a warning that during "severe winters it is impossible for anything to live there in the open." After "four long and lonesome months on the trail," the herd finally arrived at its destination in Colorado, where Burkett's crew "had the pleasure of feasting our eyes on the most beautiful range that was ever beheld by a cowboy. The gramma grass was half a knee high, and was mixed with nutritious white grass that was waist high, waiving in the breeze like a wheat field."[18] After marveling at the prairie grasses and delivering the herd, Burkett and his companions spent three days "sight-seeing" in Denver and then caught the train home to Texas.

Texas cowboys brought more than cattle when they headed up the Western Trail to the northern ranges. Dick Withers, a cowboy from near Lockhart, Texas, went up the trail for the first time in 1869 and again several times in the early '70s. By 1879 he had turned his experience into work as a trail boss for the four peak years of the second great cattle boom. From 1879 to 1882 he bossed large herds, numbering from three thousand to five thousand head, to destinations in Nebraska, Wyoming, and the Dakotas. On his last trip, in 1882, Withers guided thirty-five hundred cattle to Deadwood, South Dakota, to fill a government contract. From there he settled down to ranch in nearby Boyes, Montana.[19] Texas cowboys such as Withers, who stayed to work on northern ranches, spread the habits and techniques of the Texas range to the northern prairies. Along with longhorns, Texans brought their distinctive saddles, boots, chaps, and spurs to the cold country up north. Techniques for riding, roping, cutting, and branding, developed originally by vaqueros along the Rio Grande, now spread to the Powder River, the Belle Fourche, and the Yellowstone. In northern Wyoming and eastern Montana, cattle followed the Texas system of open ranges, roundups, and chuck wagons. In a system that minimized the costs of both capital and labor, cattle were allowed to roam freely over hundreds of miles for most of the year, to be gathered in a spring roundup, sorted and branded, and sent either back to the range or to market.

Stock growers' associations governed the roundups, including the distribution and branding of mavericks (another Texas word), and coordinated the distribution of grazing areas set aside for summer or winter use. The language, lore, and legal arrangements of Texas range country infiltrated the daily life of northern ranches.[20]

A few Texas stockmen increased the efficiency of the long drive to northern ranges by establishing ranches at the destination as well as the starting point. Dudley H. and John W. Snyder, for example, drove one of the first herds north to Nebraska in 1870 and established a headquarters for their northern operations in Cheyenne, Wyoming, the next year. Devout Methodists, the Snyder brothers, who were widely respected for their piety, established three unique and inviolable rules for their employees: no whiskey, no cards or gambling, and no swearing. After Colonel Dudley Snyder had spent the better part of a day killing newborn calves in accordance with the conventional wisdom, he became so disgusted with this "gruesome business" that he ended the practice on all subsequent drives. Instead, he used a wagon to carry the newborns. The profits from this strategy demonstrated that, at least with respect to calves, gentleness paid as well or better than cruelty. In 1877 the Snyder brothers contracted to deliver cattle to Colorado cattle baron John W. Iliff, and they became managers of his northern Colorado and Wyoming cattle estate after his untimely death a year later. Operating in both Texas and their Cheyenne headquarters, the Snyder brothers demonstrated the benefits of one family controlling all phases of the cattle operation: birth in Texas, the long drive to Wyoming, weight gain on a northern ranch, and bulk marketing for railroads and stockyards. This was Texas labor, capital, and management extending from south of San Antonio all the way to the shadow of the northern Rockies.[21]

For a time the northern range seemed to offer a second heaven for the Texas ranchers. Beef prices soared from their mid-'70s levels, peaking in 1882 with Chicago markets paying $40 or even $50 for a steer worth $3 to $6 in Texas, herded north and fattened for two years on a Wyoming ranch. An 1883 article in a cattlemen's newspaper, the *Breeder's Gazette*, noted that this $50 steer "has run on the plains and cropped the grass from the public domain for four or five years" and yielded a $40 profit courtesy of this time on the public domain. "With scarcely any expense" to the owner, a thousand such animals could net tens of thousands of dollars each year for the owner, the *Gazette* reasoned, "and that is why our cattlemen grow rich."[22] Newspaper reports echoed the theme: the grass was free and labor costs were minimal, requiring only a few cowboys, some makeshift corrals, and a branding iron. The "boundless, gateless, fenceless pastures" of the public domain, "forever emancipated from the savage sway," made it all possible.[23] The latest Gilded Age hero, the cattle baron, could expect to count his cattle in the thousands and his profits in the hundreds of thousands. Cheyenne was a "young Wall Street," where "all kinds of people are dabbling in steers." One Cheyenne man, who did not "pretend to know a maverick from a mandamus," pocketed $15,000 from buying and selling cattle he never saw.[24]

On the basis of reports such as this, cattle and capital poured into the northern ranges. The number of cattle in Wyoming soared from over half a million in 1880 to perhaps as many as 1.25 million head in 1886. Montana's cattle population was said to have surged from 250,000 in 1880 to more than 600,000 by 1883. Some of the largest herds of longhorns ever driven from Texas arrived in Montana during these years, with a few numbering between 10,000 and 20,000. Cattle came from all directions. Some drovers pushed cattle from Oregon eastward along the Oregon Trail or through the mountains of Idaho and into Montana. Still more cattle came by train from the Midwest as farmers sent barnyard stock, or "pilgrims," to new pastures in Montana and Wyoming. From 1882 to 1884, there were as many cattle heading west on the Northern Pacific as there were shipped east to the Chicago stockyards. Tens of thousands of these "pilgrim" cattle were unloaded each year in the new towns of Glendive, Miles City, and Billings, Montana—towns created by the railroad that now benefited from shipping cattle as freight in both directions.[25]

Along with this influx of cattle, investment capital from the East Coast and the British Isles flowed into the northern plains. With stories circulating that cattle companies were realizing profits ranging from 25 to 40 percent, the part-mythical, part-real cattle baron—a combination of robber baron and captain of industry—took his place alongside other Gilded Age entrepreneurs. Financed by Scottish investments, the Swan Land and Cattle Company owned thirty thousand acres and controlled the range rights to several hundred square miles and was valued at $3.7 million. John Clay, the popular Scottish cattle manager who was as familiar with the Wyoming prairie as he was with Edinburgh boardrooms and who later managed the Swan Land and Cattle Company wrote that "in Edinburgh, the ranch pot was boiling over. . . . Drawing rooms buzzed with the stories of this last of bonanzas; staid old gentlemen who scarcely knew the difference between a steer and a heifer, discussed it over their port and nuts. . . . Fortunes had been made and . . . investors did not look far into the future. The result was an era of speculation in herds. It was a minor South Sea bubble."[26]

The biggest boomer of them all was cavalry veteran James Brisbin, who in 1881 published a book with the title that neatly expressed the Gilded Age dream: *The Beef Bonanza; or, How to Get Rich on the Plains*. As Brisbin explained, the great cattle herds of Texas were "gradually drawing off North to the plains, which are the natural homes of the future cattle kings of America." In driving thousands of longhorns to the northern grasslands, the Texas drovers were realizing the "superior advantages of the Northern climate over the South." Montana, Brisbin contended, "surpasses all other sections of our great West" because its "grasses cure naturally on the ground, and even in winter, cattle and sheep, which run out all the year round, are found fat and fit for the butcher's block."[27] Brisbin claimed multiple examples of investors reaping substantial profits of 25 percent, even 40 percent. Calculating the natural reproduction of cattle and free grazing against only minimal costs, Brisbin reasoned that investments in cattle would multiply effortlessly and endlessly. A bull market indeed!

The Trails Die

Although no one noticed much at first, the air began leaking out of the bubble as early as 1882, even as beef prices were peaking. With cattle pouring into the plains from all directions, prices for northern plains beef slid slowly downward during the middle years of the decade and fell precipitously at the end of the 1880s. Meatpackers in Chicago and Kansas City were paying higher prices for well-bred cattle fattened on Illinois corn than they were for longhorns grazed on the northern plains. Contrary to Brisbin's claim that the "West will supply the people of the East," it was increasingly the Midwest rather than the Great Plains that supplied the nation's beef. In spite of national fascination with the long drives from Texas, midwestern cattle production grew faster, and Illinois alone contained more cattle than the entire West except for California and Texas.[28]

In time investors learned the painful lesson that "book cattle," the kind that yielded 40 percent profits, were not the same as real cattle. Cattle barons kept track of cattle in ledger books, where numbers multiplied at a fixed annual rate. Since rounding up and counting actual cattle would incur costs, many large ranchers dispensed with the counting and simply assumed that the numbers in the ledger books represented an actual figure. But real cattle died in subzero winters, not all heifers gave birth each year, and not all calves survived to an age when they would be ready for market. Nor did corporate balance sheets account for the degradation of grasslands. Despite the widespread notion that cattle would simply replace bison as the natural ruminants of the Plains, cattle occupied the plains differently in several important ways. They did not migrate over the distances as bison did, but instead tended to concentrate near water sources. Over a few years this meant that grasses near streams and rivers were so overgrazed that less nutritious short grass species began to replace mixed grasslands. Cattle also preferred the more nutritious big and little bluestem and so ate them first until they were gradually overrun by less nutritious native species such as ironweed, goldenrod, and gramma or even exotic invaders such as Canadian thistle or Kentucky bluegrass.[29] As the grasses became imperceptibly yet surely less palatable each year, cattle proved less successful than bison in dealing with winter storms. During a blizzard, bison would use their strong neck muscles to move their heads from side to side to push away the snow and find the grass underneath. Lacking this survival mechanism, cattle in the same weather would simply die from starvation.

The dramatic reckoning for longhorns came during the severe winter of 1886/87. This grassland tragedy was caused partly by unpredictable nature and partly by all-too-predictable human greed. The winter before had been unusually warm and was followed by a hot, dry summer on the northern plains. As fall approached, Montana cattleman Granville Stuart reported, "The earth in every direction had been trampled and hoof-beaten so that it presented a powdered appearance and every gust of wind was laden with clouds of sand and dust. Truly it looked as though every vestige of vigor and growth had been beaten out of the former grassy ranges."[30] Winter came with a blizzard in November and snow falling with scarcely any letup until March. Temperatures stayed below zero for weeks, and snow covered the ground as deep as three feet, with a crust so thick that Wyoming stagecoaches drove on top of the snow. Cattle bloodied their noses as they tried to reach the grass below and lacerated their legs as the icy granules knifed into them. Putting their backs to the wind as the buffalo had done, cattle walked, sometimes leaving blood trails behind them, until stopped by fences, drifts, exhaustion, or starvation. As the blizzards continued into February, five thousand desperate cattle drifted into Great Falls, Montana, where they bawled for food, ate newly planted tree saplings and even garbage. When the warm Chinook winds came in March, ranchers found emaciated, frozen carcasses piled in coulees, heaped along streams, and stacked against fencerows for miles. Several hundred thousand cattle died, with estimates ranging from 30 to 60 percent of the total herd. Granville Stuart pronounced it "the death knell of the range cattle business" and privately confessed: A "business that had been fascinating to me before, suddenly became distasteful. I never wanted to own again an animal that I could not feed and shelter." John Clay called it a case of "simple murder, at least for the Texas cattle. . . . Three great streams of ill-luck, mismanagement, and greed met together."[31]

If this catastrophic winter marked the end of the Texas system of open range ranching in the northern plains, the end of the great Texas cattle drives had come a few years earlier as the longhorns' biological companion, the cattle tick (*Boophilus*), continued to plague the livestock industry wherever the Texas cattle trail went. In 1884 some five thousand Texas longhorns trailed through Wyoming leaving a fierce outbreak of Texas fever in their wake. Local ranchers complained of losing upward of one hundred head of cattle per day and petitioned the state government for an end to the Texas cattle trails. In some places, ranchers took the law into their own hands and placed armed men in a position to interdict the Texas herds. The redoubtable Charles Goodnight organized such a "Winchester Quarantine" to keep tick-infested cattle from South Texas from passing through his tick-free herds in northwest Texas, while elsewhere ranchers used barbed-wire fences or ranch hands with rifles to stop or reroute herds of longhorns. Kansas farmers had pushed the quarantine line steadily westward during the 1870s, but the Western Trail through Dodge City remained open until August 1884, when Kansas governor G. W. Glick, acting on the petitions of livestock raisers in western Kansas, quarantined the entire state to Texas herds. By the end of 1885 six other western states had joined Kansas in banning Texas longhorns from trailing through their state.

In response to these growing state and local bans, Texas cattlemen proposed a national cattle trail stretching from South Texas northward to the Canadian border. Although specific routes and provisions varied, most schemes for this national bovine thoroughfare proposed a trail from five to fifty miles wide, all land coming from the public domain, with fences, bridges, and periodic way stations, all courtesy of the federal government. At the first-ever gathering of livestock growers from around the nation, a "convention of colossal proportions" dominated by Texas interests, Texas cattlemen formally proposed the idea. Although the measure passed, cattlemen from northern states wondered why their "high grade cattle" should be subject to genetic dilution from lower-quality longhorns, and why they should allow thousands of longhorns "leaving germs of disease which have already cost stockmen hundreds of thousands of dollars" to travel "through the heart of [their]grazing country."[32] National trail advocates argued that the proposed national cattle trail would comprise less than 3 percent of the land already granted to railroad companies for the building of transcontinental railroads, and that the state-by-state quarantine laws violated the Constitution's provision for federal control of interstate commerce.[33] With mixed reactions from regional cattle interests, the proposal went nowhere when introduced into Congress the following year.

The last gasp of the long drives revealed that only federal funds and land from the public domain could save them. Northern cattlemen, in contrast, championed local quarantines and states' rights. During the Civil War tens of thousands of Texans fought for the cause of a state's right to regulate its own affairs, while hundreds of thousands of Northerners struggled for the ideal of a nation unified by a federal government empowered to protect all citizens equally. Now, a mere twenty years after Appomattox, Southerners rallied for federal supremacy and limitations on the rights of states to regulate interstate commerce while Northerners relied on state and local controls to protect their livestock. Ex-Confederates championed a national trail built on public lands and federal subsidy, whereas Union veterans insisted that states had the right to manage their own economies, especially the health and safety of their own cattle herds. Kansas and Illinois still opposed Texas, but this time their views on federal supremacy and states' rights were reversed. In the politics of cattle drives, constitutional scruples that had been sacrosanct two decades earlier took a back seat. And so the cattle trails died.

Cattlemen lobbying Congress for federal protection should have ended any notion of the cattle herder as a rugged individualist. What happened next must have surprised everyone.

The Cowboy Lives

The cattle boom, one historian has concluded, was a brief period when "scrub cattle . . . helped themselves to the public's grass, paid few if any taxes, and wasted the lives of cows and men, all in the process of producing rather poor beef."[34] Although at least 5 million cattle trailed northward in the two decades after the Civil War, making this the largest forced animal migration in history, in a few years the physical traces of this great movement of cattle, horses, and men had been grassed over or plowed under. At best, the trail drives met a small portion of the nation's demand for beef; at worst, it did this at a frightening cost to men, animals, and the grassland ecosystem.

Along the way, some fortunes were made and others were lost. The trail-driving industry, according to one analysis, "made millionaires of a few, rich men of many, and left others bankrupt."[35] Some drovers successfully turned their cattle into capital and used the profits to buy land, build fences, and import improved breeding stocks.[36] Yet many others lost their earnings in a business that carried a large dose of intrinsic risk. The cattle trade enriched Kansas cattle towns for only a few years. Railroads benefitted from having cattle to fill their otherwise empty east-bound freight trains, and meatpacking industries in Chicago and Kansas City profited from the steady supply. Had Texas cattlemen been less "tradition bound" in their commitment to trail driving and more innovative in developing their own regional meatpacking industry, they may well have exercised more control over their own financial destiny.[37] In the northern ranges, the cattle-savvy Scotsman John Clay concluded that it was "doubtful if a single cent was made if you average the business as a whole. . . . The story with its flavor of romance ends in hollow failure."[38] Texans touted longhorns as breeder stock for northern ranches, but most plains cattlemen quickly crossbred the Texas cattle with short-horned breeds that offered more to the butcher, proving, as one historian suggested, that "the Plains cattle industry could do quite nicely without imported longhorns."[39]

As it turns out, Texas longhorns, taken from their semitropical ancestral home in southeastern Texas, were not well-adapted to survive the severe winters of the northern plains. An agent for the Cheyenne and Arapahoe Indians wrote from Indian Territory that the habit of providing no food for cattle during the winter was "nothing less than slow starvation, a test of stored flesh and vitality against the hard storms until the grass comes again."[40] James

Macdonald, a Scottish journalist sent to study western grazing practices to determine if American cattle represented a threat to British beef interests, called the practice a "half-civilized system of prairie cattle management," which fattened cattle on lush summer grasses only to let them starve during the harsh winters. "The prairies here and there," he concluded, "are strewn with white skeletons, and only an acclimatised Texan could contemplate with equanimity the fate of these unfortunate famished animals."[41] In some cases abuse along the trail left cattle especially unfit for the rigors of a northern winter. Although Joseph McCoy blamed this on Mexican herders, other observers claimed the same for Texans: they "have no more feeling or care for dumb brutes, either cattle or horses, than they have for a stone. Their heartless cruelty is proverbial."[42] The trail could be especially cruel if trailing contractors tried to minimize their labor and supply expenses, estimated at $500 per month, by reducing the time spent on the trail. This could cause cattle to be sore-footed or "lose flesh," which increased pain and lowered their sale value.[43]

The cattle trail also inflicted pain on the bodies of the cattle herders who pushed and prodded the animals up the trail. River crossings, lightning storms, and stampedes killed more than a few cowboys, although any accurate counting of trail fatalities is impossible. Based on the anecdotal evidence, it seems likely that trail work was almost certainly more dangerous than ranch work or other rural labors. Life on the trail was known to be a young man's occupation because of the toll it took on the body. According to George Shafer, a rancher and later governor of North Dakota, ranch and trail work caused every laborer to be a "physical wreck at the age of thirty-five years."[44] The push for efficiency carried a cost for people just as it did for cattle, including dust that caused herders to cough up black phlegm months after the drive was over; a monotonous, unhealthy diet; unsanitary water sources; and sleeping on the ground without blankets or tents.

During the two decades of the long drives, the Texas cattle herders had not done much to alter their pre–Civil War reputation as wandering vagabonds, a group of semicivilized, antisocial misfits with a penchant for violence, thievery, and binge drinking. Much of this reputation came from those who knew them firsthand. Joseph McCoy thought that the "wild, reckless conduct of cowboys while drunk . . . brought the personnel of the Texas cattle trade into great disrepute, and filled many graves with victims."[45] John Clay, who spent many seasons on the ranches of the northern ranges, described Texas cowboys employed on a Wyoming ranch as "mostly bad men who had come up the trail." Although a few were "high-class men who have risen to good positions," most were "below par . . . , light-fingered in ranch and camp, exceedingly fond of card playing, a bit brutal to their horses, quiet at their work, but noisy and treacherous under the influence of liquor."[46] One observer found nothing heroic in these "rough men with shaggy hair and wild, staring eyes, in butternut trousers stuffed into great rough boots."[47] A genteel traveler concluded that cowboys were "the plague of the West," who wandered the prairie "watching their herds, constantly at war with the Indians" and who came to town only to "get drunk and become a terror to the inhabitants."[48] Many army officers thought of cowboys as untrustworthy ruffians, as evidenced by Colonel Wesley Merritt, who described them as "idle, shiftless, and lazy."[49] This wretched reputation reached the White House in 1881, when President Chester A. Arthur called on Congress to provide troops to put down the lawlessness of "armed desperadoes known as 'Cowboys.' "[50]

On their home grounds in Texas, actual working cowboys were coming into hard times. The "beef bonanza" of the 1880s brought an influx of eastern and European capital, which created large, corporate ranches. Cowboys now found themselves permanent employees with fewer opportunities than they had had as freelance workers. Large ranches, some of them owned by foreign syndicates, bought enough land to fence in customary grazing lands and water sources, even those they did not own. Corporate ranchers used their deep pockets to string millions of acres of Illinois farmer J. F. Glidden's new invention, barbed-wire fence, effectively ending the open range grazing system, which had birthed both cowboys and longhorns. Enclosed pastures encouraged ranchers to import meatier breeds such as Herefords, and railroads that stretched into every part of the Texas countryside made the longhorns' ability to walk long distances no longer necessary. The use of more docile cattle made the old vaquero skills of the cowboy less valuable; now cowboys found themselves in the undignified position of working on foot to string fences, dig wells, or build windmills. With land and cattle owned by absentee capital and managed by professionals, roping skills mattered less than ever, and accountants carried more weight than cowhands. Corporate ranches promulgated rules that prohibited cowboys from collecting strays, owning land, or branding their own mavericks.[51] As one cowboy-turned-preacher remembered, "Between barbed wire and railroads the cowboys' days were numbered."[52] With opportunities so limited, no wonder one old Texas cowboy song lamented, "I'm going to leave old Texas now, they've got no use for the long horned cow."[53]

This difference between the romanticized past and the corporate present was reflected in the vocabulary of cattle country. Language underscored distinctions between owner and employee, between those who slept in the bunkhouse and those who slept in the ranch house. "Cattleman" applied to the mature, responsible ranch owners, the bearers of civilization and supporters of churches and colleges, while "cowboy" (no matter a man's age) implied a perpetual adolescence, evidenced by a penchant for drinking, a taste for fighting, and a general lack of restraint. Cattlemen were the patriarchs of extended families, while cowboys were drifters and loners without social ties. Cattlemen joined the Gilded Age class, which owned and managed capital, while cowboys were hired hands, working-class employees on horseback. Foreign capital, patterns of landownership, increased dependency of workers, and barbed-wire fences widened the chasm between the two classes, thus reducing social mobility and making it more difficult to move from cowboy to cattleman.

To protest this fencing off of land and opportunity, homesteaders and would-be small ranchers in 1883 started a clandestine campaign of nighttime fence cutting. Although the Fence Cutting Wars forced the Texas legislature into a few concessions, Texas Rangers infiltrated and undermined the movement, making it short-lived. In supporting the property interests of the cattlemen, one Ranger reported that the fence cutters were "cowboys or small cowmen," signifying their working-class origins and the difficulties of turning a small operation of somewhere between fifteen and two hundred head of cattle "and a few cow ponies" into a legitimate ranch.[54] For cowboys who still went up the trail, the Northern Pacific Railway laid bare the social distinction that was emerging in cattle country: cattlemen got passes to ride with the regular passengers, while cowboys were restricted to a separate compartment at the end of the train.[55]

In the end it turned out that there was more profit in cowboy stories than in cowboy labor. These disreputable cattle herders who brought cows to markets that were losing interest in them offered tempting prospects as protagonists in nostalgia-laced stories of the Western frontier. The Texas cowboys of fiction demonstrated considerably more staying power than Texas longhorns, and it was a Texas cattle herder who became the public face of the new hero. Born in Texas a few years before the Civil War and orphaned during the war,

William Levi Taylor grew up around Texas ranches and in the late 1870s went up the trail with a herd of cattle bound for the Nebraska ranch co-owned by Buffalo Bill Cody and Luther and Frank North. Known by his nickname "Buck," Taylor and his brother "Bax" (Baxter) stayed in Nebraska and hired on with the North brothers, both earning a reputation for superior skills in "busting" wild horses.

Buck Taylor's chance for fame came in 1882, when Buffalo Bill Cody staged a Fourth of July "Old Glory Blow Out" in North Platte, Nebraska. Taylor was one of the thousand cowboys who showed up to demonstrate his skills in riding horses and roping cattle. These skills used in actual roundups became the basis for rodeo (from the Spanish *rodear*, to round up) competitions of later years. A skilled rider who could stay on a bucking horse, throw a steer, and pick up a handkerchief from the ground at a full gallop, Buck Taylor was the star of the exhibition. It didn't hurt that he was also tall and handsome. The popularity of the show persuaded Cody to pursue a grander traveling event the following year, featuring "Cow-Boys Fun!" with bucking horses and displays of trick riding and roping. Taylor stood out for his prowess in riding wild horses and roping any bovine in sight. He could even rope and throw a bison. When Cody had tried to ride this particular bison, the shaggy beast threw him six feet into the air, hospitalizing him for two weeks. Taylor had a better fate. He became a popular part of Cody's show and was celebrated as "King of the Cowboys."[56]

Cody's Wild West show re-created dramatic moments from a distant frontier to entertain large urban audiences. Featuring hundreds of people and animals in an outdoor arena, Cody's extravaganza provided the illusion of authenticity for people desperate to experience the real thing. In this sense, Cody's show anticipated the Western movies of the next century. His cowboy heroes had to look the part, so they dressed not as cattle herders on the trail, but in a stage costume of ten-gallon hats, gaudy jackets, embroidered vests, red silk neckerchiefs, and hand-tooled boots with oversized spurs. According to the show's program, cowboys possessed "the noblest qualities that form the romantic hero of the poet, novelist, and historian."[57] Taylor excelled in this arena, oozing masculine domination over equines and bovine alike. His comfort and composure in the saddle led to descriptions of him as "the Centaur Ranchman of the Plains," as if to emphasize his magical unity with his horse. In the coming years the program went on to romanticize Taylor by calling him "a typical Westerner by ancestry, birth and heritage of association," who developed "sturdy qualities" during a life "replete with privations, hardship, and danger," as well as "excitements and adventures." This gentle giant, who could throw steers and break horses, was nevertheless full of "genial qualities" and "amiable as a child."[58] As if to emphasize the wholesomeness of this cowboy archetype, Taylor developed a reputation for devouring biscuits and preferring pie at every meal. For the paying audience, the appetites of the cowboy were directed toward family foods rather than sex, alcohol, or violence. He was the perfect specimen for the rehabilitation of the image of the cowboy.

Rehabilitated cowboys were not enough, however, to make Cody's show a success. The Wild West show hit its stride in 1885, when it added Annie Oakley as Little Sure Shot and numbers of Lakota Indians, including Sitting Bull, fresh from his fame at the battle of the Little Bighorn. The star power of Sitting Bull and his Lakota companions, along with the increased emphasis on firearms, altered Buck Taylor's role from trick rider and roper to knight errant, rescuing damsels in distress. The program for the Wild West show claimed the bullet and the rifle as the necessary tools of "civilization." Gun-toting cowboys were no longer the menacing ruffians who threatened violence on the streets of Abilene or Dodge City, but the heroic harbingers of a more peaceful order. Cody's cowboys now often carried twin ivory-handled pistols in initialed holsters as part of their costume, an appearance that might have gotten them arrested in any Kansas cow town. A key feature of the show was cowboys saving the stagecoach from Indian attack, a part Buck Taylor played to great enthusiasm from audiences. Creating an image of cooperation between the army and cowboys that had never actually existed, cowboys also portrayed cavalrymen in "Custer's Last Fight," with Taylor playing the role of Custer. Such shows reinforced the durable fiction that the essence of the Western experience was cowboys fighting Indians.[59]

On March 31, 1887, even as real Texas longhorns were starving and freezing by the thousands on the frozen plains of Montana and Wyoming, Cody's Wild West departed from the New York harbor bound for London to participate in Queen Victoria's Golden Jubilee. Cody's entourage included nearly two hundred horses, eighteen buffalo, and various elk, deer, mules, and Texas steers, as well as 209 performers, including Buck Taylor. By reaching London, Taylor went further up the trail than any other Texas cowboy, in both geographical and metaphorical distance. The English were impressed by this "red-shirted King of the Cowboys," who rode so skillfully. This "splendid specimen of manhood," observers gushed, not only "repeatedly picked small articles off the ground while riding at a hard gallop" but also rode bucking horses and rescued a stagecoach by sliding his body to the side of his horse so that he was "wholly hidden by his horse from the Indians" and then "rising easily to deliver his own fire."[60] In one show, after repulsing the Indians from the emigrant train, the cowboy celebration was interrupted when Taylor fractured his thigh in a collision with another horse while performing an equestrian Virginia reel. Even in the West London Hospital, Buck Taylor was "quite the hero of the hour," receiving many visitors "of high social position and culture."[61]

Encouraged by his success in England, Taylor developed his own show upon his return to the United States. Modeled on Cody's Wild West, Taylor's exhibition opened in San Francisco in 1894, featuring, according to the newspaper advertisements, a "realistic production of frontier life," with "a band of Sioux Indians" and "cowboys, Mexicans, rough riders, and crack shots." Taylor's opening met with protests from the local Humane Society, which objected to the cruelty to animals and had Taylor arrested for roping and riding steers. He was no sooner acquitted than some of the show's wild steers broke free and injured several of Taylor's fellow cowboys. The following year the show traveled to a number of northeastern cities, only to experience dwindling audiences and a variety of troubles. With his fill of stardom, the "King of the Cowboys" retired to a sedentary life in Pennsylvania.[62]

The fictional Taylor, however, lived long and prospered in a way that the real one never did, courtesy of the invention of inexpensively produced, mass market paperback novels. These dime novels mushroomed in popularity after the Civil War and featured sensationalist fantasies designed to appeal to an increasingly urbanized and industrialized society. Making use of a steam printing press, cheap paper, and a standard size and format that allowed for mass production, the novels were truly a "fiction factory" for a mass audience. Authors occasionally churned out a novel in twenty-four hours and routinely wrote a thousand words an hour and a seventy-thousand-word novel in a week. The largest firm, Beadle and Adams, hired two hundred fifty authors, published a new title every two weeks, and sold millions of copies before folding in 1898. Dime novels set in the West used a variety of frontier types for heroes, including scouts, private detectives, and buffalo hunters. Since most of the authors had never been in the West, the stories followed standard formulas, employed stock characters, and made exaggerated claims to authenticity by including elements of reality mixed in with imaginative morality tales.

One of the best-selling books was Ned Buntline's *Buffalo Bill, the King of the Border Men*, a popular success that helped to launch Cody's show career. The title may have been unintentionally clever, as Cody not only rode the border between settlements and wild Indians, civilization and savagery, as the meaning of the title intended, but also the metaphorical boundaries between Eastern markets and Western realities, Old World nobility and New World democracy, authentic elements of truth in the service of a greater fiction.[63] When dime novelists had exhausted the possibilities in earlier frontier types such as scout, hunter, and pathfinder, they turned their attention to the cowboy, who emerged as simply the last frontier character with marketable potential. This hero quickly became stereotyped into a standard mold that was instantly recognizable, easily reproduced, and sold to the public in much the same way as any other mass-produced item of the industrial revolution.[64] And when dime novelists needed a representative type for cowboys, they turned to Buck Taylor, who was after all, their king.

The first cowboy novel featuring Buck Taylor appeared in February 1887, even as Buffalo Bill Cody was preparing to ship for England. At the exact moment that the project of taking longhorns northward might have been reexamined, the heroic cowboy was about to ride off the prairie and into the pages of *Buck Taylor, King of the Cowboys; or, The Raiders and the Rangers, A Story of the Wild and Thrilling Life of William L. Taylor*. Author Prentiss Ingraham had been profoundly influenced by Cody's Wild West performances and turned to the show's cast of characters to make Taylor the first actual person to serve as the model cowboy for a fictional series. Claiming to be an authentic biography, the novels used standard fictional elements from previous frontier heroes and a lively imagination to create a character that never existed on the Chisholm Trail. The lengthy, lurid titles suggested that there was plenty of buckskin, romance, and adventure in the life of this cowboy. Like the protagonist of James Fenimore Cooper's Leatherstocking series, Natty Bumppo, the fictional Buck Taylor possessed the frontier skills to follow any tracks or start a fire in a rainstorm, just as he simultaneously understood, befriended, and sometimes fought Indians. Although a bearer of civilization, the fictional Taylor maintained an uneasy tension with conventional social codes or laws, trusting instead in his natural nobility and innate morality above that of any sheriff or court.[65] In the first novel, Taylor acquired his stature among other cowboys by besting them in fighting and bronco riding, thus assuring his place as "King" among "His Boys." The dime novels created a world where

BEADLE'S HALF DIME Library

Entered at the Post Office at New York, N. Y., at Second Class Mail Rates. Copyright, 1887, by BEADLE AND ADAMS. February 1, 1887.

Vol. XX. $2.50 a Year. PUBLISHED WEEKLY BY BEADLE AND ADAMS, No. 98 WILLIAM STREET, NEW YORK. Price, 5 Cents. No. 497.

BUCK TAYLOR

KING OF THE COWBOYS

OR,

The Raiders AND THE Rangers.

A Story of the Wild and Thrilling Life of William L. Taylor.*

BY COL. PRENTISS INGRAHAM,

AUTHOR OF "BUFFALO BILL," "WILD BILL," "TEXAS JACK," "BUCKSKIN SAM," ETC.

CHAPTER I.

THE VOLUNTEER RANGER.

A CRY of warning rung out from a man guarding a camp on a Texas prairie.

In a timber motte of several acres, around

*W. L. Taylor, of Texas, and now with Buffalo Bill's Wild West. Buck Taylor is also known as "Wild Will, the Dare Devil Rider."—THE AUTHOR.

BUCK TAYLOR.

Buck Taylor, King of the Cowboys, Beadle's Half Dime Library. Beadle's Half Dime Library, di_06925, The Dolph Briscoe Center for American History, The University of Texas at Austin

the orphaned fictional hero assumes his rightful place in the crude democracy of the frontier, a place where origins do not count for much and other cowboys effectively become the (all male) family he never had. Women, if they appeared at all, were always innocent, beautiful, transitory, and in need of assistance.[66]

The novels started with a germ of truth, but became increasingly fanciful over time. Early in the series Taylor was described, in words that set the tone for the next century of fictional and film cowboys, as tall, athletic, and handsome, the ideal representation of the Texas cowboy. Exuding admiration, Ingraham enthused, "His face was one to remember when once seen, beardless, youthful, yet full of character and fearlessness, amounting to reckless daring."[67] Later novels described the king of the cowboys in a gaudy show costume, wearing a black scarf, watch and chain, diamond pin, ruby ring, and a broad-brimmed sombrero.[68] Clearly this hero was no cattle herder plodding for months after a dusty herd of longhorns; this was a man of action who experienced the plains not as bleak solitude but rather as a joyful expanse of freedom. This hero was a man on horseback who rescued damsels in distress, punished villains, and "could follow a trail as well as an Indian, ride even better, throw a lasso unerringly, and shoot straight to dead center every time." Moreover, Taylor and his "boys," in words that would have astonished a Kansas farmer or cattle town sheriff, were "light-hearted, utterly fearless, generous, noble in the treatment of a friend or a fallen foe, and though feared by evildoers and redskins, they were admired and respected by the soldiers and the people of the settlements."[69] Perhaps the most remarkable feature of the cowboys' moral transformation from cattle trail to fictional hero was that somewhere along the way he lost his cattle. Apparently cows offered little to the fiction writer in the way of action or adventure, so the bovines that gave Taylor's "boys" their name were nearly absent from the dime novels.

What the dime novels missed in cattle, they more than made up for in horses and guns. These fictional cowboys always carried six-shooters and used them with skill, speed, and accuracy, especially while riding on a galloping horse. In a democracy of guns, which made everyone equal, it was this skill on horseback that established aristocracy, even royalty, for the "king of the cowboys." Typical of this lethal dexterity was this example from Ingraham's over-the-top prose: "It was no easy task to load that long rifle on the back of a wild horse; but Buck managed it, and turning his saddle again sent a bullet flying toward his pursuers."[70] Managing guns on horseback, combining equestrian skills with deadly weaponry, appeared as the distinguishing characteristic of cowboy virtue. What slow-moving cattle lacked in dramatic possibilities, horses and guns provided: galloping horses created excitement, a cocked gun generated suspense, and gunfire meant action. Guns sold books, as did beautiful women and a hint of romance. Marketing transformed the cowboy into a gunslinger and made him more interested in rescuing fair maidens than in following cows, a sacrifice of historical authenticity to booksellers' reality. A whiff of gunpowder and the attentions of a pretty lady provided the narrative movement that transported readers into the fantasy of freedom on the Western prairies. At the same time, Samuel Colt's popular, mass-produced .45 caliber pistol became synonymous with cowboy heroes; Colt's publicity claimed that "God created men, Colonel Colt made them equal," and that the pistol should be known as the "Peacemaker." Given the minor role that Colt's revolver played in the actual trail drives compared to its outsized role in Cody's Wild West show and in the dime novels, it might be more accurate to label this gun, as one historian suggests, the "myth-maker."[71]

Ironically, this image of the cowboy as the armed man on horseback grew in popularity at about the same time as working cowboys were under increasing pressure to disarm. Trail cowboys always dealt with municipal ordinances in cattle towns to leave their guns at the sheriff's office, but in 1882 the cattlemen's organizations in Kansas, Texas, and Wyoming passed resolutions against carrying pistols in public. According to the *Texas Livestock Journal*, "There is nothing more disgusting to business men than to see cowboys in these times of peace and safety loaded down with guns and pistols. There is no need for this display of firearms, they do not indicate courage, but cowardice. . . . This wholesale arming of cowboys is a disgrace to stock raising."[72] In the emerging class dichotomy of cattle country, cattlemen expressed the attitudes of responsible business leaders, while cowboys conveyed with their public display of guns a working-class attitude of autonomy and defiance. The narrative needs of dime novelists required that cowboys be armed, while back on the ranch and on cattle trails, the owners of cattle were becoming increasingly nervous at the prospect of an armed proletariat.[73]

Although dime novel cowboys provided an escape from the regimented world of cities and factories, a few real cowboys were beginning to act like a genuine working class, that is, they were organizing and going on strike. Cattle herders of the 1880s faced a number of daunting challenges, and the romantic myth of cowboys that was developing in the East may have made things worse. Cowboys worked in a job market that was overcrowded and seasonal. Ranches could almost always replace a herder who protested the terms of his employment, and most did not hire hands during the winter. As with other Gilded Age workers, the crafts of the trade were in less demand because fences and domestic breeds were replacing lassos and longhorns. Dime novels encouraged Easterners, especially young boys from failing farms and at least a few English aristocrats, to head out West and fulfill the romantic dreams of the free life. These new recruits entered an already crowded job market, ensuring that ranchers would not lack for replacement workers. Even so, there were a few times when cowboys organized to contest the terms of their employment. The most famous cowboy strike came in 1883, in the Texas Panhandle, when approximately two hundred cowboys demanded better wages and, rather tellingly, more nutritious food, including potatoes, onions, corn, and tomatoes. "Cowboys Strike for More Vegetables" is somehow a headline that never found its way to eastern newspapers. A third demand of the strikers was the right to "brand mavericks for themselves" and run their own herds on public lands. Within weeks the strike dissipated, as an influx of replacement workers allowed the ranch owners to fire the striking ranch hands and continue with the spring roundup. Cowboys during the 1880s attempted a few other smaller work stoppages, but these were similarly undermined by a labor market awash with men looking to be hired. Despite occasional walkouts and work slowdowns at roundups across the West, these wage laborers on horseback struggled unsuccessfully to define the conditions of their labor.[74]

This image of the cowboy as a struggling worker took a back seat to the romantic figure of dime novelists, which reached an even more refined stature when large-scale cattle ranchers and their investors from the East and Europe began romanticizing the cattle industry. As investors chased the "beef bonanza" on the open range, their more literary friends found unexpected virtues in cattle herders. John Clay, the Scot who worked for Scottish investors and worried that some Texas cowboys used a branding iron a little freely in order to build up their own herds, nevertheless thought that, compared with the "caste" system of Scotland, the American West offered a "champagne air." The Western landscape had "a freedom, a romance, a sort of mystic halo hanging over those green, grassy, swelling divides that was impregnated, grafted into your system. . . . It was another world" of sublime natural beauty, where both cattle and capital could grow with ease.[75] John Arnot, who moved from Scotland to Dodge City in 1884 wrote, "It was the life of freedom that drew the adventurous of the world to the cattle ranges of the West." This was the "heroic age of the great West."[76]

Perhaps the greatest publicist for the otherworldly beauty and freedom of the cattle country was Teddy Roosevelt, who turned his brief time in the Dakotas into a series of lectures, articles, and books championing ranch life for its "toil and hardship and hunger and thirst," as well as "the glory of work and the joy of living." Although a local newspaper described him as "playing cowboy," Roosevelt reported that he was quite proud of his new buckskin clothes, which made him "a regular cowboy dandy."[77] Cowboys were, the future president wrote, "as hardy and self-reliant as any men who ever breathed." Although some might "cut mad antics" on drunken sprees, most were "self-contained men, perfectly frank and simple," who displayed "whole-souled hospitality" toward strangers and were "much better fellows and pleasanter companions" than other frontier types and incomparably better than "the mechanics and workmen of a great city." The work of cattle herders could be sometimes toilsome, Roosevelt admitted, but was nevertheless "superbly health-giving, and is full of excitement and adventure." The cowboy possessed, Roosevelt claimed in words that sound more like a mirror of himself than an accurate social lens, "few of the emasculated, milk-and-water moralities admired by the pseudo-philanthropists; but he does possess, to a very high degree, the stern, manly qualities that are invaluable to a nation." Roosevelt's mythical cowboy was "brave, hospitable, hardy, and adventurous, he is the grim pioneer of our race; he prepares the way for the civilization from before whose face he must himself disappear."[78]

It fell to Roosevelt's Wyoming friend, Owen Wister, to transform the president's glowing prose into a fully fictionalized hero in the 1902 novel *The Virginian*, which became the best-selling book of that year and provided the model for cowboys in fiction and film for decades to come. Like Cooper's Leatherstocking and so many dime novel heroes before him, Wister's ideal cowboy stood for frontier virtues of manliness and freedom, which were tragically but inevitably disappearing. Wister's nameless cowboy hero had a major upgrade from dime novel cowboys, however, in his social standing. The reader learns early that this hero possesses an innate nobility, not to mention rugged good looks, that sets him apart from everyone else: "No dinginess of travel or shabbiness of attire could tarnish the splendor that radiated from his youth and strength. . . . Had I been the bride," the books narrator confesses in a tone somewhere between admiration and lust, "I should have taken the giant, dust and all." Like the dime novel cowboys, Wister's hero proves his superiority by rising above "the boys" in manly competition (card playing, storytelling, horseback riding) and most importantly by his ability to draw fast and shoot straight. During the course of the novel the hero not only demonstrates his superiority over other men, he romances the lovely schoolmarm from the East, participates in an extralegal (but morally justified, as Wister writes it) lynching of a cattle thief, kills the villain in a shootout, and demonstrates social mobility by moving from drifting ranch hand to foreman to ranch owner. His triumph, Wister claims, is because in the "true democracy" of the American West, the "best man" will win and "true democracy and true aristocracy" will become the same thing.[79] He is the bearer of civilization who himself is never domesticated. Most of all, like the dime novel cowboy, the hero of *The Virginian* is unburdened by any actual livestock.

Wister also transformed the dime novel hero, as well as the actual cattle herders who went up the Chisholm or Western trails, by whitening and ennobling him. For Wister, the cowboy was "the American descendant of Saxon ancestors" with the same chivalric virtues as a medieval knight. These virtues were presumably heightened for Wister in contrast with the vaquero, "this small, deceitful alien" who had, in Wister's view, contributed little to the cattle kingdom.[80] In Wister's hands, African American contributions to cowboy life disappeared, and the entire Hispanic herding tradition existed only as a moral foil, a degenerate race that heightened the dignity of white cowboys. As nature's nobleman, Wister's cowboy hero had the innate moral autonomy to stand against the crowd and the martial and manly qualities to bring the nineteenth-century past into the twentieth-century present. During a time of worrisome urbanization and soul-killing industrialization, the medieval man on horseback could still ride up the trail from Texas and into the American psyche.

John A. Lomax, the most important collector of cowboy songs, understood how these songs tapped into the ancient "Anglo-Saxon spirit." Growing up on a farm in Bosque County, Texas, near a branch of the Chisholm Trail, he learned to love cowboy songs at the age of four, when a cattle herder's night singing awakened him. Fascinated by the sounds, the motion, and the haunting beauty of the passing longhorns and the songs of the herders, he soon began to write them down. As an adult, he made it his life's work to find and collect cowboy songs that came from the "wild, far-away places of the big and still unpeopled West." These songs, he realized, took their shape on the long drive from Texas to Kansas, as herders sang to soothe the restless longhorns, especially at night or when the herd threatened to stampede, and provided one of the few forms of entertainment around the campfire. Tunes were adopted from Methodist hymns, minstrel shows, and popular ballads, and lyrics were invented that reflected the herders' ambivalent feelings about the trail:

the freedom, excitement, and adventure, and also the boredom, hardship, and longing for home.[81] Lomax learned one of the oldest and most authentic trail songs, "The Old Chisholm Trail," from an old-timer who claimed to have sung it all the way from San Antonio to Dodge City and added a new verse every day. With a rhyming couplet and recurring refrain, the words could express almost any mood of the trail: the adrenalin rush of the stampede, the danger of river crossings, the satisfaction of hard work well done, the pleasure of working with trustworthy trail hands, or even the determination to quit the trail: "I'll sell my horse and I'll sell my saddle; You can go to hell with your longhorn cattle." One of the most famous songs that Lomax recorded, "Git Along Little Dogies," took the soothing tune of an old Irish lullaby, while the words spoke to the long trail ("Wyoming will be your new home") even as they suggested a cruel loneliness about the fate of the cattle ("It's your misfortune and none of my own.")[82]

These songs and many others, forged on the trail and recorded early in the twentieth century, contained enough diverse elements to feed a century of popular music. In the 1930s a second generation of cowboy singers, including Gene Autry, came alive on the silver screen as "singing cowboys," invigorating Western movies with syrupy sweet songs and "Ten Cowboy Commandments," which presented cowboys as the bearers of middle-class, Christian morality, more cattleman than cowboy. In the 1970s a very different version of the cowboy emerged with the Outlaw Country singers, such as Waylon Jennings ("My Heroes Have Always Been Cowboys") and Willie Nelson ("Mamas, Don't Let Your Babies Grow Up to Be Cowboys"). The cowboy of these songs was more suited to the rebellious spirit of the times, an alienated loner, in touch with nature but out of step in society. What Autry's respectable role model and the Outlaw's misanthropic outcast shared was an apparent lack of interest in cows. For these cowboys, longhorns and cattle trails had taken a back seat to guitars and guns. In that vein, Garth Brooks's 1993 hit, "The Cowboy Song," is a refreshing change, even as it replayed a familiar nostalgia. "Pushin horns weren't easy like the movie said it was," the song begins, locating listeners on a difficult trail and not the movie house or dance hall. The journey meets with work that was "hot and tired and nasty," as well as flooding rivers, lost steers, terror, and death, but the cowboy is "just chasin' what he really loves" and "wishin' to God that he'd been born a hundred years ago."[83]

This backward look at the cowboy as an exemplar of a simpler and more durable set of virtues informed not only music but also twentieth-century film versions of the fictional cowboy. The lure of the cowboy helped to make the American film industry successful. Between 1910 and the 1930, fully one in five American films was a Western.[84] These early films drew on the fictional cowboy of the dime novels more than on the memories of trail experiences, and they quickly became reduced to genre films, with stock characters and simple moral messages. Their being known as "horse operas" suggested that, in the tradition of Cody's Wild West show, the hero remained connected with animals, nature, and the grand landscapes of the West, but only a few of these movies made the cattle drive itself the focus of the story. An early classic of trail Westerns is Howard Hawks's *Red River*. John Wayne plays an unstable hero who abandons his friends on a wagon train in order to start a ranch, kills a Mexican who has prior claim to the land, miraculously starts a large cattle herd from a single cow, bullies his trail crew so brutally that they revolt, and generally treats people and animals around him like objects, to be manipulated for his single-minded purpose of getting his cattle to Abilene. Viewers may differ as to whether Wayne's character grows enough to justify the happy ending, but there is no doubt that there are damaged people and wasted lives along the trail.[85]

The cattle trail took a darker, if immensely popular, turn in Larry McMurtry's 1985 Pulitzer Prize winning novel *Lonesome Dove*, an epic of the trail from Texas to Montana. In the novel and the Emmy Award–winning television miniseries, McMurtry revived not only the Western, but especially the cattle trail Western, as an art form. Some 40 million viewers watched each night as two former Texas Rangers risked everything in order to drive a herd of cattle, mostly stolen from Mexico, to the lush pastures of Montana. They manifest good humor, courage, and loyalty, but McMurtry gives the most revealing line to a woman: "All you two done was ruin one another, not to mention those close to you." McMurtry's brilliance is to combine myth and antimyth, courage and complexity, heroism and tragedy, all in a compelling story that seems to ask the questions: Does the cattle trail ennoble those who choose to undertake it? Or does it damage and even destroy them? Through McMurtry's vision, the cattle trail became in the twentieth century one of the essential narratives of the American West, a story of challenge, growth, injury, success and failure.[86]

At the beginning of the century, one year before *The Virginian* was published, when a political assassination meant that Vice President Theodore Roosevelt would become the next president, Ohio Senator Mark Hanna famously lamented, "Now look! That damned cowboy is president."[87] But it was much worse than Hanna believed; that cowboy, damned or otherwise, was not only in the White House but would influence American politics and popular culture for the rest of the new century. For the young boys who followed cattle up the trail, the experience often proved to be an initiation into manhood, a source of identity for the rest of one's life. For the nation that idolized the cowboy image, these herders became a source of national identity in the new century. According to Roosevelt, "we who have felt the charm of the life, and have exulted in its abounding vigor and its bold, restless freedom" can glean lasting inspiration from "the pleasantest, healthiest, and most exciting phase of American existence."[88] Of all the Gilded Age success stories, of all the Horatio Alger characters who went from rags to riches, the cowboy's journey from a morally reprobate ruffian stealing cattle along the Rio Grande border to a place in the Oval Office and a star of the silver screen may be the most remarkable trail of all.

ACKNOWLEDGMENTS

This book would not have been possible without the encouragement and advice of Bob Brugger, editor emeritus at Johns Hopkins University Press. He supported me from the beginning and shared his patience and wisdom all along. Thanks also to Elizabeth Demers, Laura Davulis, and their associates at the press for seeing the book to completion. Their professionalism and commitment to excellence have made it a pleasure to work with them. The series editors for How Things Worked, Robin Einhorn and Richard R. John, also deserve credit for conceptualizing the project and supporting the work. Special thanks to Professor John for his detailed comments, which have helped make this a better book. In that vein I also want to thank two anonymous reviewers, who read the manuscript carefully and offered thoughtful suggestions that have improved the final product. Finally, I have a deep admiration for the painstaking labors of Barbara Lamb, who copyedited the manuscript and saved me from many errors.

My research would not have been possible without the exceptional work of Bethany Schatzke and the rest of the library staff at Rocky Mountain College. With great cheerfulness Beth found many obscure sources on Interlibrary Loan that proved invaluable, demonstrating that in our digital age a small library can have a very large reach. Thanks also to the students at Rocky Mountain College, who remind me on a daily basis of what makes for good history. In Austin, Texas, researcher Susan Burneson located some important sources in the University of Texas archives. And thanks to my sister, Eunice Kerbs, who hosted me during my research visit to the archives in Kansas and helped me understand how things look from the center of the continent.

Most of all, my gratitude and love go to Danell Jones, an accomplished writer who still found the time to help me with every phase of this project. Although she claims no special knowledge of cattle or cowboys, I benefited enormously from her intelligent conversation and unflagging enthusiasm for these topics. She also read every word of the manuscript, some chapters several times, and shaped it into something leaner and more lucid. She brings grace, style, and intelligence to everything she does, and if this book has any of those qualities, it is due to her influence.

NOTES

Prologue

1. George C. Duffield, "Driving Cattle from Texas to Iowa, 1866," *Annals of Iowa* 14, no. 5 (1925): 248, 249.

2. Duffield, "Driving Cattle," 251.

3. Duffield, "Driving Cattle," 252, 253, 254.

4. Duffield, "Driving Cattle," 259, 262.

CHAPTER ONE: How Cowboys and Longhorns Came to Texas

1. E. C. "Teddy Blue" Abbott and Helena Huntington Smith, *We Pointed Them North: Recollections of a Cowpuncher* (1939; repr., Norman: University of Oklahoma Press, 1955), 64.

2. Richard W. Slatta, *Cowboys of the Americas* (New Haven, CT: Yale University Press, 1990), 9.

3. Alfred Crosby, *Ecological Imperialism: The Biological Expansion of Europe, 900–1900* (Cambridge: Cambridge University Press, 1986), 177–179; Elinor G. K. Melville, *A Plague of Sheep: Environmental Consequences of the Conquest of Mexico* (Cambridge: Cambridge University Press, 1994), 158–164.

4. David Dary, *Cowboy Culture: A Saga of Five Centuries* (Lawrence: University Press of Kansas, 1981), 13.

5. Pita Kelekna, *The Horse in Human History* (Cambridge: Cambridge University Press, 2009), 371.

6. J. Frank Dobie, *The Mustangs* (Boston: Little, Brown, 1952), 99–100; Jack Jackson, *Los Mestenos: Spanish Ranching in Texas, 1721–1821* (College Station: Texas A&M University Press, 1986), 78; Bill Jones, *Louisiana Cowboys* (Gretna, LA: Pelican, 2007), 19.

7. Slatta, *Cowboys of the Americas*, 18–22, 39–44; Lawrence Clayton, Jim Hoy, and Jerald Underwood, *Vaqueros, Cowboys, and Buckaroos* (Austin: University of Texas Press, 2001), 25–33.

8. Dary, *Cowboy Culture*, 21–35.

9. Andrew Sluyter, *Black Ranching Frontiers: African Cattle Herders of the Atlantic World, 1500–1900* (New Haven, CT: Yale University Press, 2012), 96.

10. Terry G. Jordan, *North American Cattle-Ranching Frontiers: Origins, Diffusion, and Differentiation* (Albuquerque: University of New Mexico Press, 1993), 13.

11. Brooks Blevins, *Cattle in the Cotton Fields: A History of Cattle Raising in Alabama* (Tuscaloosa: University of Alabama Press, 1998), 19; Mart A. Stewart, "'Whether Wast, Deodand, or Stray': Cattle, Culture, and the Environment in Early Georgia," *Agricultural History* 65, no. 3 (1991): 1–28.

12. Terry G. Jordan, *Trails to Texas: Southern Roots of Western Cattle Ranching* (Lincoln: University of Nebraska Press, 1981), esp. chap. 6; Jordan, *North American Cattle-Ranching Frontiers*, 117.

13. Kathryn Newfont, *Blue Ridge Commons: Environmental Activism and Forest History in Western North Carolina* (Athens: University of Georgia Press, 2012), 33.

14. Jordan, *North American Cattle-Ranching Frontiers*, 49; Ty Cashion, *A Texas Frontier: The Clear Fork Country and Fort Griffin, 1849–1887* (Norman: University of Oklahoma Press, 1996), 64, 73.

15. T. R. Fehrenbach, *Lone Star: A History of Texas and the Texans* (New York: Macmillan, 1968), 257, 447–448; Gary Clayton Anderson, *The Conquest of Texas: Ethnic Cleansing in the Promised Land* (Norman: University of Oklahoma Press, 2005), 5–7, 41–42, 124, 140.

16. Jacqueline M. Moore, *Cow Boys and Cattle Men: Class and Masculinities on the Texas Frontier, 1865–1900* (New York: New York University Press, 2010), 2.

17. Stephen L. Moore, *Savage Frontier: Rangers, Rifleman, and Indian Wars in Texas* (Plano: Republic of Texas Press, 2002), 1: 170; David Montejano, *Anglos and Mexicans in the Making of Texas, 1836–1986* (Austin: University of Texas Press, 1987), 30.

18. "Stock-Raising," *Texas Almanac, 1861*, 149.

19. Dary, *Cowboy Culture*, 84.

20. Andrew R. Graybill, *Policing the Great Plains: Rangers, Mounties, and the North American Frontier, 1875–1910* (Lincoln: University of Nebraska Press, 2007), 81; Robert Utley, *Lone Star Justice: The First Century of The Texas Rangers* (Oxford: Oxford University Press, 2002), 107–119.

21. Jerry Thompson, *Cortina: Defending the Mexican Name in Texas* (College Station: Texas A&M University Press, 2007), 202.

22. Walter Prescott Webb, quoted in Graybill, *Policing the Great Plains*, 95.

23. J. Frank Dobie, *The Longhorns* (1941; repr., Austin: University of Texas, 2007), 28.

24. *Texas Almanac, 1861*, 148–149; quoted in Vernon R. Maddux, *John Hittson: Cattle King on the Texas and Colorado Frontier* (Nivot: University Press of Colorado, 1994), 100–101.

25. Modern genetic testing has confirmed that longhorns inherited 80 percent or more of their genes from Spanish cattle, with the rest coming from British breeds. John E. Rouse, *The Criollo: Spanish Cattle in the Americas* (Norman: University of Oklahoma Press, 1977), 192–194; Joshua Specht, "The Rise, Fall, and Rebirth of the Texas Longhorn: An Evolutionary History," *Environmental History* 21 (2016): 348.

26. Edmund Russell, *Evolutionary History: Uniting History and Biology to Understand Life on Earth* (Cambridge: Cambridge University Press, 2011), 21–22, 179.

27. Jackson, *Los Mestenos*, 9–10.

28. Dobie, *Longhorns*, 12–13.

29. Virginia Dejohn Anderson, "Animals into the Wilderness: The Development of Livestock Husbandry in the Seventeenth-Century Chesapeake," in *The American South: A Reader*, ed. Paul S. Sutter and Christopher J. Manganiello (Athens: University of Georgia Press, 2009), 44–51; Steven Stoll, *Larding the Lean Earth: Soil and Society in Nineteenth-Century America* (New York: Hill & Wang, 2002), 20–21.

30. Dobie, *Longhorns*, xv.

31. Daniel Boorstin, *The Americans: The Democratic Experience* (New York: Vintage, 1974), 7.

32. Catherine Johns, *Cattle: History, Myth, Art* (London: British Museum Press, 2011), 9.

33. Dobie, *Longhorns*, 36–37; Sue Flanagan, *Trailing the Longhorns: A Century Later* (Austin: Madrona Press, 1974), 10.

34. *Texas Almanac, 1857*, 122.

35. Flanagan, *Trailing the Longhorns*, 10; Jimmy M. Skaggs, *Prime Cut: Livestock Raising and Meatpacking in the United States, 1607–1983* (1986; repr., College Station: Texas A&M University Press, 2000), 26.

36. James Cox, *Historical and Biographical Record of the Cattle Industry and the Cattlemen of Texas* (Saint Louis: Woodward & Tiernan, 1895), 562.

37. Tom Candy Ponting, with notes and introduction by Herbert O. Brayer, *Life of Tom Candy Ponting: An Autobiography* (Evanston, IL: Branding Iron Press, 1952), 41, 42.

38. Harvey A. Levenstein, *Revolution at the Table: The Transformation of the American Diet* (New York: Oxford University Press, 1988), 21–22.

39. Dary, *Cowboy Culture*, 114.

40. Wayne Gard, *The Chisholm Trail* (Norman: University of Oklahoma Press, 1954), 31, 32.

41. Claire Strom, *Making Catfish Bait Out of Government Boys: The Fight against Cattle Ticks and the Transformation of the Yeoman South* (Athens: University of Georgia Press, 2010), 9–21.

42. Paul Wallace Gates, *Agriculture and the Civil War* (New York: Alfred A. Knopf, 1965), 7–8.

43. Tamara Myner Haygood, "Cows, Ticks, and Disease: A Medical Interpretation of the Southern Cattle Industry," *Journal of Southern History* 52, no. 4 (1986): 551–564.

44. Dary, *Cowboy Culture*, 121.

45. Cox, *Historical and Biographical Record*, 74, 81.

46. Gard, *Chisholm Trail*, 36.

47. Odie B. Faulk, "Ranching in Spanish Texas," *Hispanic Historical Review* 45, no. 2 (1965): 257–266; Terry G. Jordan, "The Origin of Anglo-American Cattle Ranching in Texas: A Documentation of Diffusion from the Lower South," *Economic Geography* 45, no. 1 (1969): 72.

48. Gates, *Agriculture and the Civil War*, 176–177.

49. Blevins, *Cattle in the Cotton Fields*, 30–32; Clara M. Love, "History of the

Cattle Industry in the Southwest," *Southwestern Historical Quarterly* 19, no. 4 (1916): 383–384.

50. US Department of the Interior, Department of Indian Affairs, *Annual Report of the Commissioner of Indian Affairs, 1865* (Washington, DC: Government Printing Office, 1865), 32–33; Clara Sue Kidwell, *The Choctaws in Oklahoma: From Tribe to Nation, 1855–1970* (Norman: University of Oklahoma Press, 2007), 70–71; Norman Arthur Grabner, "History of Cattle Ranching in Eastern Oklahoma," *Chronicles of Oklahoma* 21 (1943): 300–303; Michael F. Doran, "Antebellum Cattle Herding in the Indian Territory," *Geographical Review* 66, no. 1(1976): 53.

51. Mary Jane Warde, *When the Wolf Came: The Civil War and Indian Territory* (Fayetteville: University of Arkansas Press, 2013), 217, 135; see also Annie Heloise Abel, *The American Indian and the End of the Confederacy, 1863–1866* (Cleveland, OH: Arthur H. Clark, 1925; repr., Lincoln: University of Nebraska Press, 1993), 96–97.

52. Dary, *Cowboy Culture*, 124–133; Maddux, *John Hittson*, 72; Glen Sample Ely, *Where the West Begins: Debating Texas Identity* (Lubbock: Texas Tech University Press, 2011), 63.

53. Graybill, *Policing the Great Plains*, 120; Dary, *Cowboy Culture*, 140–141.

54. Lawrie Tatum, quoted in Graybill, *Policing the Great Plains*, 25.

55. Pekka Hamalainen, *The Comanche Empire* (New Haven, CT: Yale University Press, 2008), 320–330; for the argument that the frontier retrenchment was exaggerated, even mythological, see Anderson, *Conquest of Texas*, 328.

CHAPTER TWO: How the Cattle Market Boomed and Busted

1. Tex Bender, *Ten Years a Cowboy* (Chicago: Rhodes & McClure, 1890), 386.

2. James W. Freeman, ed., *Prose and Poetry of the Livestock Industry of the United States* (Denver: National Live Stock Historical Association, 1905), 431.

3. James Cox, *Historical and Biographical Record of the Cattle Industry and the Cattlemen of Texas* (Saint Louis: Woodward & Tiernan, 1895), 45.

4. *Texas Almanac, 1868*, 111, 113.

5. Joe B. Frantz and Julian Ernest Choate Jr., *The American Cowboy, Myth and Reality* (Norman: University of Oklahoma Press, 1955), 101.

6. *Texas Almanac, 1867*, 197–198; *Texas Almanac, 1870*, 126.

7. Wayne Gard, *The Chisholm Trail* (Norman: University of Oklahoma Press, 1954), 87–88.

8. *Texas Almanac, 1869*, 180.

9. Daniel Boorstin, *The Americans: The Democratic Experience* (New York: Vintage, 1974), 9; Heather Cox Richardson, *West from Appomattox: The Reconstruction of America after the Civil War* (New Haven, CT: Yale University Press, 2007), 33–35; Carl H. Moneyhon, *Texas after the Civil War: The Struggle of Reconstruction* (College Station: Texas A&M University Press, 2004), 159–161.

10. Will Hale, *Twenty-Four Years a Cowboy and Ranchman in Southern Texas and Old Mexico* (Norman: University of Oklahoma Press, 1959), 55; Edward Everett Dale,

The Range Cattle Industry: Ranching on the Great Plains from 1865 to 1925 (Norman: University of Oklahoma Press, 1930), 6.

11. Lee Moore, *Letters from Old Friends and Members of the Wyoming Stock Growers Association* (Cheyenne: S. A. Bristol, 1923), 33.

12. J. Frank Dobie, *A Vaquero of the Brush Country* (Boston: Little, Brown, 1929), 14; L. B. Sanderson, "Habits and Customs of Early Texans," in *The Trail Drivers of Texas*, ed. J. Marvin Hunter (1924; repr., Austin: University of Texas Press, 1985), 184; William J. Bennett, "Sixty Years in Texas," in Hunter, *Trail Drivers*, 121.

13. J. Frank Dobie, *The Longhorns* (1941; repr., Austin: University of Texas Press, 2007), 52.

14. David Dary, *Cowboy Culture: A Saga of Five Centuries* (Lawrence: University Press of Kansas, 1981), 138.

15. Luther A. Lawhon, "The Men Who Made the Trail," in Hunter, ed., *Trail Drivers of Texas*, 196.

16. W. C. Cochran, "Story of the Early Days: Indian Troubles and Cattle Business of Palo Pinto and Adjoining Counties," p. 33, in Box 2Q480, Briscoe Research Center, University of Texas, Austin.

17. Cox, *Historical and Biographical Record*, 65–66.

18. W. S. James, *Cow-Boy Life in Texas; or, Twenty-Seven Years a Mavrick* (Chicago: M. A. Donahue, 1893), 64.

19. Lewis Atherton, *The Cattle Kings* (1961; repr., Lincoln: University of Nebraska Press, 1972), 33; Frantz and Choate, *American Cowboy*, 101; J. Evetts Haley, *Charles Goodnight: Cowman and Plainsman* (Norman: University of Oklahoma Press, 1936), 111–112.

20. Freeman, *Prose and Poetry*, 620; David Montejano, *Anglos and Mexicans in the Making of Texas, 1836–1986* (Austin: University of Texas Press, 1987), 87.

21. Don Worcester, *The Chisholm Trail: High Road of the Cattle Kingdom* (1980; repr., New York: Indian Head Books, 1994), 6–7.

22. Dobie, *Vaquero*, 15, 16, 19; C. W. Ackerman, "Exciting Experiences on the Frontier and on the Trail," in Hunter, *Trail Drivers*, 154.

23. *Texas Almanac, 1861*, 150–151.

24. Bennett, "Sixty Years in Texas," in Hunter, *Trail Drivers*; George N. Steen, "When a Man's Word Was as Good as a Gilt-Edged Note," in Hunter, *Trail Drivers*, 139.

25. Cox, *Historical and Biographical Record*, 62–64.

26. Manfred R. Wolfenstine, *The Manual of Brands and Marks* (Norman: University of Oklahoma Press, 1970), 18, 31, 52; Boorstin, *Americans*, 24–25.

27. Blake Allmendinger, *The Cowboy: Representations of Labor in an American Work Culture* (New York: Oxford University Press, 1992), 4–5.

28. Walter Prescott Webb, *The Great Plains* (New York: Grosset & Dunlap, 1931), 216; see also Jimmy M. Skaggs, *Prime Cut: Livestock Raising and Meatpacking in the United States, 1607–1983* (College Station: Texas A&M University Press, 2000), 50–52.

29. Dale, *Range Cattle Industry*, 34.

30. Joseph G. McCoy, *Historic Sketches of the Cattle Trade* (Kansas City, MO: Ramsey, Millett & Hudson, 1874), 30–36.

31. Worcester, *Chisholm Trail*, 10.

32. Freeman, *Prose and Poetry*, 432.

33. J. M. Daugherty, "Harrowing Experience with Jayhawkers," in Hunter, *Trail Drivers of Texas*, 696–699; Cox, *Historical and Biographical Record*, 352–253; Dary, *Cowboy Culture*, 171–174; Gard, *Chisholm Trail*, 51.

34. Michael Kennedy, "Tall in the Saddle: First Trail Drive to Montana Territory," in *Cowboys and Cattlemen*, ed. Michael Kennedy (New York: Hastings House, 1964), 103–113; Ernest Staples Osgood, *The Day of the Cattleman* (Chicago: University of Chicago Press, 1929), 21.

35. Haley, *Charles Goodnight*, 121.

36. Haley, *Charles Goodnight*, 147.

37. Atherton, *Cattle Kings*, 184–185; "Shanghai Pierce," in Hunter, *Trail Drivers*, 923–924.

38. *Texas Almanac, 1870*, 124–126; Dary, *Cowboy Culture*, 169–170; Gard, *Chisholm Trail*, 55.

39. Freeman, *Prose and Poetry*, 434.

40. McCoy, *Historic Sketches*, 37.

41. Richard White, *Railroaded: The Transcontinentals and the Making of Modern America* (New York: W. W. Norton, 2011), 50.

42. Gard, *Chisholm Trail*, 67, 58.

43. McCoy, *Historic Sketches*, 40, 54, 21.

44. Gard, *Chisholm Trail*, 68.

45. McCoy, *Historic Sketches*, 56.

46. McCoy, *Historic Sketches*, 50, 44; Gard, *Chisholm Trail*, 66.

47. McCoy, *Historic Sketches*, 53.

48. McCoy, *Historic Sketches*, 107.

49. McCoy, *Historic Sketches*, 65.

50. Terry Anderson and Peter J. Hill, *The Not So Wild West: Property Rights on the Frontier* (Stanford: University of Stanford Press, 2004), 147.

51. Claire Strom, *Making Catfish Bait Out of Government Boys: The Fight against Cattle Ticks and the Transformation of the Yeoman South* (Athens: University of Georgia Press, 2010), 21.

52. "The Spanish Fever," *Emporia News*, August 28, 1868, 1.

53. McCoy, *Historic Sketches*, 152–153.

54. McCoy, *Historic Sketches*, 179.

55. McCoy, *Historic Sketches*, 179–182; Gard, *Chisholm Trail*, 93–94.

56. McCoy, *Historic Sketches*, 202, 226.

57. Jimmy M. Skaggs, *The Cattle-Trailing Industry: Between Supply and Demand, 1866–1890* (1973; repr., Norman: University of Oklahoma Press, 1991), 4; *Emporia News*, February 17, 1871, 2; *Emporia News*, May 19, 1871, 3; "The Texas Cattle Trade," *Wichita City Eagle*, October 24, 1872, 1.

58. Skaggs, *Cattle-Trailing Industry*, 1–5, 123; McCoy, *Historic Sketches*, 78–79.

59. J. F. Ellison, "Sketch of Col. J. F. Ellison," in Hunter, *Trail Drivers*, 476–478; Skaggs, *Cattle-Trailing Industry*, vii, 1–11, 59–60; Col. Ike T. Pryor, "The Cost of Moving a Herd to Northern Markets," in Hunter, *Trail Drivers*, 367–368.

60. Harold E. Briggs, *Frontiers of the Northwest: A History of the Upper Missouri Valley* (New York: Peter Smith, 1950), 199.

61. Louis Pelzer, *The Cattleman's Frontier* (Glendale, CA: Arthur H. Clark, 1936), 55.

62. "Texas Cattle Fever," *White Cloud Kansas Chief*, November 2, 1872, 2.

63. *Emporia News*, July 14, 1871, 3; July 28, 1871, 3; and September 22, 1871, 3; *Leavenworth Weekly Times*, September 15, 1870, 5; *Saline County Journal*, March 14, 1871, 3; "A Cure for the Texas Fever," *White Cloud Kansas Chief*, August 10, 1871, 4; "The Cattle Act," *Leavenworth Weekly Times*, July 3, 1873, 4.

64. *Wichita City Eagle*, January 23, 1873, 2; Skaggs, *Trail-Driving Industry*, 91.

65. White, *Railroaded*, 468.

66. McCoy, *Historic Sketches*, 226; Dary, *Cowboy Culture*, 190; Cox, *Historical and Biographical Record*, 88.

67. McCoy, *Historic Sketches*, 227, 195; Cox, *Historical and Biographical Record*, 88–89; Freeman, *Prose and Poetry*, 462.

68. *Emporia News*, March 22, 1872, 1.

69. Freeman, *Prose and Poetry*, 464; Atherton, *Cattle Kings*, 158–159.

70. Cox, *Historical and Biographical Record*, 93; McCoy, *Historic Sketches*, 251.

71. Cox, *Historical and Biographical Record*, 55, 89; Freeman, *Prose and Poetry*, 464; McCoy, *Historic Sketches*, 252; Richard White, "Animals and Enterprise," in *The Oxford History of the American West*, ed. Clyde A. Milner, Carol A. O'Connor, and Martha A. Sandwiess (New York: Oxford University Press, 1994), 260; James Belich, *Replenishing the Earth: The Settler Revolution and the Rise of the Anglo-World, 1783–1939* (Oxford: Oxford University Press, 2009), 88, 337–338.

72. Dale, *Range Cattle Industry*, 14; Doby, *Longhorns*, ix.

CHAPTER THREE: How to Organize the Largest, Longest Cattle Drive Ever

1. Charles Goodnight, "Managing a Trail Herd in the Early Days," *Frontier Times* 6, no. 5 (March 1929): 250.

2. J. B. Cranfill, "Bill Poage's Drive to Cheyenne in 1874," 7, J. B. Cranfill Cattle Scrapbook, box 3L120, Dolph Briscoe Center for American History, University of Texas at Austin.

3. E. C. "Teddy Blue" Abbott and Helena Huntington Smith, *We Pointed Them North: Recollections of a Cowpuncher* (1939; repr., Norman: University of Oklahoma Press, 1955), 53.

4. Jimmy M. Skaggs, "John Thomas Lytle: Cattle Baron," *Southwestern Historical Quarterly* 71, no. 1 (1967), 51.

5. J. Evetts Haley, *Charles Goodnight: Cowman and Plainsman* (Norman: University of Oklahoma Press, 1936), 121–122.

6. The high estimate of thirty-five thousand cowboys who went up the trail comes

from George W. Saunders, in *The Trail Drivers of Texas*, ed. J. Marvin Hunter (1924; repr., Austin: University of Texas Press, 1985), 453 and is almost certainly exaggerated. The low figure of twelve thousand comes from William W. Savage Jr., *The Cowboy Hero: His Image in American History and Culture* (Norman: University of Oklahoma Press, 1979), 6–9. Jacqueline M. Moore, *Cow Boys and Cattle Men: Class and Masculinities on the Texas Frontier, 1865–1900* (New York: New York University Press, 2010), 39, argues that the only thing certain is that the higher numbers are wrong, whereas Jimmy M. Skaggs, *Prime Cut: Livestock Raising and Meatpacking in the United States, 1607–1983* (1986; repr., College Station: Texas A&M University Press, 2000), 56, settles on thirty thousand as a reasonable number.

7. L. B. Anderson, "Habits and Customs of Early Texans," in Hunter, *Trail Drivers*, 185.

8. Moore, *Cow Boys and Cattle Men*, 38–39; Jimmy M. Skaggs, *The Cattle-Trailing Industry: Between Supply and Demand, 1866–1890* (1973; repr., Norman: University of Oklahoma Press, 1991), 52–53; J. B. Pumphrey, "The Pumphrey Brothers' Experience on the Trail," in Hunter, *Trail Drivers*, 26; S. B. Brite, "A Thorny Experience," in Hunter, *Trail Drivers*, 47–48.

9. George W. Saunders, "Reflections of the Trail," in Hunter, *Trail Drivers*, 453.

10. For a discussion of this debate, see Sara R. Massey, "Preface," in *Black Cowboys of Texas*, ed. Sara R. Massey (College Station: Texas A&M University Press, 2000), xiii–xiv.

11. Abbott and Smith, *We Pointed Them North*, 33–34; Moore, *Cow Boys and Cattle Men*, 41; William D. Carrigan and Clive Webb, *Forgotten Dead: Mob Violence against Mexicans in the United States, 1848–1928* (New York: Oxford University Press, 2013), 6, 30, 44–50.

12. James Smallwood, *Time of Hope, Time of Despair: Black Texans during Reconstruction* (Port Washington, NY: Kennikat Press, 1981), 45; Michael N. Searles, "In Search of the Black Cowboy in Texas," in *The African American Experience in Texas: An Anthology*, ed. Bruce A. Glasrud and James M. Smallwood (Lubbock: Texas Tech University Press, 2007), 86–89.

13. Alwyn Barr, "Introduction," in Massey, *Black Cowboys of Texas*, 10.

14. Abbott and Smith, *We Pointed Them North*, 33; Searles, "In Search of the Black Cowboy in Texas," 90–98.

15. Moore, *Cow Boys and Cattle Men*, 136.

16. *The Trail Riders of Texas* includes no Indian narratives, while the Works Progress Administration Federal Writers' Project Life History Interviews of Texas ranch hands includes only one Indian, George T. Steirs, and he was a ranch hand and Pony Express rider who never worked as a trail rider. See the Federal Writers' Project online as part of the Library of Congress American Memory project, at http://www.loc.ammem.wpaintro.txcat.html.

17. James S. Brisbin, *The Beef Bonanza; or, How to Get Rich on the Plains* (Norman: University of Oklahoma Press, 1959), 66; William W. Savage Jr., "Indian Ranchers," in *Ranch and Range in Oklahoma*, ed. Jimmy M. Skaggs (Oklahoma City: Oklahoma

Historical Society, 1978), 31–35; Peter Iverson, *When Indians Became Cowboys* (Norman: University of Oklahoma Press, 1994), chap. 5.

18. George Duffield, "Driving Cattle from Texas to Iowa, 1866," *Annals of Iowa* 14, no. 5 (1924): 254.

19. Andrew C. Isenberg, *Wyatt Earp: A Vigilante Life* (New York: Hill & Wang, 2013), 38.

20. Robert V. Hine and John Mack Faragher, *Frontiers: A Short History of the American West* (New Haven, CT: Yale University Press, 2007), 126.

21. John W. Barber and Henry Howe, *All the Western States and Territories* (Cincinnati, OH: Howe's Subscription Book Concern, 1868), 684.

22. Joyce Gibson Roach, "Cowgirls and Cattle Queens," in *Texas Women on the Cattle Trails*, ed. Sara R. Massey (College Station: Texas A&M University Press, 2006), 21.

23. Samuel Dunn Houston, "When a Girl Masqueraded as a Cowboy and Spent Four Months on the Trail," in Hunter, *Trail Drivers*, 71–77.

24. Jack Bailey, *A Texas Cowboy's Journal: Up the Trail to Kansas in 1868*, ed. David Dary (Norman: University of Oklahoma Press, 2006), 10, 16, 23, 26, 54.

25. Phyllis A. McKenzie, "Margaret Hefferman Dunbar Hardy Borland," in Massey, *Texas Women on the Cattle Trails*, 89; *Emporia News*, July 18, 1873, 3.

26. Mrs. A. Burks, "A Woman Trail Driver," in Hunter, *Trail Drivers*, 295–305; Roach, "Cowgirls and Cattle Queens," in Massey, *Texas Women on the Cattle Trails*, 53–54.

27. Moore, *Cow Boys and Cattle Men*, 143–145.

28. Bill Stein, "Harriet (Hattie) L. Standefer Cluck," in Massey, *Texas Women on the Cattle Trails*, 66–78.

29. Goodnight, "Managing a Trail Herd," 250–252.

30. Joseph G. McCoy, *Historic Sketches of the Cattle Trade of the West and Southwest* (Kansas City, MO: Ramsey, Millet & Hudson, 1874), 95.

31. James Cox, *Historical and Biographical Record of the Cattle Industry and the Cattlemen of Texas* (Saint Louis: Woodward & Tiernan, 1895), 192; J. Frank Dobie, *The Longhorns* (1941; repr., Austin: University of Texas Press, 2007), 72.

32. David Dary, *Cowboy Culture: A Saga of Five Centuries* (Lawrence: University Press of Kansas, 1981), 192.

33. Abbott and Smith, *We Pointed Them North*, 62, 63.

34. Goodnight, "Managing a Trail Herd," 250–251.

35. McCoy, *Historic Sketches*, 95; Goodnight, "Managing a Trail Herd," 250–251.

36. Haley, *Charles Goodnight*, 256; Joshua Specht, "The Rise, Fall, and Rebirth of the Texas Longhorn: An Evolutionary History," *Environmental History* 21 (2016): 343–363.

37. Dobie, *Longhorns*, 267–270.

38. Goodnight, "Managing a Trail Herd," 52; Abbott and Smith, *We Pointed Them North*, 36.

39. Temple Grandin, "Behavioural Principles of Handling Cattle and Other Grazing Animals under Extensive Conditions," in *Livestock Handling and Transport*, ed.

Temple Grandin, 3d. ed. (Wallingford, UK: Center for Agriculture and Biosciences International, 2007), 63–68.

40. Dobie, *Longhorns*, 283, 72.

41. Haley, *Charles Goodnight*, 136; Branch Isbell, "Days That Were Full of Thrills," in Hunter, *Trail Drivers*, 573; John James Haynes, "His Father Made Fine 'Bowie' Knives," in Hunter, *Trail Drivers*, 246.

42. Dobie, *Longhorns*, 109.

43. John Baylis Fletcher, *Up the Trail in '79*, ed. Wayne Gard (Norman: University of Oklahoma Press, 1966), 15–20.

44. A. W. Capt, "The Early Cattle Days in Texas," in Hunter, *Trail Drivers*, 364.

45. G. W. Mills, "Experiences 'Tenderfeet' Could Not Survive," in Hunter, *Trail Drivers*, 236; W. F. Cude, "Trail Driving to Kansas and Elsewhere," in Hunter, *Trail Drivers*, 215; Fletcher, *Up the Trail*, 24–25.

46. Fletcher, *Up the Trail*, 28; Cude, "Trail Driving to Kansas," in Hunter, *Trail Drivers*, 215.

47. Title IX, Offenses against the Public Peace, chap. 4, "Unlawfully Carrying Arms," *The Penal Code of the State of Texas* (Austin: State Printing Office, 1887), 42; Lewis Atherton, *The Cattle Kings* (1961; repr., Lincoln: University of Nebraska Press, 1972), 40–42; C. W. Ackermann, "Exciting Experiences on the Frontier and on the Trail," in Hunter, *Trail Drivers*, 154–155; Fletcher, *Up the Trail*, 27.

48. A. Huffmeyer, "Catching Antelope and Buffalo on the Trail," in Hunter, *Trail Drivers*, 262; Mills, "Experiences 'Tenderfeet' Could Not Survive," in Hunter, *Trail Drivers*, 231.

49. Fletcher, *Up the Trail*, 28.

50. *Guide Map of the Great Texas Cattle Trail from the Red River Crossing to the Old Reliable Kansas Pacific Railway* (Kansas City, MO: Kansas Pacific Railway, 1874), 8.

51. C. H. Rust, "What Has Become of the Old Fashioned Boy?" in Hunter, *Trail Drivers*, 40; "The Chisholm Trail," *Wichita Daily Eagle*, Mar. 14, 1893, 8.

52. McCoy, *Historic Sketches*, 93.

53. Byron Price, "Prairie Policemen: The United States Army's Relationship to the Cattle Industry in Indian Territory, 1866–1893," in Skaggs, *Ranch and Range in Oklahoma*, 53.

54. Huffmeyer, "Catching Antelope and Buffalo on the Trail," in Hunter, *Trail Drivers*, 265; Wayne Gard, *The Chisholm Trail* (Norman: University of Oklahoma Press, 1954), 130.

55. George N. Steen, "When a Man's Word Was as Good as a Gilt-Edged Note," in Hunter, *Trail Drivers*, 39–40. For other examples, see Mills, "Experiences 'Tenderfeet' Could Not Survive," 234, and Huffmeyer, "Catching Antelope and Buffalo on the Trail," 265, both in Hunter, *Trail Drivers*.

56. Fletcher, *Up the Trail*, 31.

57. Mills, "Experiences 'Tenderfeet' Could Not Survive," 234; Huffmeyer, "Catching Antelope and Buffalo on the Trail," 264; E. A. Robuck, "Dodging Indians Near Packsaddle Mountains," 33; and Cude, "Trail Driving to Kansas and Elsewhere,"

215–216, A. W. Capt, "The Early Cattle Days in Texas," 365–366, all in Hunter, *Trail Drivers*.

58. "Courage and Hardihood on the Old Texas Cattle Trail," in Hunter, *Trail Drivers*, 130.

59. Mills, "Experiences 'Tenderfeet' Could Not Survive," in Hunter, *Trail Drivers*, 238–240.

60. Richard A. Withers, "The Experience of an Old Trail Driver," in Hunter, *Trail Drivers*, 314.

61. C. W. Ackerman, "Exciting Experiences on the Frontier and on the Trail," in Hunter, *Trail Drivers*, 156–157.

62. George W. Brock, "When Lightning Set the Grass on Fire," in Hunter, *Trail Drivers*, 222.

63. A. W. Capt, "The Early Cattle Days in Texas," in Hunter, *Trail Drivers*, 365.

64. Cranfill, "Bill Poage's Drive to Cheyenne in 1874," 9.

65. Robuck, "Dodging Indians Near Packsaddle Mountain," in Hunter, *Trail Drivers*, 32.

66. Abbott and Smith, *We Pointed Them North*, 68.

67. Duffield, "Driving Cattle from Texas to Iowa, 1866," 242–262.

68. Bailey, *Texas Cowboy's Journal*, 13, 35.

69. McCoy, *Historic Sketches*, 138.

70. Cox, *Historical and Biographical Record*, 90–91.

CHAPTER FOUR: How Kansas Survived the Longhorn Invasion

1. *Dodge City Times*, June 2, 1877, 1; *Dodge City Times*, June 16, 1877; accessed through the Library of Congress's Chronicling America: Historic American Newspapers, at http: chroniclingamerica.loc.gov; Minnie Dubbs Millbrook, "North from Dodge: Troubles along the Trail," *Kansas Quarterly* 6, no. 4 (1974): 6–7.

2. James D. Harvey Papers and G. W. Glick Papers, Record Group 252, Records of the Governor's Office, Kansas State Historical Society, Topeka.

3. H. Craig Miner, *Wichita: The Early Years, 1865–1880* (Lincoln: University of Nebraska Press, 1982), 55.

4. Wayne Gard, *The Chisholm Trail* (Norman: University of Oklahoma Press, 1954), 83–84.

5. E. C. "Teddy Blue" Abbott and Helena Huntington Smith, *We Pointed Them North* (1939; repr., Norman: University of Oklahoma Press, 1955), 7, 23–24.

6. A. Huffmeyer, "Catching Antelope and Buffalo on the Trail," in *The Trail Drivers of Texas*, ed. J. Marvin Hunter (1924; repr., Austin: University of Texas Press, 1985), 266; George W. Saunders, "Reflections of the Trail," in Hunter, *Trail Drivers*, 435; J. M. Hunkins, "Reminiscences of Old Trail Driving," in Hunter, *Trail Drivers*, 114.

7. E. R. Rachal, "A Long, Hard Trip," in Hunter, *Trail Drivers*, 807.

8. Chisholm Trail Tracings, Warren L. Matthews Papers, Kansas State Historical Society, Topeka.

9. Mrs. A. Burks, "A Woman Trail Driver," in Hunter, *Trail Drivers*, 303.

10. Life Sketch of Mrs. Pauline (Floeder) Wickham, Lilla Day Monroe Collection of Pioneer Stories #163, box 16, folder 1, Kansas Historical Society. Accessed at http://www.kansasmemory.org/item/211613.

11. J. E. Pettus, "Had Less Trouble with Indians Than with Grangers on the Trail," in Hunter, *Trail Drivers*, 526.

12. J. B. Cranfill, "Bill Poage's Drive to Cheyenne in 1874," 13–14, J. B. Cranfill Cattle Scrapbook, box 3L120, Dolph Briscoe Center for American History, University of Texas at Austin.

13. W. T. (Bill) Jackman, "Where They Put a Trail Boss in Jail," in Hunter, *Trail Drivers*, 856–858.

14. Gus Black, "Had Plenty of Fun," 542, and A. F. Carvajal, "Reminiscences of the Trail," in Hunter, *Trail Drivers*, 841.

15. Abbott and Smith, *We Pointed Them North*, 34, 69; James Smallwood, "James Kelly: The Ebony Gun," in *Black Cowboys of Texas*, ed. Sara R. Massey (College Station: Texas A&M University Press, 2000), 148–149.

16. *Emporia News*, March 17, 1871, 3.

17. Kansas Pacific Railway, *Guide Map of the Great Texas Cattle Trail*, 1874. Accessed at http://books.google.com.

18. Frank S. Geil and William Rochette letters, Warren L. Matthews, "Trails," 127, Warren L. Matthews Papers, KSHS.

19. Rodney O. Davis, "Before Barbed Wire: Herd Law Agitations in Early Kansas and Nebraska," *Journal of the West* 6 (January 1967): 41–52.

20. Saunders, "Reflections," in Hunter, *Trail Drivers*, 435.

21. Matthews, "Trails," 129, Warren L. Matthews Papers, KSHS.

22. Robert R. Dykstra, *The Cattle Towns* (New York: Alfred A. Knopf, 1968), 6.

23. Charles F. Gross letter to J. B. Edwards, April 13, 1922, in J. B. Edwards Papers, Manuscript Collection 1256, Kansas State Historical Society, Topeka.

24. M. A. Withers, "Killing and Capturing Buffalo in Kansas," in Hunter, *Trail Drivers*, 98.

25. J. F. Ellison, "Sketch of J. F. Ellison," in Hunter, *Trail Drivers*, 477.

26. James Cox, *Historical and Biographical Record of the Cattle Industry and the Cattlemen of Texas* (Saint Louis: Woodward & Tiernan, 1895), 305; Gard, *Chisholm Trail*, 105; Jimmy M. Skaggs, *The Cattle-Trailing Industry: Between Supply and Demand, 1866–1890* (1973; repr., Norman: University of Oklahoma Press, 1991), 5, 32–33.

27. Cox, *Historical and Biographical Record*, 309, 352; James W. Freeman, ed., *Prose and Poetry of the Livestock Industry of the United States* (Denver: National Live Stock Historical Association, 1905), 295.

28. Freeman, *Prose and Poetry*, 435; "Driving Texas Cattle to Abilene, Kansas," *Abilene Daily Chronicle*, December 22, 1870.

29. David Galenson, "The Profitability of the Long Drive," *Agricultural History* 51, no. 4 (1977): 737–758.

30. James W. Whitaker, *Feedlot Empire: Beef Cattle Feeding in Illinois and Iowa, 1840–1900* (Ames: Iowa State University Press, 1975), 63.

31. Dykstra, *Cattle Towns*, 76.

32. Joseph G. McCoy, *Historic Sketches of the Cattle Trade of the West and Southwest* (Kansas City, MO: Ramsey, Millett & Hudson, 1874), 226, 204.

33. Dykstra, *Cattle Towns*, 77–78.

34. McCoy, *Historic Sketches*, 195.

35. J. B. Edwards, "Early Days in Abilene," edited and published by C. W. Wheeler, reprinted in the *Abilene Daily Chronicle*, 1938, 3.

36. McCoy, *Historic Sketches*, 250; Dykstra, *Cattle Towns*, 82–83.

37. McCoy, *Historic Sketches*, 137, 204; Edwards, "Early Days in Abilene," 8; Dykstra, *Cattle Towns*, 87–88.

38. Cox, *Historical and Biographical Record*, 178; Freeman, *Prose and Poetry*, 555; Abbott and Smith, *We Pointed Them North*, 7; Gard, *Chisholm Trail*, 107.

39. McCoy, *Historic Sketches*, 138.

40. R. J. Jennings, "Cowboys Dressed Up at the End of the Trail," in Hunter, *Trail Drivers*, 535–536; G. O. Burrows, "High-Heeled Boots and Striped Breeches," in Hunter, *Trail Drivers*, 120.

41. Charles A. Siringo, *A Texas Cowboy* (Lincoln: University of Nebraska Press, 1979), 42; Abbott and Smith, *We Pointed Them North*, 40.

42. Ben Drake, "Ate Terrapin and Dog Meat, and Was Glad to Get It," in Hunter, *Trail Drivers*, 625.

43. Jackman, "Where They Put a Trail Boss in Jail," in Hunter, *Trail Drivers*, 860; Mary Ellen Jones, *Daily Life on the Nineteenth-Century American Frontier* (Westport, CT: Greenwood Press, 1998), 168.

44. Daniel Justin Herman, *Hell on the Range: A Story of Honor, Conscience, and the American West* (New Haven, CT: Yale University Press, 2010), 95; Jacqueline M. Moore, *Cow Boys and Cattle Men: Class and Masculinity on the Texas Frontier, 1865–1900* (New York: New York University Press, 2010), 170.

45. Dykstra, *Cattle Towns*, 89–92; George L. Cushman, "Abilene, First of the Kansas Cow Towns," *Kansas Historical Quarterly* 9, no. 3 (1940): 240–258.

46. *Wichita City Eagle*, April 19, 1872, 3; Dykstra, *Cattle Towns*, 97–98.

47. McCoy, *Historic Sketches*,131, 138.

48. Gard, *Chisholm Trail*, 163.

49. Alfred Iverson, "Buried a Cowboy in a Lonely Grave on the Prairie," in Hunter, *Trail Drivers*, 456–457; J. L. McCaleb, "My First Five-Dollar Bill," in Hunter, *Trail Drivers*, 486–497; John James Haynes, "His Father Made Fine 'Bowie' Knives," in Hunter, *Trail Drivers*, 245; L. D. Taylor, "Some Thrilling Experiences of an Old Trailer," in Hunter, *Trail Drivers*, 504.

50. Gard, *Chisholm Trail*, 166; on the culture of honor, see Bertram Wyatt-Brown, *The Shaping of Southern Culture: Honor, Grace, and War, 1760s–1890s* (Chapel Hill: University of North Carolina Press, 2001); Herman, *Hell on the Range*, xiv-xv; Moore, *Cow Boys and Cattle Men*, 115.

51. Joseph W. Snell, *Painted Ladies of the Cowtown Frontier* (Kansas City, MO: Kansas City Posse of the Westerners, 1965), 11–13.

52. Snell, *Painted Ladies*, 21; Dykstra, *Cattle Towns*, 102–106; Gard, *Chisholm Trail*, 163–165.

53. Gary L. Cunningham, "Gambling in the Kansas Cattle Towns: Prominent and Somewhat Honorable Profession," *Kansas History* 5 (Spring 1982): 11–13; Carol Leonard and Isidor Wallimann, "Prostitution and Changing Morality in the Frontier Cattle Towns of Kansas," *Kansas History* 2 (Spring 1979): 42–43; Miner, *Wichita*, 105.

54. Dykstra, *Cattle Towns*, 297–302.

55. *Abilene Chronicle*, June 15, 1871, and July 20, 1871; Charles F. Gross to J. B. Edwards, April 20, 1922, in the J. B. Edwards Papers, Manuscript Collection 1256, KSHS; Leonard and Wallimann, "Prostitution and Changing Morality," 43–44.

56. Dykstra, *Cattle Towns*, 304.

57. Dykstra, *Cattle Towns*, 306; McCoy, *Historic Sketches*, 231.

58. Gard, *Chisholm Trail*, 187.

59. Dykstra, *Cattle Towns*, 41.

60. Richard White, *Railroaded: The Transcontinentals and the Making of Modern America* (New York: W. W. Norton, 2011), 211, 465.

61. Dykstra, *Cattle Towns*, 81.

62. John D. Waltner, "The Process of Civilization on the Kansas Frontier, Newton, Kansas, 1871–1873," M.A. thesis, University of Kansas, 1968, 30–32.

63. L. B. Anderson, "Habits and Customs of Early Texans," in Hunter, *Trail Drivers*, 186.

64. *Topeka Daily Commonwealth*, August 15, 1871, and November 2, 1871.

65. James R. Mead, *Hunting and Trading on the Great Plains, 1859–1875* (Wichita: Rowfant Press, 2008), 232–236; Miner, *Wichita*, 67.

66. J. H. Baker Diary, Jonathon Hamilton Baker Papers, box 2Q419, Eugene C. Barker Texas History Center, University of Texas at Austin.

67. Gard, *Chisholm Trail*, 147.

68. Dykstra, *Cattle Towns*, 161–172.

69. *Wichita City Eagle*, December 12, 1872; Miner, *Wichita*, 79–81.

70. *Wichita City Eagle*, March 20, 1873.

71. Matthews, "Trails," 128, Warren L. Matthews Papers, KSHS.

72. *Wichita City Eagle*, October 24, 1872.

73. Miner, *Wichita*, 80, 84.

74. Dykstra, *Cattle Towns*, 83; *Wichita City Eagle*, 12, 1872.

75. *Wichita City Eagle*, October 24, 1872; Miner, *Wichita*, 79–80.

76. Andrew C. Isenberg, *Wyatt Earp: A Vigilante Life* (New York: Hill & Wang, 2013), 81.

77. *Wichita City Eagle*, October 4, 1872; Gard, *Chisholm Trail*, 165, 186, 197–198; C. Robert Haywood, *Victorian West: Class and Culture in Kansas Cattle Towns* (Lawrence: University Press of Kansas, 1991), 21.

78. Gard, *Chisholm Trail*, 186.

79. Isenberg, *Wyatt Earp*, 81; Leonard and Wallimann, "Prostitution and Changing Morality," 40.

80. *Wichita City Eagle*, January 23, 1873.

81. Dykstra, *Cattle Towns*, 146; Roger D. McGrath, *Gunfighters, Highwaymen, and Vigilantes* (Berkeley: University of California Press, 1984), 267–268; Isenberg, *Wyatt Earp*, 85; Randolph Roth, Michael D. Maltz, and Douglas L. Eckberg, "Homicide Rates in the Old West," *Western Historical Quarterly* 42 (Summer 2011): 173–195.

82. Miner, *Wichita*, 101.

83. *Abilene Chronicle*, May 12, 1870; Dykstra, *Cattle Towns*, 122–123.

84. Cushman, "Abilene," 248; Gard, *Chisholm Trail*, 170.

85. L. D. Taylor, "Some Thrilling Experiences of an Old Trailer," in Hunter, *Trail Drivers*, 503.

86. Freeman, *Prose and Poetry*, 509.

87. Cushman, "Abilene," 250; Gard, *Chisholm Trail*, 168.

88. *Kansas Daily Commonwealth*, June 14 and September 26, 1871.

89. Herman, *Hell on the Range*, xiv, 12–13; Moore, *Cow Boys and Cattle Men*, 175–178.

90. Abbott and Smith, *We Pointed Them North*, 24; Richard Maxwell Brown, "Violence," in *The Oxford History of the American West*, ed. Clyde A. Milner, Carol A. O'Connor, and Martha A. Sandwiess (New York: Oxford University Press, 1994), 401; Moore, *Cow Boys and Cattle Men*, 175.

91. Lewis Atherton, *The Cattle Kings* (1961; repr., Lincoln: University of Nebraska Press, 1972), 40–42.

92. Branch Isbell, "Days That Were Full of Thrills," in Hunter, *Trail Drivers*, 574, 578.

93. Freeman, *Prose and Poetry*, 517.

94. McCoy, *Historic Sketches*, 138.

95. Edwards, "Early Days in Abilene," 3.

96. Haywood, *Victorian West*, 24

97. Anne M. Butler, *Daughters of Joy, Sisters of Misery: Prostitutes in the American West* (Urbana: University of Illinois Press, 1987), 16, 46; Snell, *Painted Ladies*, 12, 16–19.

98. Isenberg, *Wyatt Earp*, 80–82; Edwards, "Early Days in Abilene," 8.

CHAPTER FIVE: How the Trails Died and the Cowboy Lived On

1. Jacqueline M. Moore, *Cow Boys and Cattle Men: Class and Masculinities on the Texas Frontier, 1865–1890* (New York: New York University Press, 2010), 24–25.

2. Edward Everett Dale, *The Range Cattle Industry: Ranching on the Great Plains from 1865 to 1925* (Norman: University of Oklahoma Press, 1930), 44. For similar versions of this origin story, see Joseph Nimmo, *Report in Regard to the Range and Cattle Business of the United States* (Washington, DC: Government Printing Office 1885), 5; Frederic L. Paxson, "The Cow Country," *American Historical Review* 22, no. 1(1916): 66; Ernest Staples Osgood, *The Day of the Cattleman* (Chicago: University of Chicago Press, 1929), 43–44.

3. Osgood, *Day of the Cattleman*, 52–55; Paul L. Hedren, *After Custer: Loss and*

Transformation in Sioux Country (Norman: University of Oklahoma Press, 2011), 114–119.

4. Ike T. Pryor, "The Cost of Moving a Herd to Northern Markets," in *The Trail Drivers of Texas*, ed. J. Marvin Hunter (1924; repr., Austin: University of Texas Press, 1985), 367; Osgood, *Day of the Cattleman*, 90–91.

5. James Cox, *Historical and Biographical Record of the Cattle Industry and the Cattlemen of Texas and Adjacent Territory* (Saint Louis: Woodward & Tiernan, 1895), 89; James W. Freeman, ed., *Prose and Poetry of the Live Stock Industry of the United States* (Denver: National Livestock Historical Association, 1905), 464.

6. Richard Slotkin, *Gunfighter Nation: The Myth of the Frontier in Twentieth-Century America* (1992; repr., New York: Harper Collins, 19982), 18; see also James Belich, *Replenishing the Earth: The Settler Revolution and the Rise of the Anglo-World, 1783–1939* (Oxford: Oxford University Press, 2009), 237–238.

7. Freeman, *Prose and Poetry*, 663.

8. Osgood, *Day of the Cattleman*, 43–44; Richard White, *Railroaded: The Transcontinentals and the Making of Modern America* (New York: W. W. Norton, 2011), 469–470.

9. Andrew C. Isenberg, *The Destruction of the Bison* (Cambridge: Cambridge University Press, 2000), 23.

10. J. Evetts Haley, *Charles Goodnight: Cowman and Plainsman* (Norman: University of Oklahoma Press, 1936), 145–146.

11. William Hornaday, quoted in White, *Railroaded*, 463.

12. William Temple Hornaday, *The Extermination of the American Bison* (1889; repr., Washington, DC: Smithsonian Institution, 2002), 466–469; Isenberg, *Destruction of the Bison*, 130–138.

13. Richard Irving Dodge, *The Plains of North America*, ed. Wayne R. Kine (Newark: University of Delaware Press, 1989), 150.

14. Osgood, *Day of the Cattleman*, 53; Dale, *Range Cattle Industry*, 43.

15. Richard White, "Animals and Enterprise," in *The Oxford History of the American West*, ed. Clyde A. Milner, Carol A. O'Connor, and Martha A. Sandwiess (New York: Oxford University Press, 1994), 254; Osgood, *Day of the Cattleman*, 38.

16. Jimmy M. Skaggs, *The Cattle-Trailing Industry: Between Supply and Demand, 1866–1890* (1973; repr., Norman: University of Oklahoma Press, 1991), 34.

17. Dale, *Range Cattle Industry*, 63–64; Edward Everett Dale, *Cow Country* (Norman: University of Oklahoma Press, 1942), 14; Byron Price, "Prairie Policemen: The United States Army's Relationship to the Cattle Industry in Indian Territory, 1866–1893," in *Ranch and Range in Oklahoma*, ed. Jimmy M. Skaggs (Oklahoma City: Oklahoma Historical Society, 1978), 50–51.

18. T. J. Burkett Sr., "On the Fort Worth and Dodge City Trail," in Hunter, *Trail Drivers*, 926–930.

19. Richard (Dick) Withers, "The Experience of an Old Trail Driver," in Hunter, *Trail Drivers*, 305–316.

20. David Dary, *Cowboy Culture: A Saga of Five Centuries* (Lawrence: University Press of Kansas, 1981), 240–243; Hedren, *After Custer*, 114–115.

21. D. H. Snyder, "Made Early Drives," in Hunter, *Trail Drivers*, 1029–1031; John M. Sharpe, "Experiences of a Texas Pioneer," in Hunter, *Trail Drivers*, 721–729; Newspaper clippings, Colonel Dudley H. Snyder and D. H. Snyder Reminiscence, Snyder (Dudley Hiram) Family Collection, box 3K425, Dolph Briscoe Center for American History, University of Texas at Austin.

22. Osgood, *Day of the Cattleman*, 94, 86.

23. Hedren, *After Custer*, 114; Dary, *Cowboy Culture*, 242.

24. Osgood, *Day of the Cattleman*, 96.

25. Osgood, *Day of the Cattleman*, 92–93; White, *Railroaded*, 470; Hedren, *After Custer*, 120.

26. Osgood, *Day of the Cattleman*, 96–101; John Clay, *My Life on the Range* (1924; repr., New York: Antiquarian Press, 1961), 35.

27. James S. Brisbin, *The Beef Bonanza; or, How to Get Rich on the Plains* (1881; repr. Norman: University of Oklahoma Press, 1959), 68–70, 158.

28. Brisbin, *Beef Bonanza*, 50; White, *Railroaded*, 476–677.

29. White, *Railroaded*, 474–475; William Cronon, *Nature's Metropolis: Chicago and the Great West* (New York: W. W. Norton, 1992), 220–221.

30. Paul C. Phillips, ed., *Forty Years on the Frontier as Seen in the Journals of Reminiscences of Granville Stuart* (Cleveland, 1925), 2:230–231.

31. Phillips, *Forty Years*, 237; Clay, *My Life on the Range*, 178.

32. Cox, *Historical and Biographical Record*, 103; Skaggs, *Cattle-Trailing Industry*, 110.

33. Nimmo, *Report in Regard to the Range and Cattle Business*, 30–31.

34. Charles L. Wood, *The Kansas Beef Industry* (Lawrence: Regents Press of Kansas, 1980), 2.

35. David Galenson, "The Profitability of the Long Drive," *Agricultural History* 51, no. 4 (1977): 737–758; Harry S. Drago, *Great American Cattle Trails* (New York: Dodd, Mead, 1965), 100.

36. "Branding Iron, Nerve Established Ranches in West Texas in Early Days," *Pioneer* (Fort Stockton, TX), October 5, 1934, in "Cattle Clippings," Van Dale (Earl) Collection, box 3K425, Eugene C. Barker Texas History Center, University of Texas at Austin; Wayne Gard, *The Chisholm Trail* (Norman: University of Oklahoma Press, 1954), 261–263; Jimmy M. Skaggs, *The Cattle-Trailing Industry: Between Supply and Demand, 1866–1890* (1973; repr., Norman: University of Oklahoma Press, 1991 (Norman: University of Oklahoma Press, 1991), 123; Galenson, "Profitability of the Long Drive," 737–758.

37. Skaggs, *Cattle-Trailing Industry*, 124.

38. Clay, *My Life on the Range*, 180–181.

39. Terry Jordan, *North American Cattle-Ranching Frontiers* (Albuquerque: University of New Mexico Press, 1993), 274.

40. White, *Railroaded*, 475.

41. James Macdonald, *Food from the Far West* (London: William P. Nimmo, 1878), 271, 46.

42. Joseph McCoy, *Historic Sketches of the Cattle Trade of the West and Southwest* (Kansas City, MO: Ramsey, Millett & Hudson, 1874), 86.

43. Jim East to J. Evetts Haley, 5, in Van Dale (Earl) Collection, box 2H480, Eugene C. Barker Texas History Center, University of Texas at Austin.

44. White, *Railroaded*, 476.

45. McCoy, *Historic Sketches*, 141

46. Clay, *My Life on the Range*, 234, 268.

47. Henry Nash Smith, *Virgin Land: The American West as Symbol and Myth* (Cambridge, MA: Harvard University Press, 1950), 109; Raymond B. Wrabley Jr., "Drunk Driving or Dry Run: Cowboys and Alcohol on the Cattle Trail," *Kansas History: A Journal of the Central Plains* 30 (Spring 2007): 41.

48. Edmond Mandat-Grancey, *Cow-Boys and Colonels* (London, 1887; repr., Philadelphia: J. B. Lippincott, 1963), 15.

49. James R. Wagner, "Cowboy: Origin and Early Use of the Term," in *The Cowboy Way*, ed. Paul R. Carlson (Lubbock: Texas Tech University Press, 2000), 15.

50. Smith, *Virgin Land*, 110.

51. Moore, *Cow Boys and Cattlemen*, 26–35.

52. W. S. James, *Cowboy Life in Texas; or, 27 Years a Mavrick* (Chicago: M. A. Donohue, 1893), 116.

53. Jim Bob Tinsley, *He Was Singin' This Song* (Orlando: University Presses of Florida, 1981), 224–227.

54. Dary, *Cowboy Culture*, 322.

55. Moore, *Cow Boys and Cattlemen*, 2–7, 21–22.

56. Don Russell, *The Lives and Legends of Buffalo Bill* (Norman: University of Oklahoma Press, 1960), 290–298.

57. Louis Warren, *Buffalo Bill's America* (New York: Vintage Books, 2005), 224; Don Russell, "The Cowboy: From Black Hat to White," in *The Cowboy: Six-Shooters, Songs, and Sex*, ed. Charles W. Harris and Buck Rainey (1976; repr., Norman: University of Oklahoma Press, 2002), 9.

58. William W. Savage Jr., *The Cowboy Hero: His Image in American History and Culture* (Norman: University of Oklahoma Press, 1979), 110.

59. Slotkin, *Gunfighter Nation*, 74–77; Roger A. Hall, *Performing the American Frontier, 1870–1906* (Cambridge: Cambridge University Press,) 139–141; Warren, *Buffalo Bill's America*, 223.

60. "What our Prince and Princesses Saw of 'Buffalo Bill's' Show," from Penny Illustrated and Times (London: England); "Mr. Gladstone at the American Exhibition," both reprinted at The William F. Cody Archive: Documenting the Life and Times of Buffalo Bill, at http:codyarchive.org.

61. "Accident at the American Exhibition" and "King of the Cowboys," at http: codyarchive.org.

62. *San Francisco Morning Call*, April 13, 15, 17, and 21, 1894; *New York Sun*, May 10, 1895; *New York Tribune*, September 29, 1895, accessed at http://chroniclingamerica.loc.gov.

63. Daryl Jones, *The Dime Novel Western* (Bowling Green, OH: Popular Press, 1978); Karen R. Jones and John Wills, *The American West: Competing Visions* (Edinburgh: Edinburgh University Press, 2009), 73–77; Jeremy Agnew, *The Creation of the Cowboy Hero: Fiction, Film and Fact* (Jefferson, NC: McFarland, 2015), 31–32.

64. Savage, *Cowboy Hero*, 109–110.

65. Richard W. Etulain, *Telling Western Stories: From Buffalo Bill to Larry McMurtry* (Albuquerque: University of New Mexico Press, 1999), 24.

66. Prentiss Ingraham, *Buck Taylor: King of the Cowboys*, Beadle's Dime Novels (New York: Beadle & Adams, 1887), 2–3.

67. Prentiss Ingraham, *Buck Taylor, the Saddle King; or, The Lasso Ranger League*, Beadle's Dime Novels (New York: Beadle & Adams, 1891), 2.

68. W. French, "The Cowboy in the Dime Novel," *Texas Studies in English* 30 (1951): 230; see also Smith, *Virgin Land*, 110–111.

69. Prentiss Ingraham, *The Cowboy Clan; or, The Tigress of Texas*, Beadle's Dime Novels, (New York: Beadle & Adams, 1891), 7; see also French, "The Cowboy," 231.

70. Ingraham, *Buck Taylor: King of the Cowboys*, 5.

71. Savage, *Cowboy Hero*, 113; Jones and Wills, *The American West*, 65–66.

72. Quoted in Clifford P. Westermeier, ed., *Trailing the Cowboy: His Life and Lore as Told by Frontier Journalists* (Caldwell, ID: Claxton Printers, 1955), 113.

73. Jack Weston, *The Real American Cowboy* (New York: Schocken Books, 1985), 61–63, 95–99; Robert E. Ziegler, "The Cowboy Strike of 1883," in Carlson, *The Cowboy Way*, 77–93.

74. David E. Lopez, "Cowboy Strikes and Unions," *Labor History* 18, no. 3 (1977): 325–340.

75. Clay, *My Life on the Range*, 2–3.

76. John Arnot autobiographical interview, Van Dale (Earl) Collection, box 2H471, Eugene C. Baker Texas History Center, University of Texas at Austin.

77. White, *Railroaded*, 476; Jones and Wills, *The American West*, 72.

78. Theodore Roosevelt, *Ranch Life and the Hunting-Trail* (New York: Century, 1899), 9–10, 71, 56, 100.

79. Owen Wister, *The Virginian: The Horseman of the Plains* (New York: Macmillan, 1902), 5, 147.

80. Owen Wister, "The Evolution of the Cow-Puncher," *Harper's Monthly*, September 1895, 617, 608.

81. E. C. "Teddy Blue" Abbott and Helen Huntington Smith, *We Pointed Them North: Recollections of a Cowpuncher* (1939; repr. Norman: University of Oklahoma Press, 1955), 220–223; Tinsley, *He Was Singin' This Song*, 17.

82. John A. Lomax, *Adventures of a Ballad Hunter* (New York: Macmillan, 1947), 19–20, 41–45; John A. Lomax, *Cowboy Songs and Other Frontier Ballads* (New York: Macmillan, 1910), xxv, 4–7, 28–38. It's worth noting that although Lomax collected and printed these songs, they were widely sung and in some cases recorded elsewhere. Owen Wister had recorded several verses of "Git Along Little Dogies," and even the blues singer Lead Belly had a version of "The Old Chisholm Trail."

83. Savage, *Cowboy Hero*, chap. 5; Richard Aquila, "A Blaze of Glory: The Mythic West in Pop and Rock Music," in *Wanted Dead or Alive: The American West in Popular Culture*, ed. Richard Aquila (Urbana: University of Illinois Press, 1986), chap. 7; Garth Brooks, "The Cowboy Song," lyrics at http://www.azlyrics.com/lyrics/garthbrooks/thecowboysong.html

84. Moore, *Cow Boys and Cattlemen*, 212.

85. Jane Tompkins, *West of Everything: The Inner Life of Westerns* (New York: Oxford University Press, 1992), 114–118.

86. William Bloodworth, "Writers of the Purple Sage: Novelists and the American West," in Aquila, *Wanted Dead or Alive*, 63; Elliott West, "On the Trail with Gus and Call: *Lonesome Dove* and the Western Myth," in *The Essential West: Collected Essays* (Norman: University of Oklahoma Press, 2012), 277–289.

87. Jones and Wills, *The American West*, 74.

88. Roosevelt, *Ranch Life and the Hunting-Trail*, 24.

SUGGESTED FURTHER READING

Those interested in reading more about cattle trails in the American West are fortunate to find many primary accounts in print. The most important accounts of trail experiences are E. C. "Teddy Blue" Abbott and Helena Huntington Smith, *We Pointed Them North: Recollections of a Cowpuncher* (1939; repr., Norman: University of Oklahoma Press, 1955); Charles A. Siringo, *A Texas Cowboy* (Lincoln: University of Nebraska Press, 1979); and the collection of reminiscences edited by J. Marvin Hunter, *The Trail Drivers of Texas* (1924; repr., Austin: University of Texas Press, 1985). These can be rounded out with a selection of lesser known storytellers, including Tex Bender, *Ten Years a Cowboy* (Chicago: Rhodes & McClure,1890); Will Hale, *Twenty-Four Years a Cowboy and Ranchman in Southern Texas and Old Mexico* (Norman: University of Oklahoma Press, 1959); W. S. James, *Cow-Boy Life in Texas; or, Twenty-Seven Years a Mavrick* (Chicago: M. A. Donahue, 1893); and Lee Moore, *Letters from Old Friends and Members of the Wyoming Stock Growers Association* (Cheyenne: S. A. Bristol, 1923).

All of these accounts were remembered after the fact, so nostalgia and mythical elements sometimes creep into the narratives. These recollections are usefully contrasted with the brutally honest diaries written during the drive itself, especially those by George C. Duffield, "Driving Cattle from Texas to Iowa, 1866," *Annals of Iowa* 14 (April 1925); Jack Bailey, *A Texas Cowboy's Journal: Up the Trail to Kansas in 1868*, edited by David Dary (Norman: University of Oklahoma Press, 2006); and John Baylis Fletcher, *Up the Trail in '79*, edited by Wayne Gard (Norman: University of Oklahoma Press, 1966).

Although not focused on the trail experience, Joseph G. McCoy, *Historic Sketches of the Cattle Trade* (Kansas City, MO: Ramsey, Millett & Hudson, 1874), and John Clay, *My Life on the Range* (1924; repr., New York: Antiquarian Press, 1961), provide important firsthand documentation for many facets of the early cattle era. McCoy and Clay participated in, but also criticized, the cattle industry. Two important early overviews of the cattle kingdom from semiofficial sources that celebrate everything about Texas cattle are James W. Freeman, ed., *Prose and Poetry of the Livestock Industry of the United States* (Denver: National Live Stock Historical Association, 1905), and James Cox, *Historical and Biographical Record of the Cattle Industry and the Cattlemen of Texas* (Saint Louis: Woodward & Tiernan, 1895).

The indispensable academic accounts of the cattle trails are Wayne Gard, *The Chisholm Trail* (Norman: University of Oklahoma Press, 1954); Don Worcester, *The*

Chisholm Trail: High Road of the Cattle Kingdom (1980; repr., New York: Indian Head Books, 1994); and Jimmy M. Skaggs, *The Cattle-Trailing Industry* (1973; repr., Norman: University of Oklahoma Press, 1991). The topic has drawn the attention of a number of talented historians, including Walter Prescott Webb, *The Great Plains* (New York: Grosset & Dunlap, 1931); Lewis Atherton, *The Cattle Kings* (Bloomington: University of Indiana Press, 1959); Terry G. Jordan, *North American Cattle-Ranching Frontiers: Origins, Diffusion, and Differentiation* (Albuquerque: University of New Mexico Press, 1993); Terry G. Jordan, *Trails to Texas: Southern Roots of Western Cattle Ranching* (Lincoln: University of Nebraska Press, 1981); Ernest Staples Osgood, *The Day of the Cattleman* (Chicago: University of Chicago Press, 1929); and Edward Everett Dale, *The Range Cattle Industry: Ranching on the Great Plains from 1865 to 1925* (Norman: University of Oklahoma Press, 1930).

For a broader view of cowboys over different times and places, see David Dary, *Cowboy Culture: A Saga of Five Centuries* (Lawrence: University Press of Kansas, 1981), and Richard W. Slatta, *Cowboys of the Americas* (New Haven, CT: Yale University Press, 1990). To gain a fuller context for understanding the Texas cowboys, read Jack Jackson, *Los Mestenos: Spanish Ranching in Texas, 1721–1821* (College Station: Texas A&M University Press, 1986); Bill Jones, *Louisiana Cowboys* (Gretna, LA: Pelican, 2007); Andrew Sluyter, *Black Ranching Frontiers: African Cattle Herders of the Atlantic World, 1500–1900* (New Haven, CT: Yale University Press, 2012); and Lawrence Clayton, Jim Hoy, and Jerald Underwood, *Vaqueros, Cowboys, and Buckaroos* (Austin: University of Texas Press, 2001). See also J. Frank Dobie, *A Vaquero of the Brush Country* (Boston: Little, Brown, 1929).

Biographies of crucial participants include J. Evetts Haley, *Charles Goodnight: Cowman and Plainsman* (Norman: University of Oklahoma Press, 1936); Jimmy M. Skaggs, "John Thomas Lytle: Cattle Baron," *Southwestern Historical Quarterly* 71, no. 1 (1967); and Andrew C. Isenberg, *Wyatt Earp: A Vigilante Life* (New York: Hill & Wang, 2013). Information on African Americans in cattle drives comes from Sara R. Massey, ed., *Black Cowboys of Texas* (College Station: Texas A&M University Press, 2000); James Smallwood, *Time of Hope, Time of Despair: Black Texans during Reconstruction* (Port Washington, NY: Kennikat Press, 1981); and Michael N. Searles, "In Search of the Black Cowboy in Texas," in *The African American Experience in Texas: An Anthology*, edited by Bruce A. Glasrud and James M. Smallwood (Lubbock: Texas Tech University Press, 2007). Although there is not much information about Native American participation in driving cattle northward, there are a few important sources about native ranches, including Peter Iverson, *When Indians Became Cowboys* (Norman: University of Oklahoma Press, 1994), and William W. Savage Jr., in "Indian Ranchers," *Ranch and Range in Oklahoma*, edited by Jimmy M. Skaggs (Oklahoma City: Oklahoma Historical Society, 1978). An important collection of women's experiences on the cattle trails is *Texas Women on the Cattle Trails*, edited by Sara R. Massey (College Station: Texas A&M University Press, 2006).

The animals who made the trails possible have been the subject of much writing over the years. A useful place to start is with J. Frank Dobie's sometimes sentimental *The Longhorns* (1941; repr., Austin: University of Texas Press, 2007). For a fuller context of cattle, see Catherine Johns, *Cattle: History, Myth, Art* (London: British Museum Press, 2011); John E. Rouse, *The Criollo: Spanish Cattle in the Americas* (Norman: University of Oklahoma Press, 1977); and Joshua Specht, "The Rise, Fall, and Rebirth of the Texas Longhorn: An Evolutionary History," *Environmental History* 21 (2016). For treatments of the horse, see J. Frank Dobie, *The Mustangs* (Boston: Little, Brown, 1952), and the more recent overview by Pita Kelekna, *The Horse in Human History* (Cambridge: Cambridge University Press, 2009). These sources can be read in conjunction with Richard White, "Animals and Enterprise," *The Oxford History of the American West*, edited by Clyde A. Milner, Carol A. O'Connor, and Martha A. Sandwiess (New York: Oxford University Press, 1994), and Donald E. Worcester, *The Texas Longhorn: Relic of the Past, Asset for the Future* (College Station: Texas A&M University Press, 2000). On the demise of the longhorns' bovine predecessor, see Andrew C. Isenberg, *The Destruction of the Bison* (Cambridge: Cambridge University Press, 2000).

Studies of particular aspects of the cattle trails have flourished in recent years. On the masculinity of trail drivers and the important distinction between labor and management implied in the title, see Jacqueline M. Moore, *Cow Boys and Cattle Men: Class and Masculinities on the Texas Frontier, 1865–1900* (New York: New York University Press, 2010). Another important view of the cowboy as laborer comes from Blake Allmendinger's *The Cowboy: Representations of Labor in an American Work Culture* (New York: Oxford University Press, 1992). A provocative recent study of honor culture in cattle country is Daniel Justin Herman's *Hell on the Range: A Story of Honor, Conscience, and the American West* (New Haven, CT: Yale University Press, 2010). For a historical view of how meat goes from trail to slaughterhouse to table, see Jimmy M. Skaggs, *Prime Cut: Livestock Raising and Meatpacking in the United States, 1607–1983* (1986; repr., College Station: Texas A&M University Press, 2001). For the history and science of Texas fever, see Claire Strom, *Making Catfish Bait Out of Government Boys: The Fight against Cattle Ticks and the Transformation of the Yeoman South* (Athens: University of Georgia Press, 2010). A global context for understanding the cattle bonanza of the American West, as well as other nineteenth-century economic booms, is presented in James Belich's *Replenishing the Earth: The Settler Revolution and the Rise of the Anglo World, 1783–1939* (New York: Oxford University Press, 2009). Finally, in *Railroaded: The Transcontinentals and the Making of Modern America* (New York: W. W. Norton, 2011), Richard White provides a thoroughly researched treatment of how railroads made cattle and other Western businesses possible even as they fueled the boom-and-bust cycle that both created and destroyed the cattle trails.

The classic study of social life at trail's end is Robert R. Dykstra, *The Cattle Towns* (New York: Alfred A. Knopf, 1968), which is updated and supplemented by H. Craig Miner, *Wichita: The Early Years, 1865–1880* (Lincoln: University of Nebraska Press, 1982), and C. Robert Haywood, *Victorian West: Class and Culture in Kansas Cattle Towns* (Lawrence: University Press of Kansas, 1991). On prostitution in these towns, consult Anne M. Butler, *Daughters of Joy, Sisters of Misery: Prostitutes in the American West*

(Urbana: University of Illinois Press, 1987); Anne Seagraves, *Soiled Doves: Prostitution in the Early West* (Hayden, ID: Wesanne Publications, 1994); Joseph W. Snell, *Painted Ladies of the Cowtown Frontier* (Kansas City, MO: Kansas City Posse of the Westerners, 1965); and Carol Leonard and Isidor Wallimann, "Prostitution and Changing Morality in the Frontier Cattle Towns of Kansas," *Kansas History* 2 (Spring 1979).

Aspects of Texas history, so crucial to understanding the cattle trails, are covered in T. R. Fehrenbach's standard, but somewhat outdated, *Lone Star: A History of Texas and the Texans* (New York: Macmillan, 1968). This should be read alongside more recent interpretations, including Heather Cox Richardson, *West from Appomattox: The Reconstruction of America after the Civil War* (New Haven, CT: Yale University Press, 2007); Gary Clayton Anderson, *The Conquest of Texas: Ethnic Cleansing in the Promised Land* (Norman: University of Oklahoma Press, 2005); Glen Sample Ely, *Where the West Begins: Debating Texas Identity* (Lubbock: Texas Tech University Press, 2011); and David Montejano, *Anglos and Mexicans in the Making of Texas, 1836–1986* (Austin: University of Texas Press, 1987).

Important interpretations of selected facets of Texas history include Carl H. Moneyhon, *Texas after the Civil War: The Struggle of Reconstruction* (College Station: Texas A&M University Press, 2004), and Ty Cashion, *A Texas Frontier: The Clear Fork Country and Fort Griffin, 1849–1887* (Norman: University of Oklahoma Press, 1996). For the Texas Rangers, see Andrew R. Graybill, *Policing the Great Plains: Rangers, Mounties, and the North American Frontier, 1875–1910* (Lincoln: University of Nebraska Press, 2007), and Robert Utley, *Lone Star Justice: The First Century of the Texas Rangers* (Oxford: Oxford University Press, 2002).

Mythmaking about the cowboy's life on the trail started early. Versions establishing mythical elements of the story include James S. Brisbin, *The Beef Bonanza; or, How to Get Rich on the Plains* (Norman: University of Oklahoma Press, 1959); Theodore Roosevelt, *Ranch Life and the Hunting-Trail* (New York: Century, 1899); and Roosevelt's friend Owen Wister, *The Virginian: The Horseman of the Plains* (New York: Macmillan, 1902). For studies of this mythmaking process, consult Henry Nash Smith, *Virgin Land: The American West as Symbol and Myth* (Cambridge, MA: Harvard University Press, 1950); Richard Slotkin, *Gunfighter Nation: The Myth of the Frontier in Twentieth-Century America* (1992; repr., Norman: University of Oklahoma Press, 1998); and Richard W. Etulain, *Telling Western Stories: From Buffalo Bill to Larry McMurtry* (Albuquerque: University of New Mexico Press, 1999). The early dime novel Westerns are difficult to find in print, but they make fascinating reading. Look for Prentiss Ingraham, *Buck Taylor: King of the Cowboys*, Beadle's Dime Novels (New York: Beadle & Adams, 1887), or Prentiss Ingraham, *Buck Taylor, the Saddle King; or, The Lasso Ranger League*, Beadle's Dime Novels (New York: Beadle & Adams, 1891). For detailed studies of these early fictional cowboys, consult Daryl Jones, *The Dime Novel Western* (Bowling Green, OH: Popular Press, 1978); Karen R. Jones and John Wills, *The American West: Competing Visions* (Edinburgh: Edinburgh University Press, 2009); and Jeremy Agnew, *The Creation of the Cowboy Hero: Fiction, Film and Fact* (Jefferson, NC: McFarland, 2015).

Insightful studies of the cowboy hero, each with a distinct perspective, include Joe B. Frantz and Julian Ernest Choate Jr., *The American Cowboy, Myth and Reality* (Norman: University of Oklahoma Press, 1955); William W, Savage Jr., *The Cowboy Hero: His Image in American History and Culture* (Norman: University of Oklahoma Press, 1979); and Jack Weston, *The Real American Cowboy* (New York: Schocken Books, 1985).

The range of scholarship on specific aspects of cowboy mythology is demonstrated in the recent anthologies of Paul R. Carlson, ed., *The Cowboy Way* (Lubbock: Texas Tech University Press, 2000), and Richard Aquila, ed., *Wanted Dead or Alive: The American West in Popular Culture* (Urbana: University of Illinois Press, 1986). A spirited defense of the best in the cowboy tradition comes in Paul A. Starrs, *Let The Cowboy Ride: Cattle Ranching in the American West* (Baltimore: Johns Hopkins University Press, 1998). Jane Tompkins, *West of Everything: The Inner Life of Westerns* (Oxford: Oxford University Press, 1993), provides a readable brand of literary criticism, including a deft analysis of the classic trail movie *Red River*. For more on how the cowboy has fared in movies over the decades, see Michael Coyne, *The Crowded Prairie: American National Identity in the Hollywood Western* (London: I. B. Tauris, 1998). The seminal work on the cowboy in song is the autobiography of John A. Lomax, *Adventures of a Ballad Hunter* (New York: Macmillan, 1947), as well as his collection of songs, John A. Lomax, *Cowboy Songs and Other Frontier Ballads* (New York: Macmillan, 1910).

INDEX